LEARNING VISUAL BASIC.NET THROUGH APPLICATIONS

D1709363

LEARNING VISUAL BASIC.NET THROUGH APPLICATIONS

CLAYTON E. CROOKS II

CHARLES RIVER MEDIA, INC.

Hingham, Massachusetts

CHARLES RIVER MEDIA, INC.
20 Downer Avenue, Suite 3
Hingham, Massachusetts 02043
781-740-0400
781-740-8816 (FAX)
info@charlesriver.com
www.charlesriver.com

This book is printed on acid-free paper.

Clayton E. Crooks II. *Learning Visual Basic.NET Through Applications*.
ISBN: 1-58450-242-8

Library of Congress Cataloging-in-Publication Data

Crooks, Clayton E.
  Learning Visual Basic.NET through applications / Clayton E. Crooks II.
    p. cm.
  ISBN 1-58450-242-8 (paperback with CD-ROM : alk. paper)
  1. BASIC (Computer program language) 2. Microsoft Visual BASIC.
  3. Microsoft .NET. 4. Application software—Development. I. Title.
  QA76.73.B3 C737 2003
  005.26'8—dc21
                          2002014120

Printed in the United States of America
02 7 6 5 4 3 2 First Edition

CHARLES RIVER MEDIA titles are available for site license or bulk purchase by institutions, user groups, corporations, etc. For additional information, please contact the Special Sales Department at 781-740-0400.

Requests for replacement of a defective CD-ROM must be accompanied by the original disc, your mailing address, telephone number, date of purchase, and purchase price. Please state the nature of the problem, and send the information to CHARLES RIVER MEDIA, INC., 20 Downer Avenue, Suite 3, Hingham, Massachusetts 02043. CRM's sole obligation to the purchaser is to replace the disc, based on defective materials or faulty workmanship, but not on the operation or functionality of the product.

This book is dedicated to Amy, my wife and best friend,
and my son Clayton III, who relinquished immeasurable amounts of time
with their husband and father so that this book could be written.

CONTENTS

x   Contents

ACKNOWLEDGMENTS

There are many people who have been involved with the development of this book and because of their hard work and dedication, you are now holding it. First, I'd like to thank everyone at Charles River Media, and especially Dave Pallai, for the opportunity to write this book. Your patience with this project has been greatly appreciated. I'd also like to individually thank Kelly Robinson for his help and advice with coordinating the manuscript.

I'd also like to thank my parents, Clayton and Donna, and the rest of my family for putting up with me during these long projects. Thank you for being so understanding.

PREFACE

Visual Basic.NET is the newest incarnation of the ever-popular Microsoft development language. While the IDE and some of the language will look familiar to you, there have been countless changes that have been made to VB. You can spend a lifetime attending conferences, reading how-to books or magazine articles, but unless you actually write programs, your skill level will never increase. As the vast majority of people learn better by following examples, this book will give you some of the basic information about VB.NET with later chapters focusing on the development of a complete application in each chapter instead of focusing on a single topic. Not only will this be a more stimulating way for beginners to learn Visual Basic, but intermediate or advanced users can simply skip to a specific chapter in the book that covers a project they are interested in.

While there are many books about programming in general and specifically Visual Basic, most of them tend to focus entire chapters on a particular topic. While learning about controls and TextBoxes is a must for any Visual Basic programmer, the theory is only somewhat useful. That's where this book comes in.

With the exception of Visual Basic itself, this book and CD-ROM contain everything you need to complete the projects, as they don't rely on any commercial controls or add-ons. The following list of projects will help you understand what you'll find in this book.

- Creating an MP3 Player that can play standard MP3 music files.
- Unique Interface Designs: Using the .NET framework to create a user interface, with irregularly shaped forms and buttons, giving a variety of effects to normally dull Visual Basic forms.
- Slots: You will build a fully functional game of Visual Basic slots.
- Word Processor: Develop a fully functional Word Processor.
- Encryption and Decryption: Add encryption and decryption to the Word Processor.

- Calculator: Build a simple calculator that accepts inputs of values and outputs a result.
- System Information: Using WMI to retrieve information about your system such as BIOS, CPU, etc.
- Email: Sending email in VB.NET.
- Screen Capture: A screen capture application.
- Image Convertor: Create a conversion utility that allows you to save images in various formats using drag-and-drop.
- Web Browser: Microsoft's Web Browser control gives us programmatic control over Internet Explorer and using this technology, we create a multiple document interface browser.
- Paint Program: Develop a Visual Basic Paint Program that has a wide range of drawing and painting tools.
- Many more…

1

INTRODUCTION TO VISUAL BASIC.NET

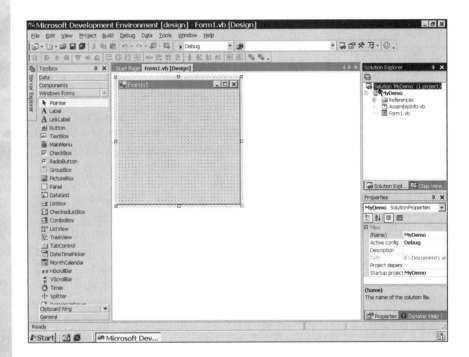

Although this book is based on developing projects, it's important to have at least a basic understanding of the Visual Basic.NET development environment and programming language. As a result, this chapter introduces you to Visual Basic and guides you through the creation of your first Visual Basic program. Topics that you'll be exposed to include the fundamentals of the Visual Basic Integrated Development Environment (IDE); the basic language; variables; and the built-in components.

 Throughout this book, unless I state Visual Basic 6 or VB 6 specifically, you can safely assume that any reference to VB or Visual Basic is related to the new Visual Basic 7. This latest version is referred to commonly as Visual Basic.NET.

If you are already well versed in VB.NET or earlier versions of Visual Basic, some of this chapter deals with topics that are undoubtedly familiar to you. Although most of the concepts have remained the same, the IDE has been changed and I'll touch on many new ideas in this opening chapter. If you're a beginner or intermediate programmer and new to VB.NET, this chapter will help you build a solid foundation onto which you can base your future Visual Basic learning.

HISTORY OF VISUAL BASIC

Visual Basic has been in existence for over 10 years now after debuting in the spring of 1991. It received a tremendous amount of press coverage that propelled it into what is now the most widely used programming environment in the world. The first couple of versions were very simple and probably weren't useful for much more than prototyping an application you planned to write with something else. In subsequent releases—beginning with database connectivity in VB 3—Microsoft added features that transformed the tool that many considered a toy into a very useable product. Version 4 provided a limited ability to create objects, and with Versions 5 and 6 came additional object-oriented features. Now, with VB.NET, Visual Basic has been altered yet again and with these changes comes a shift in the way you'll develop applications.

We'll look further at the language changes and how to upgrade VB 6 projects to .NET in Chapter 2. For now, I'll introduce you to the VB IDE.

THE INTEGRATED DEVELOPMENT ENVIRONMENT

I'll begin by looking at the VB IDE, which is primarily responsible for its vast popularity. It provides everything you need to develop applications easily and includes a Graphical User Interface or GUI (pronounced *Gooey*).

Like many Windows applications, there are several ways that you can open Visual Basic. First, and probably the easiest, is accessing it through the Start menu. The exact path required to access this shortcut is dependent upon your installation and may differ on individual machines. Another option is to create a shortcut on your desktop, which will execute Visual Basic when you double-click on it. There are several additional options such as double-clicking on files that are associated with the environment, so you should simply use the option that best suits your individual needs.

If you have experience with previous versions of Visual Basic, the first thing you'll notice is the lack of the familiar New Project window being displayed on startup. Instead, you're presented with a new Start page that will appear very much like Figure 1.1.

The Start page is displayed at first startup showing the My Profile option, which allows you to set the environment so that it reflects your personal settings. Customization is an important option as it can help reduce

FIGURE 1.1   The Start page is displayed at startup.

your learning curve and make your job much easier. You'll notice that there are three settings you can change in the Profile portion of the page:

- Keyboard Scheme
- Window Layout
- Help Filter

Because you're using Visual Basic, you can set the Profile drop-down to read Visual Basic Developer. Doing so will make changes to the other options for you by setting the options to Visual Basic preferences automatically. You can see the changes reflected in Figure 1.2.

There are several other interesting items on the Start page that are new to this version of Visual Basic. First, there's the Headlines option, which will pull information from the Internet for you and display it inside the environment. You can see an example of the Headlines tab in Figure 1.3.

The information on this tab consists of features of a new OS (operating system), technical articles and white papers that give specific details for topics, and a knowledge base that allows you to search through thou-

FIGURE 1.2   Visual Basic preferences are automatically selected when you set the profile.

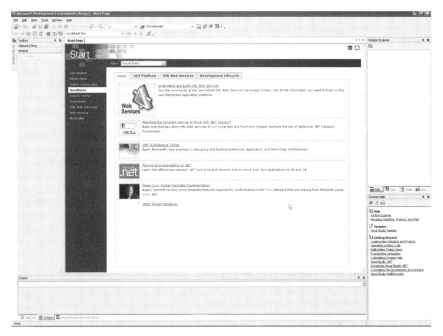

FIGURE 1.3   Headlines are retrieved from the Internet and displayed in the IDE.

sands of topics. Having this information available directly in the IDE is a tremendous time-saver.

The Get Started item, which can be seen in Figure 1.4, allows you to view the projects you have been working on quickly in a very convenient format. You can open any of the files listed on the Project tab by simply clicking on them. You can also start a new project by clicking on the New Project button.

For most of the projects in this book, you'll develop standard Windows executable files. In previous versions, you would have selected the Standard EXE project from the Project Window. The new VB.NET Project window, which can be seen in Figure 1.5, has several new options including Windows Application, which is similar to the Standard EXE project in VB 6.

When you create the project, you're required to give it a name and location in the dialog boxes that are listed beneath the project types. Once you have set the appropriate options, you can click the OK button to create the project.

Once you click OK, the VB.NET IDE will be displayed; it looks similar to Figure 1.5. One thing you may notice immediately is the change in file

FIGURE 1.4   The Get Started item displays previous projects.

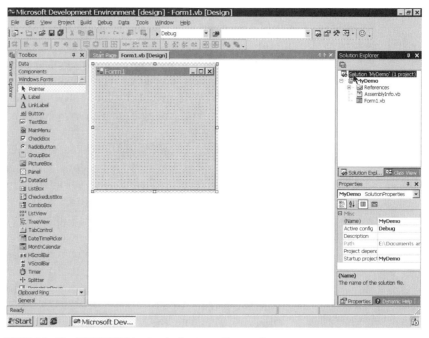

FIGURE 1.5   The VB.NET IDE looks similar to earlier versions.

extensions for VB Forms, which contained an extension of .FRM. In VB.NET, items that are used in a project are given the extension .VB. Also given a new extension is a class which also uses the .VB extension.

As you can see in Figure 1.5, fundamentally, the Visual Basic IDE is a collection of menus, toolbars, and windows that come together to form the GUI. There are several main windows that appear in the default Visual Basic IDE, along with various toolbars. The menus include standard Windows menus like a File menu and many menus that are specific to VB.NET. There are also a wide range of toolbars that you have access to. In the upcoming sections, we'll look at these in detail.

The Menus

As you can see in Figure 1.6, the Visual Basic IDE contains a menu bar and title bar that appear very similar to most Windows applications. The title bar serves as a quick reminder of what you're doing inside the IDE. For instance, unless you've changed something, the title bar should currently read similar to WindowsApplication—Microsoft Visual Basic.NET [design]—Form1.vb [design]. This text is displayed at the top of the IDE when you start a new project.

File   Edit   View   Tools   Window   Help

FIGURE 1.6   Menu and title bars provide information similar to most Windows programs.

The menu bar provides functions that you would expect from any standard Windows application. For instance, the File menu allows you to load and save projects; the Edit menu provides Cut, Copy, and Paste commands that are familiar to most Windows users; and the Window menu allows you to open and close windows inside the IDE. All menu options work as they do in any other Windows application, so they don't need introduction. You shouldn't be overly concerned with all of the options at this time because I'll be spending some time on them throughout the book.

The Toolbars

VB.NET provides toolbars that allow you to quickly access commonly used functions. There are several toolbars, some of which are displayed by default, while some are hidden. You can also create your own custom toolbars if the need arises.

Standard Toolbar

The Standard toolbar, which is displayed in Figure 1.7, is also comparable to the vast majority of Windows applications. It provides shortcuts to many of the commonly used functions provided by Visual Basic. Along with the Standard toolbar, Microsoft has provided several additional built-in toolbars that can make your job a little easier. To add or remove any of the toolbars, you can right-click on the menu bar or you can select Toolbars from the View menu.

FIGURE 1.7   Toolbars provide shortcuts to many of the common functions.

Individual Toolbars

The individual toolbars include the Debug, Edit, and Form toolbars. The Debug toolbar, which is visible in Figure 1.8, is utilized for resolving errors in your program and provides shortcuts to commands that are found in the Debug menu.

FIGURE 1.8   Shortcuts in the Debug toolbar are helpful when finding errors in your program.

The Layout Toolbar

The Layout toolbar (see Figure 1.9) includes many of the commands in the Format menu and is useful when you're arranging controls on a form's surface. For instance, you can quickly and easily align objects or center them horizontally or vertically on a form.

FIGURE 1.9   The Layout toolbar displays buttons specific to editing features.

Whether you decide to display these toolbars is purely a matter of personal taste as the functions they provide are generally available in menu options. Several factors, such as your screen size and resolution, may make their use impractical.

Customizing Toolbars

You can create a custom toolbar or customize the appearance of the built-in toolbars by following these steps.

1. Right-click on any toolbar, and then select the Customize option to display the Customize window that appears (see Figure 1.10).
2. Click the New button and type a name for the new toolbar. The name will appear in the toolbar list. Make sure that its check box is selected.
3. Click the Commands tab, which displays a list of available menu commands. From the list of categories and commands, select the options you would like to have on your toolbar. The changes are automatically saved, so continue placing options on the toolbar until you are finished and then simply close the window.
    You can now use your toolbar like any other.

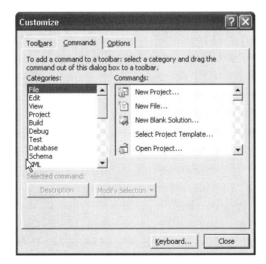

FIGURE 1.10 The Customize window allows you to create or customize a toolbar.

THE WINDOWS

In addition to the menus and toolbars, there are several windows that you need to become familiar with in order to get a basic grasp of the Visual Basic IDE. The Form Designer displays the basic building blocks of a typical Visual Basic application. The Toolbox window displays some of the built-in Visual Basic controls. You can set properties of the components and forms with the Properties window. Lastly, the Solutions Explorer displays the objects that make up the project you're working and you can position and view the forms with the Form Designer window.

The Toolbox

The Toolbox, which can be seen in Figure 1.11, is probably the window that you will become familiar with the quickest as it provides access to all

FIGURE 1.11 Standard controls as well as
ActiveX controls are displayed in the Toolbox.

of the standard controls that reside within the Visual Basic runtime itself. These controls, know as *intrinsic controls,* can be sorted by right-clicking on the Toolbox and choosing Sort Items Alphabetically from the pop-up menu (Table 1.1).

Table 1.1   VB.NET Controls

CONTROL	DESCRIPTION
Pointer	The pointer is the only item on the Toolbox that isn't a control. You can use it to select controls that have already been placed on a form.
Button	Much like the TextBox, CommandButtons are used for input on almost every frame. They are used as standard buttons for input such as OK or Cancel.
CheckBox	If you need the ability to select True/False or Yes/No, the CheckBox control is the correct control.
CheckedListBox	Displays a list of items that can display a check mark next to items in the list.
Color Dialog	Dialog that allows users to choose colors.
ComboBox	ComboBox controls are similar to a ListBox controls but they only provide support for a single selection.
ContextMenu	Gives users access to frequently used menu commands
CrystalReportViewer	Allows a Crystal Report to be viewed in an application.
DataGrid	Displays data in a tabular view.
DateTimePicker	Chooses a single item from date/time.
DomainUpDown	Displays and sets a text string from a list of choices.
ErrorProvider	Allows you to show the end user that something is wrong.
FontDialog	Dialog box for fonts.
GroupBox	Provides grouping for other controls.
HelpProvider	Used to associate a Hyper Text Markup Language (HTML) help file.
HScrollBar	The HScrollBar and VScrollBar controls let you create scroll bars but are used infrequently because many controls provide the ability to display their own scroll bars.
ImageList	Used to display images on other controls.
Label	The Label control is used to display text information that doesn't need to be edited by an end user. It's often displayed next to additional controls to label their use.
LinkLabel	Web style links for your programs.

(continues)

Table 1.1   *(continued)*

CONTROL	DESCRIPTION
ListBox	This control contains a list of items allowing an end user to select one or more items.
ListView	Displays a list of items with icons.
MainMenu	Menu for your programs.
MonthCalendar	Displays a calendar from which dates can be picked.
NumericUpDown	Displays and sets numeric values.
OpenFileDialog	Dialog box for opening files.
PageSetupDialog	Dialog box for setting up pages.
Panel	A panel for your program.
PictureBox	You use the PictureBox to display images in several different graphics formats such as .BMP, .GIF, and .JPEG among others.
PrintDialog	Dialog box for printing.
PrintDocument	Used for printing.
PrintPreviewControl	Preview for printing.
PrintPreviewDialog	Dialog box for print preview.
ProgressBar	Indicates progress of an action.
RadioButton	Selects from a small set of exclusive choices.
RichTextBox	Displays RichText files on a form.
SaveFileDialog	Dialog box for saving files.
Splitter	Used to resize docked controls at runtime.
StatusBar	Displays various types of information.
TabControl	Used to display tabs such as those that appear in a notebook.
TextBox	Used for input or displaying text.
Timer	The Timer control is an oddity when compared to other controls in that it isn't displayed at runtime. It's used to provide timed functions for certain events.
ToolBar	Toolbar for your application.
TrackBar	Also known as a "Slider" control. Used to navigate large amounts of data.
TreeView	Displays a hierarchy of nodes.
VScrollBar	The HScrollBar and VScrollBar controls let you create scroll bars but are used infrequently because many controls provide the ability to display their own scroll bars.

Some of the intrinsic controls are used more frequently than others and you're likely to become acquainted with them much faster. For example, the Button and Label controls are used in almost all Visual Basic applications. While some are very important, others may provide functionality that can be replaced by far superior controls.

Additional controls—known as *ActiveX controls*, *OCX controls*, or *OLE custom controls*—provide extra functionality and can be added to the Toolbox for use in a project. These components are provided by many third-party companies or may have been provided by Visual Basic, itself. Many times, these controls provide extended functionality that makes them much more powerful than the intrinsic controls. That being said, the built-in varieties offer a few advantages that cannot be overlooked. For instance, if you use a third-party control, you'll need to distribute it with your application.

Form Designer

You need a place to assemble your controls, which is the function of forms. As you can see in Figure 1.12, the forms you work with are displayed inside the Form Designer window. When they're displayed in this way, you can place and manipulate controls.

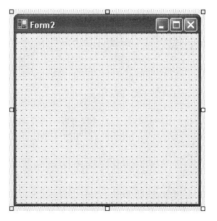

FIGURE 1.12 During development, the Form Designer displays the form you're working on.

Code Window

Every form has a Code window, which is where you write the code for your program. The Code window can be opened in a variety of ways such as double-clicking on a form or choosing Code from the View menu. Figure 1.13 displays a sample Code window.

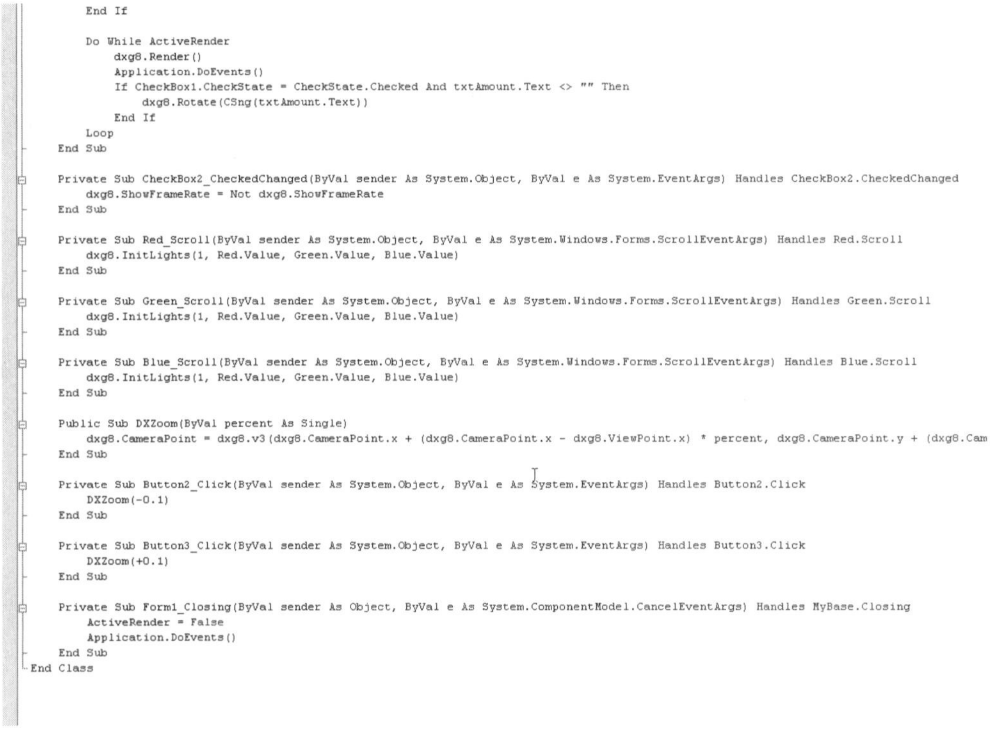

```
    End If

    Do While ActiveRender
        dxg8.Render()
        Application.DoEvents()
        If CheckBox1.CheckState = CheckState.Checked And txtAmount.Text <> "" Then
            dxg8.Rotate(CSng(txtAmount.Text))
        End If
    Loop
End Sub

Private Sub CheckBox2_CheckedChanged(ByVal sender As System.Object, ByVal e As System.EventArgs) Handles CheckBox2.CheckedChanged
    dxg8.ShowFrameRate = Not dxg8.ShowFrameRate
End Sub

Private Sub Red_Scroll(ByVal sender As System.Object, ByVal e As System.Windows.Forms.ScrollEventArgs) Handles Red.Scroll
    dxg8.InitLights(1, Red.Value, Green.Value, Blue.Value)
End Sub

Private Sub Green_Scroll(ByVal sender As System.Object, ByVal e As System.Windows.Forms.ScrollEventArgs) Handles Green.Scroll
    dxg8.InitLights(1, Red.Value, Green.Value, Blue.Value)
End Sub

Private Sub Blue_Scroll(ByVal sender As System.Object, ByVal e As System.Windows.Forms.ScrollEventArgs) Handles Blue.Scroll
    dxg8.InitLights(1, Red.Value, Green.Value, Blue.Value)
End Sub

Public Sub DXZoom(ByVal percent As Single)
    dxg8.CameraPoint = dxg8.v3(dxg8.CameraPoint.x + (dxg8.CameraPoint.x - dxg8.ViewPoint.x) * percent, dxg8.CameraPoint.y + (dxg8.Cam
End Sub

Private Sub Button2_Click(ByVal sender As System.Object, ByVal e As System.EventArgs) Handles Button2.Click
    DXZoom(-0.1)
End Sub

Private Sub Button3_Click(ByVal sender As System.Object, ByVal e As System.EventArgs) Handles Button3.Click
    DXZoom(+0.1)
End Sub

Private Sub Form1_Closing(ByVal sender As Object, ByVal e As System.ComponentModel.CancelEventArgs) Handles MyBase.Closing
    ActiveRender = False
    Application.DoEvents()
End Sub
End Class
```

FIGURE 1.13   Visual Basic code is written in the Code window.

Solution Explorer

The Solution Explorer can be seen in Figure 1.14 and is provided to help you manage projects. The Solution Explorer is a hierarchical tree-branch structure that displays projects at the top of the tree. The components that make up a project—such as forms—descend from the tree. This makes navigation quick and easy as you can simply double-click on the part of the project you'd like to work on. For instance, if you have a project with several forms, you can simply double-click on the particular form you want to view. Doing so provides quick and easy means of navigation.

FIGURE 1.14   You'll quickly realize the usefulness of the Solution Explorer.

The Solution Explorer also provides additional functions. For example, you can add new forms by right-clicking on an open area of the Solution Explorer window, and selecting Add Form from the pop-up Context menu that can be seen in Figure 1.15.

Properties Window

The Properties window is used for the configuration of the controls you place on a form as well as the form, itself. All of the standard Visual Basic controls have properties and the majority of ActiveX controls do as well. As you can see in Figure 1.16, the window displays the available properties for an individual control or the forms that they are placed on. These properties can be changed as you design an application or you can alter them in code.

FIGURE 1.15 Pop-up menus make available countless valuable features in the IDE.

FIGURE 1.16 The Properties window allows you to adjust properties for many Visual Basic objects.

CHAPTER REVIEW

In this chapter, we looked at some of the history of Visual Basic, from its early days as a tool used mainly for prototyping, to its present standard that has made it the most popular development tool available today. We looked at the VB.NET development environment and went through some of the basic features of the IDE.

In the next chapter, we'll continue our look at VB.NET by looking at its new features. In subsequent chapters, we'll go over the basic features of the Upgrade Wizard that walks you through the process of converting VB 6 files to VB.NET. Finally, we'll put together the information from the first chapters to build our first project in VB.NET, the standard Hello World! application.

2

WORKING WITH VB.NET

The previous chapter looked at the VB.NET IDE in some detail. You'll expand on what you learned in the previous chapter by detailing some of the differences between VB 6 and Visual Basic.NET. First, you'll look at how to use the Upgrade Wizard to move your products from VB 6 to VB.NET. Then you'll see the changes that have been made to the programming language.

WORKING WITH BOTH VISUAL BASIC 6 AND VISUAL BASIC.NET

The Visual Basic.NET and Visual Basic 6 IDEs can be used on the same computer and can even execute simultaneously. This is something very new as previous versions of Visual Basic would cause considerable problems for one another if they were installed on the same machine. Additionally, applications written and compiled in Visual Basic.NET and Visual Basic 6 can be installed and executed on the same computer. Although the projects in this book have been written for Visual Basic.NET, they can be written so that they will work in VB 6.

Upgrading Version 6 Projects to Visual Basic.NET

Because of the new changes associated with Visual Basic.NET, VB 6 code will need to be upgraded before it can be used. Fortunately, the vast majority of time, this is very easy as it happens automatically when you open a Visual Basic 6 project in Visual Basic.NET. This is not a perfect upgrade, however, and you'll often be left with a list of tasks that the wizard could not handle on its own.

An Upgrade Wizard, which can be seen in Figure 2.1, steps you through the upgrade process and creates a new Visual Basic.NET project. The existing Visual Basic 6 project is left unchanged. If you have Visual Basic Version 5 projects, it's best to upgrade them to 6 before moving on to VB.NET.

When your project is upgraded, the language is modified for any syntax changes and your Visual Basic 6 forms are converted to Windows Forms. Depending on your application, you may need to make minor changes to your code after it is upgraded. Many times this can be necessary because certain features either aren't available in Visual Basic.NET or the features have altered significantly enough to warrant manual changes.

Once your project is upgraded, Visual Basic.Net provides an upgrade report to help you make changes and review the status of your project. The items are displayed as tasks in the new Task List window,

FIGURE 2.1   The Upgrade Wizard makes it easy to convert Version 6 projects to Visual Basic.NET.

so you can easily see what changes are required. You can navigate to the code statement by double-clicking on the task. Many times, the document recommendations simply represent good programming practices, but they also identify the Visual Basic 6 objects and methods that are no longer supported.

PROBLEMS WITH CODE UPGRADES

When your VB 6 code is upgraded to Visual Basic.NET, it follows a specific set of rules. The following rules list some basic information that you should keep in mind if you're currently planning to upgrade VB 6 projects to .NET.

Variant to Object

Previous versions of Visual Basic supported the Variant data type, which could be assigned to any primitive type. In fact, Variant is the default data type if a variable wasn't declared in VB 6. VB.NET converts variants to the Object data type.

Integer to Short

In Visual Basic.NET, the data type for 16-bit whole numbers is now Short. The data type for 32-bit whole numbers is now Integer and Long is now 64 bits.

Here are a few examples:

VB 6	VB.NET
Dim A As Integer	Dim A As Short
Dim B as Long	Dim B as Integer
N/A	Dim A As Long
Variant	N/A (Use new 'Object')
Currency	N/A (Use Decimal or Long)
N/A	Decimal
String	String (doesn't support fixed-length strings)

APIs

The vast majority of application programming interface (API) calls expect 32-bit values if they take numeric arguments. Keeping in mind the previous section, you can see that problems are sure to arise. For instance, in VB 6, a 32-bit value is a Long data type while in .NET, a Long is 64 bits. You'll have to use Integer as the data type in .NET to make the calls correctly. According to Microsoft documentation, many APIs will no longer be callable from VB or may have replacements.

The Upgrade Wizard tries to correct API calls by creating wrappers for them. This is not a good idea as it makes your code more difficult to follow. Additionally, it's a good idea to become accustomed to the necessary changes. You should look at every API call individually to make any changes you need.

Here's an example of an API call under each:

VB 6:

```
Private Declare Function GetVersion Lib "kernel32" () As Long
Function GetVer()
```

```
    Dim Ver As Long
    Ver = GetVersion()
    MsgBox ("System Version is " & Ver)
End Function
```

VB.NET:

```
    Private Declare Function GetVersion Lib "kernel32" () As
Integer
    Function GetVer()
        Dim Ver As Integer
        Ver = GetVersion()
        MsgBox("System Version is " & Ver)
    End Function
```

Newly Introduced Keywords

VB.NET introduces several new keywords that have no counterpart in VB
6. Table 2.1 details some of them.

Table 2.1   New Keywords in VB.NET

KEYWORD	NOTES
Catch	New error handling—indicates code to use to process errors.
Char	New character data type.
Finally	New error handling—indicates code to use to run, regardless of errors.
Imports	Makes an object hierarchy (namespace) available in a module.
Inherits	Points to a base class for inheritance.
MustOverride	Indicates that any class that derives from this class must supply an override for this member.
MyBase	References the base class for use by subclass' code.
Namespace	Specifies a namespace for a module.
Overloads	Indicates that there's more than one version of a function and the compiler can distinguish among them by the input parameters.
Overrides	Indicates that a member overrides the identically named member in the base class.
Overridable	A member can be overridden in any class derived from the base class.
Protected	This member is only available to classes derived from this class.
ReadOnly	Used in a property that contains only a "Get."

(continues)

Table 2.1   *(continued)*

KEYWORD	NOTES
Shared	All instances of a class should share a variable in a class.
Throw	New error handling—used to raise an error.
Try	New error handling—starts code with error handling enabled.
Webmethod	Tags a method as part of a Web service that's available publicly.
WriteOnly	Used in a property that contains only a "Set."

Removed from .NET

Like the additions from the previous section, there are also some items that have been removed in VB.NET. The following list details some of the removed keywords and functions:

- VarPtr
- ObjPtr
- StrPtr
- LSet
- GoSub
- Let
- Is Missing
- DefBool
- DefByte
- DefLng
- DefCur
- DefSng
- DefDbl
- DefDec
- DefDate
- DefStr
- DefObj
- DefVar
- On x Goto

Table 2.2 details some commands that have equivalents in VB.NET.

Table 2.2   Commands with Equivalents in VB.NET

VB 6	VB.NET NAMESPACE	METHOD/PROPERTY
Circle	System.Drawing.Graphics	DrawEllipse
Line	System.Drawing.Graphics	DrawLine
Atn	System.Math	Atan
Sgn	System.Math	Sign
Sqr	System.Math	Sqrt
Lset	System.String	PadRight
Rset	System.String	PadLeft
Rnd	Microsoft.VisualBasic.Compatibility.VB6	Rnd
Round	Microsoft.VisualBasic.Compatibility.VB6	Round
DoEvents	System.Winform.Application	DoEvents

This is certainly not an exhaustive list as there are sure to be other things that have been added and removed. However, this list should serve as a good focal point for your work. There are a couple of additional commands that are no longer supported. One in particular is the `Set` command, which has been removed so that the following code in VB 6

```
Set objObject = objAnotherObject
```

will be changed to this:

```
objObject = objAnotherObject
```

Another widely used command that has been changed is `Debug`, which was used as follows in VB 6:

```
Debug.Print
```

in VB.NET this will now be like so:

```
Debug.Write
Debug.WriteLine
```

Arrays

The use of arrays in VB.NET has also changed. In VB 6, if you declare an array like the following, you would get 11 items from 0 to 10:

```
Dim number(10) as Integer
```

Within VB.NET, the same array would only give you 10 items from 0 to 9.

Default Properties

In Visual Basic 6, a control or object had a default property that wouldn't need to be specified. For instance, if you wanted to set a TextBox equal to a string, you would simply use this:

```
txtInformation = "This is a string"
```

Visual Basic.NET doesn't support default properties. So instead, you have to make sure to specify it as follows:

```
txtInformation.Text = "This is a string"
```

References to Form Controls

Controls in Visual Basic 6 were *public*. That is, you could simply reference a control on Form 1 inside the Code window on Form 2 by simply using form1.textbox1.text. In VB.NET, you'll have to create a public Let and Get property procedure for every control property you'd like to access.

Get and Let are now combined in VB.NET, so instead of being two separate property procedures, you create one. The following are simple examples that indicate the differences between VB 6 and VB.NET.

VB 6 code:

```
Property Get PropertyA() As Integer
    m_PropertyA = PropertyA
End Property

Property Let PropertyA(NewValue As Integer)
    m_PropertyA = NewValue
End Property
```

VB.NET Code:

```
Property PropertyA() As Short
  Get
      m_PropertyA = MyPropertyA
  End Get
  Set
      m_PropertyA = Value
  End Set
End Property
```

Forms and Controls

Visual Basic.NET Forms are now called Windows Forms. The following list will give you an idea of the differences between Version 6 and .NET forms:

- Windows Forms don't support the object linking and embedding (OLE) container control.
- Windows Forms only support true-type and open-type fonts.
- There are no shape controls in Windows Forms. Shape controls have been upgraded to labels.
- Drag-and-drop properties of VB 6 don't work on Windows Forms.
- Windows Forms have no support for Dynamic Data Exchange (DDE).
- There's no line control in Windows Forms.
- Windows Forms don't have access to form methods such as `Circle` or `Line`.
- Windows Forms don't support the `PrintForm` method.
- Clipboards are different and cannot be upgraded from Version 6 to .NET.

CHAPTER REVIEW

In this chapter, we looked at some of the changes that have been made to VB.NET. There are complete books written on this subject so this chapter shouldn't be considered an all-inclusive list of changes. However, it should provide you with the ideas that have been altered and it will help you in subsequent chapters.

In the next chapter, we're going to spend a little time looking at the Visual Basic.NET framework. Once we have a little more background information, we'll move on to writing several complete applications in VB.NET.

3

BASICS OF THE .NET FRAMEWORK

U sing the .NET Framework, Microsoft Visual Basic developers can build robust applications that were very difficult to write in previous versions of Visual Basic. The .NET Framework is Microsoft's latest offering in the world of cross-platform development. As such, there have been many changes to the VB language and even the philosophy of developing applications in VB.NET has been forever altered. While the changes are very positive for VB programmers, they can be a little difficult to become accustomed to.

The .NET Framework is essentially a combination of the Common Language Runtime (CLR) and the standard classes that are available to .NET programmers. The CLR is the execution environment for all programs in the .NET Framework. It's similar in nature to the Java Virtual Machine (JVM). The runtime classes provide hundreds of prewritten services that clients can use as the basic building blocks for an application. In this chapter, we'll look at these key concepts in a little more detail.

COMMON LANGUAGE RUNTIME

The CLR is the new runtime environment shared by every .NET application. Its purpose is to manage code execution along with all of the services that .NET provides.

The CLR is very similar to the concepts used in other languages such as the VB6 runtime library, a Java virtual machine, or even the Microsoft Foundation Class (MFC) library for C++.

One of the nice features of .NET is that there are many languages that can take advantage of this same runtime—currently, C# (*C-Sharp*), VB, and C++. It's the purpose of this runtime to execute the code for any language that was developed for the runtime. Code that was developed for the .NET runtime is called *managed code*, which can be simply thought of as a relationship between the language and the runtime itself. Because all .NET languages use this same runtime, there's no longer a need for language specific runtimes. Further enhancing this is the ability of C# programmers and VB programmers to share their code with no extra work.

With the shared runtime, there's a common file format for .NET executable code, which is called the Microsoft Intermediate Language (MSIL, or just IL). IL is a semi-compiled language that's compiled into native code by .NET when the program is executed. This is similar to what all versions of Visual Basic used to do prior to Version 5. This previous method for compiling was known as *pseudocode* or *P-Code*. With the CLR, the best features of pseudocode and compiled languages are available.

The following list details some of the benefits of using the CLR:

- Consistent programming model: All application services are offered via a common object-oriented programming (OOP) model. This differs from past programming models where some functions are accessed via dynamic linking libraries (DLLs) while others are accessed via Component Object Model (COM) objects.

- Simplified programming model: By removing archaic requirements of the Win32 application programming interface (API), .NET seeks to simplify the development process significantly. More specifically, a developer will no longer be required to delve into GUIDs, HRESULTS, and so on.

- DLL problems: When programmers are using DLLs, they are always concerned with installing components for a new application that can overwrite components of an old one. The old application will often exhibit strange behavior or stop functioning altogether because the DLL has changed the way it works. The .NET architecture removes this common problem and if the application runs after its installation, then the application should always run without the headaches caused by DLL versions.

- Platforms: Today, there are many different flavors of Windows including the three Windows XX variations (Windows 95, Windows 98, and Windows ME), Windows NT 4.0, Windows 2000, Windows XP, and Windows CE. Most of these systems run on x86 CPUs, with the exception of Windows CE devices, which work with Million Instructions Per Second (MIPS) and StrongArm processors. A .NET application that consists of managed code can execute on any platform that supports the .NET CLR. This opens some interesting possibilities for the Windows platform and could further be enhanced if the .NET platform is ever ported to platforms such as Linux or the Mac OS.

- Reuse of code/Language integration: .NET allows languages to be integrated with one another. For example, it's now entirely possible to create a class in C++ that derives from a class first implemented in Visual Basic. The Microsoft Common Language Specification ensures that all .NET languages are implemented in a manner that will allow this. While there are currently the three .NET languages (C#, VB, and C++), there are sure to be many more available in the near future with companies other than Microsoft producing compilers that also target the .NET CLR.

- Resource management: A common error among applications occurs when a developer forgets to free up resources once they're no longer needed. This can cause a great deal of inconsistency in an application and is sometimes one of the most difficult bugs to track down. Again, the .NET CLR comes to our rescue by automatically tracking resource usage.

- Types: The .NET CLR can verify that all your code is *type safe*, which simply means that allocated objects are always accessed in compatible ways. This actually helps in eliminating many common programming errors but it is also advantageous because of the protection of exploitation of buffer overruns used by many hackers.

- Error handling: One of the most difficult aspects of programming in Windows is the various ways that error messages can be reported. For example, some will return an HRESULT while others may return a Win32 error code. In .NET, all errors are reported via exceptions, which greatly simplify maintaining code.

- Deployment: This could go side-by-side with the DLL problems mentioned already. Windows-based applications in the past were incredibly difficult to install and deploy. There can be many files including data plus several DLL files and registry settings to deal with, to name a few of the more common examples. .NET components are no longer referenced in the Registry and installing most of them can be as simple as copying the files to a directory. Uninstalling can sometimes be a more difficult task, but with .NET, you can simply delete those same files that you installed.

- Common Type System: The CLR greatly simplifies cross-language communication through the introduction of the *Common Type System* (*CTS*). The CTS defines all of the basic types that can be used in the .NET Framework and the operations that can be performed on those types. Although an application can create a more complex type, it must be built from one of the CTS defined types, which are classes that derive from a base class called System.Object. We'll look at the CTS in more detail in the next chapter.

THE FOUNDATION FOR .NET DEVELOPMENT

Recall that you can think of the .NET Framework as a foundation on which you build and run applications. Having such a foundation makes it easier to build applications while using a consistent, simplified programming model. In earlier versions of VB, we spent a great deal of time using the Win32 API to do things that we could not access natively in the standard VB functions. These include operations such as accessing registry keys or creating irregularly shaped forms. Another option was third-party ActiveX controls that are actually very easy to use but they are often expensive for a single project.

This flexibility offered in the Win32 API was a blessing for VB programmers, allowing access to a variety of functions that were otherwise unavailable. Unfortunately, with this power also came a great deal of problems and confusion. Learning the API can be difficult as the calls are complex and many times the available examples were written for C++. This made calling the API very error prone, often resulting in crashed computers and lost hours of coding.

Another problem was the deployment of these applications. Once you finally managed to have the API calls working, you then had to deploy the appropriate DLL files with the correct version numbers. You can quickly see why this common framework makes sense from a development standpoint. You still have access to most of the powerful features of the API without actually knowing how to implement them. And deployment is now very simple as you don't need to concern yourself with how to handle the various DLL files.

API to VB.NET

While the API has not become obsolete, you'll need to have a quick way to access the various classes that implement the functions you've used in the past. The following BitBlt API call details some of a common .NET equivalent. BitBlt performs a bit-block transfer of the color data corresponding to a rectangle of pixels from the specified source device context into a destination device context. Here's a sample API call and .NET equivalent:

WinAPI:

```
Declare Function BitBlt Lib "gdi32" Alias "BitBlt" ( _
        ByVal hDestDC As Long, _
        ByVal x As Long, _
        ByVal y As Long, _
        ByVal nWidth As Long, _
        ByVal nHeight As Long, _
        ByVal hSrcDC As Long, _
        ByVal xSrc As Long, _
        ByVal ySrc As Long, _
        ByVal dwRop As Long _
    ) As Long
```

.NET:

```
System.Drawing.Graphics.DrawImage
```

CHAPTER REVIEW

In this chapter, we looked at some of the basics of the CLR, CST, and the overall .NET Framework. The Framework itself is a topic that encompasses so much information that we could devote an entire volume to its study.

In the next chapter, we're going to look at some of the syntax of the VB.NET programming language. We'll also take an even greater look at the differences between VB 6 and .NET.

4

INTRODUCTION TO THE VB.NET LANGUAGE

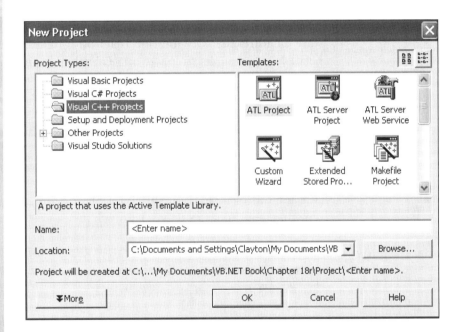

Although this book is focused on the creation of applications, it's important that you have a fundamental understanding of the VB.NET language. So, this chapter will introduce you to some of the basic principles. For those of you with programming experience, you can probably skim over this chapter and move on. For those without any programming experience, this chapter will help you with some of the basic concepts used in most VB applications.

VARIABLES

Variables are used in almost every VB application. They are simply used to store data in a memory location that you can access and manipulate as needed. For example, suppose you're developing an application that adds two numbers together. When writing the code, you could temporarily store the values of the two numbers in separate variables and then a third variable could hold the resulting value. Instead of referring to an actual memory location, VB allows us to use a variable name that we can declare to refer to these values.

Declaring a variable is as simple as creating a name along with a specific data type. When you declare a variable, Visual Basic allocates a certain amount of memory for the variable to store the data. It's the data type that determines exactly how much memory is being put aside.

 If you don't specifically declare a data type, VB.NET will assign it to the Object *data type. This is not a suggestion to do so. As for readability, you should always declare the data type even if it is of type* Object.

Table 4.1 details some of the variable types, the range of values they can store, and the memory that's allocated.

Table 4.1   VB.NET Variable Types

TYPE	SIZE	RANGE
Boolean	4 bytes	True or False
Byte	1 byte	0–255 unsigned
Char	2 bytes	0–65,535 unsigned
Date	8 bytes	1/1/1 CE to 12/31/9999
Decimal	12 bytes	+/–79,228,162,514,264,337,593,543,950,335 with no decimal point;

(continues)

Table 4.1   *(continued)*

TYPE	SIZE	RANGE
		+/–7.9228162514264337593543950335 with 28 places to the right of the decimal; smallest nonzero number is +/–0.0000000000000000000000000001
Double	8 bytes	–1.79769313486231E308 to –4.94065645841247E-324 for negative values; 4.94065645841247E-324 to 1.79769313486232E308 for positive values
Integer	4 bytes	–2,147,483,648 to 2,147,483,647
Long	8 bytes	–9,223,372,036,854,775,808 to 9,223,372,036,854,775,807
Object	4 bytes	Any object type
Short	2 bytes	–32,768 to 32,767
Single	4 bytes	–3.402823E38 to –1.401298E-45 for negative values; 1.401298E-45 to 3.402823E38 for positive values
String	10 bytes	+ 0 to approximately 2 billion Unicode characters (characters in string * 2)

With some of this basic information out of the way, we'll look at how variables are actually declared using the Dim keyword as in previous versions of Visual Basic. The following are some common examples of declaring variables:

```
Dim x as Single
Dim txt as String
Dim str as string
Dim oObj as Object
```

By default, when you declare a variable in VB, it's initialized to a standard value. Numeric variables are set to 0, strings are initialized to an empty string, " ", and object variables are initialized to nothing. In VB.NET, you can now initialize variables to something other than their defaults when you declare them.

Here are a few examples of initializing variables when declaring them:

```
Dim x as Single = 1.5
Dim txt as String = "Bob"
Dim Answer as Boolean = "True"
```

Variable declarations are usually very simple although they can get a little more complicated when you invoke an object's constructors. Different constructors use different arguments to initialize the object. For example, suppose you need to initialize a string with 50 asterisks (*). You could manually type in 50 of them and it would work just fine, although you can use a String variable constructor as follows:

```
Dim txt3 As New String("*", 50)
```

You can see that this is much easier than attempting to type out 50 asterisks and is much more readable as well.

When multiple variables are declared on the same line, then each variable type is the same as the rest of the variables on the line. For example:

```
Dim x,y,z as Integer
```

This will give x, y, z the Integer data type. You can take this a step further as well:

```
Dim x,y,z as Integer, a,b as String
```

This will set the x, y, z types to Integer and a, b types to String. In earlier versions of VB, these types of declarations could have caused some problems, so this is a welcome addition.

COMMON TYPE SYSTEM

Before moving on, we'll look at a more exhaustive list of the data types supported in the .NET CTS. It's worth noting that the CTS data types are either structures (which are value types) or classes (which are reference types). The data types are as follows:

Boolean

```
CTS Type: System.Boolean
Type: Value (Structure)
Storage: 2 bytes
Value range: True or False
```

Byte

```
CTS Type: System.Byte
Type: Value (Structure)
```

```
Storage: 1 byte
Value range: 0 to 255 (unsigned)
```

Char

```
CTS Type: System.Char
Type: Value (Structure)
Storage: 2 bytes
Value range: A character code from 0 to 65,535 (unsigned)
```

Date

```
CTS Type: System.DateTime
Type: Value (Structure)
Storage: 8 bytes
Value range: January 1, 1 CE to December 31, 9999
```

Decimal

```
CTS Type: System.Decimal
Type: Value (Structure)
Storage: 12 bytes
Value range: +/-79,228,162,514,264,337,593,543,950,335 with no
decimal point; +/-
7.9228162514264337593543950335 with 28 places to the right of
the decimal; smallest
nonzero number is +/-0.0000000000000000000000000001
53
```

Double (double-precision floating point)

```
CTS Type: System.Double
Type: Value (Structure)
Storage: 8 bytes
Value range: -1.79769313486231E308 to -4.94065645841247E-324
for negative values;
4.94065645841247E-324 to 1.79769313486232E308 for positive
values
```

Integer

```
CTS Type: System.Int32
Type: Value (Structure)
Storage: 4 bytes
Value range: -2,147,483,648 to 2,147,483,647
```

Long (long integer)

```
CTS Type: System.Int64
Type: Value (Structure)
Storage: 8 bytes
Value range: -9,223,372,036,854,775,808 to
9,223,372,036,854,775,807
```

Object

```
CTS Type: System.Object
Type: Reference (Class)
Storage: 4 bytes
Value range: Any type can be stored in an Object variable.
```

Short

```
CTS Type: System.Int16
Type: Value (Structure)
Storage: 2 bytes
Value range: -32,768 to 32,767
```

Single (single precision floating point)

```
CTS Type: System.Single
Type: Value (Structure)
Storage: 4 bytes
Value range: -3.402823E38 to -1.401298E-45 for negative values;
1.401298E-45 to
3.402823E38 for positive values
```

String (variable-length)

```
CTS Type: System.String
Type: Reference (Class)
Storage: 10 bytes + (2 * string length)
Value range: 0 to approximately 2 billion Unicode characters
```

User-Defined Type (structure)

```
CTS Type: (inherits from System.ValueType)
Type: Value (Structure)
Storage: Sum of the sizes of its members
Value range: Each structure member has range determined by its
data type and is independent of the ranges of the other members.
```

SCOPE

The *scope* of a variable determines where in a program it's visible to the code. Variables and constants both have a scope, which allows a programmer to decide when a variable can be referred to in the rest of the program. Variables were discussed earlier in this chapter and constants will be discussed later in this chapter.

Block-Level and Procedure-Level Scope

If a variable is declared inside a block of code, then the variable has *block-level scope*. This basically means that the variable is visible only within that block of code. A block of code, in this instance, refers to a part of a program that is terminated by a loop. Loops are covered in more detail in the next chapter.

Look at the following example that would give an error if it were executed:

```
If x <> 0 Then
Dim intAmount As Integer
intAmount = 50
End If
MsgBox CStr(intAmount)
```

This would give an error because the value of `intAmount` cannot be seen outside of the block of code encompassed by the `If…End If` loop.

If you declare a variable inside a procedure but not within the constraints of a loop, the variable is said to have *procedure-level scope*. This allows us to utilize the variable within the procedure, but once you get outside of it, the variable is again invisible to the rest of the program. A nice feature of procedure-level variables is that you don't really have to worry as much about naming them because each procedure can name their variables exactly the same. However, because you cannot see these variables outside of the procedure, the code doesn't cause a problem.

Module-Level and Project-Level

Module-level and *project-level* declarations can get a little more confusing as the modules themselves are declared using one of the following access modifiers:

- Private
- Public
- Friend

Don't concern yourself with these ideas at this time. However, remember that if you declare a module as a `Friend`, and then declare a variable as a `Public` inside the module, the variable will take on the attributes of the module in which it was declared and thus it has a `Friend` scope.

A variable that is declared in the declarations section of a standard module using the `Private` access modifier has module-level scope. The variable is visible in the entire module, but when you're outside of the module, it is invisible to the rest of the program code.

Now, if you were to create the same variable by using the `Friend` access modifier, the variable would be visible in the entire project (project-level scope). It's not visible to other projects, however.

A third possibility exists if you declare the same variable as a `Public` modifier in which case the module would also need to be `Public`. The variable is visible to this project and any additional projects that reference it.

Lifetime

Many people confuse a variable lifetime with its scope but the differences are actually very clear. The *lifetime* of a variable refers to the time that a variable is valid during program execution. As you know, scope refers to where the variable can be seen by other code. A *static variable* is a special type of variable, which has a lifetime that exists during the entire program execution. Previous versions of VB lacked this feature although you could implement a workaround.

CONSTANTS

Constants are similar to variables although the value that is assigned to a constant doesn't get changed during program execution. You can use constants instead of hard coding the values directly into your code as it's much easier to make changes to your code if you approach it in this manner.

For example, suppose you're developing an application that uses the value of Pi (3.1415) for calculations. Instead of adding the value 3.1415 to every line that uses it for a calculation, you can store it in a variable. Look at the following code example:

```
Const X as Double = 3.1415
Dim Y as Integer
Dim Answer as Double

For Y = 1 to 100
```

```
Answer = Const * Y
Next Y
```

You could have replaced `Const` with the actual value `3.1415` in the `Answer = ` line. This would be very easy for such a simple example. However, suppose you use this value in 40 or 50 calculations in different modules and procedures in your code. Now, assume that you've been asked to shorten `3.1415` to `3.14` for the calculations. You could change this in a single location in your program by changing the `X` constant or you could go through hundreds of lines of code searching for `3.1415`. While you would eventually change all of them, using a constant saves a great deal of time and is much more reliable.

STRUCTURES

Now that we've looked at declaring variables using the built-in data types, we're going to examine the ability to create your own custom data types using a structure. A structure contains members that can be any data type. The members each have their own names allowing you to reference them individually. The following example creates a structure called `Customer`:

```
Structure Customer
Dim ID As Long
Dim Name As String
Dim Address As String
Dim City As String
Dim State As String
End Structure
```

Once you've created a structure, you can use it within your program. The following example gives you an idea of how to use these structures:

```
Dim cust as Customer

Cust.ID = 1000
Cust.Name = "Clayton Crooks"
Cust.Address = "12345 South Main Street"
```

These lines created a variable called `cust` as type `Customer`. We then had access to the individual members and assigned them values of `"Clayton Crooks"`, `1000`, and `"12345 South Main Street"`.

CONVERTING BETWEEN DATA TYPES

In a project, you'll often be faced with the prospect of converting data from one format to another. For example, suppose you have an integer value that you'd like to store in a TextBox. You'll need to convert the data from an Integer to a string. The process of converting the values is known as *casting* or simply *conversion*. A cast can be one of two distinct types: *widening* or *narrowing*. A widening cast is one that converts to a data type that can handle all of the existing data. That is, if you convert from Short to Integer, the Integer data type can handle everything that was stored in the Short data type. Therefore, no data is lost. The narrowing cast is obviously the opposite of this where data is lost in the conversion process.

VB.NET handles data conversions in one of two ways: *explicitly* or *implicitly*. An implicit conversion occurs without interaction from the developer. For example, look at the following code:

```
Dim X as Long
X = 99
```

While the value 99 that is stored in X is obviously an integer, it's implicitly converted to a Long for storage in the variable. VB.Net did this on its own without any interaction. Explicit conversion requires calling one of the many VB.NET conversion functions. The following list details them:

CBool
    Example: newValue = CBool(oldValue)
    DescriptionConvert a data type to Boolean.
    Description: Converts any valid String or numeric expression to Boolean. If a numeric value is converted, it will result in True if the value is nonzero or False if the value is zero.

CByte
    Example: newValue = CByte(oldValue)
    Description: Converts a numeric data type from 0 to 255 to a byte. Any fractions are rounded.

CChar
    Example: newValue = CChar(oldValue)
    Description: Returns the first character of a string that is passed to it.

CCur

    Example: newValue = CCur(oldValue)

    Description: Converts a data type to Currency.

CDate

    Example: newValue = CDate(oldValue)

    Description: Converts a data type to Date or Time.

CDbl

    Example: newValue = CDbl(oldValue)

    Description: Converts a data type to Double.

CInt

    Example: newValue = CInt(oldValue)

    Description: Converts a data type to Integer while rounding fractional portions.

CShort

    Example: newValue=CShort(oldValue)

    Description: Rounds any fractional part while converting to a Short.

CSng

    Example: newValue = CSng(oldValue)

    Description: Converts a data type to Single.

CStr

    Example: newValue = CStr(oldValue)

    Description: Converts a data type to String.

ARRAYS

When you develop applications, you're often faced with the need to store multiple instances of like data. An *array* is a set of variables that are represented by a single name. The individual variables are called *elements* and they are distinguished from one another via an index number.

Arrays have a lower bound and an upper bound and have changed slightly in Visual Basic.NET. This is one of those areas where VB 6 programmers will need to be careful. The lower bounds for an array is always 0, and unlike previous versions of VB, you cannot change the lower bound. For example, suppose you have an array of 20 elements. This would suggest that the lower bound is 0 and the upper bound is 9.

Declaring an array is similar to declaring other variables:

```
Dim Name(50) As String
```

This would create an array of 50 elements that were each a string. The lower bound would be 0 and the upper bound would be 49.

Like variables, you can also initialize the array when you declare it. The following code declares an array of integers and initializes the values:

```
Dim Num1(5) As Integer = {9,8,7,6,5}
```

Alternately, you could also declare this as follows:

```
Dim Num1() As Integer = {9,8,7,6,5}
```

This dimensions the variable to the appropriate number of elements, automatically.

You can access the individual elements of an array as you would other variables. For instance, you could do the following:

```
Num1(3) = 0
```

This would set the third element to a 0.

Multi-Dimensional Arrays

An array isn't limited to a single dimension. It can have multiple dimensions that allow you to create a grid. VB.NET can have up to 60 dimensions although that's probably unrealistic for any real-world use. The following example gives you an idea of dimensioning an array:

```
Dim grid(3, 3) As Integer
```

To access the information in this array to retrieve or assign values, you use the combination of numbers to identify the element, as shown here:

```
grid(0, 0) = 1
grid(1, 1) = 0
```

You can also declare an array with uneven elements. For example, if you wish to declare an array that holds the following data

```
1    2    3    4    5
1    2    3    4    5
1    2    3    4    5
```

you would use this code:

```
Dim arr(3,5) As Integer
```

To initialize a multi-dimensional array when you declare it, you leave the parentheses (()) empty with the exception of a comma (,) for each additional array dimension. For example, to initialize an array, you could use something like this:

```
Dim arr(,) As String = {{"1", "1", "1"}, {"2", "2", "2"}}
```

Dynamic Arrays

In VB.NET, all arrays are dynamic. The declared size is only the initial size of the array, which can be changed as needed. (Please note that you cannot change the dimensions of an array after declaration.) To change the size of an array, you use the ReDim statement. The process of changing the size of an array is known as *redimensioning*. This is confusing as we've already mentioned that you cannot actually redimension an array.

 There are two functions that can help when redimensioning arrays: UBound *and* LBound. UBound *returns the upper limit while* LBound *returns lower bound.*

It's actually very simple to redimension an array. Let's start with an array dimensioned as follows:

```
Dim Nums(10, 10) As Integer
```

To redemension this, you can use the following:

```
ReDim Nums (100,100) as Integer
```

When you redimension an array, all of the data in it is lost. If you need the data, you can use the Preserve keyword to keep the existing data. If you use the Preserve keyword, you can only change the last coordinate:
This is ok

```
ReDim Preserve Nums (10,100) as Integer
```

while this isn't:

```
ReDim Preserve Nums (100,100) as Integer
```

In VB 6, you could have an array of controls that were very similar to the arrays we've been looking at. The new changes to the event model make control arrays a thing of the past. This is because the event model in Visual Basic .NET allows any event handler to handle events from multiple controls. For example, if you had multiple Button *controls on a form (called* Button1 *and* Button2*), you could handle the click events for both of them as follows:*

Private Sub MixedControls_Click (ByVal sender As System.Object, ByVal e As System.EventArgs) Handles Button1.Click, Button2.Click

LOOPS

When you develop applications in VB.NET, you need a way to manage the execution of the programs. For example, you might need to execute code a certain number of times, or you may need to check a condition to see if you should be executing the code. For both cases, we use loops.

If...Then...Else

If...Then...Else loops allow you to test a condition before executing a block of code. For the block of code to execute, the condition must evaluate to True. Let's take a look at an example of an If...Then statement:

```
Dim X as Integer


X = 0
If X < 1 Then
     X = 6
End If
```

This simply checks the value of X and if it is less than the value of 1, it assigns the value 6 to it. The program code execution would then continue with the next step.

Another example, allows us to look at the If...Then...Else statement:

```
Dim Cost1 As Integer
Dim Cost2 As Integer
Dim BuyIt As Boolean
```

```
Cost1 = 50
Cost2 = 75

If Cost1 < Cost2 Then
BuyIt = False
Else If Cost2>=Cost1 Then
BuyIt = True
End If
```

The preceding code is a very simplistic example but serves its purpose to show how the `ElseIf` statement can be added to check multiple conditions. For `If…Then` statements, you need to use comparison operators to check the various conditions. In the preceding example, we used the less than (<), greater than (>), and equal to (=) comparison operators. The following list gives you some ideas of the various types:

=   Equal to
<   Less than
<= Less than or equal to
>   Greater than
>= Greater than or equal to
<> Not equal to

There are two additional operators that are worth mentioning: Like and Is. The Like operator compares a string to a string pattern instead of an exact copy of the string. The Is operator compares two object references to see if they point to the same object. When you use the Like operator, you can use wildcards for pattern matching. They are as follows:

?	Matches a single character.
*	Matches all or none of the characters.
#	Matches a single digit.
[character list]	Matches any single character in the character list.
[! Character list]	Matches any single character not in the character list.

The Like operator gives you many options when looking for patterns in a string. By testing the result of the condition, you can return a value of `True` if it's found; otherwise, a value of `False` is returned.

Table 4.2 provides a few examples.

Table 4.2   Like Operator Results

VALUE	OPERATOR	CONDITION	RESULT
"pqrs"	Like	"p*p"	False
"pqrs"	Like	"p*s"	True
"pqr"	Like	"p?r"	False
"pqr"	Like	"p?r"	True
"pqr"	Like	"p#r"	False
"pqr"	Like	"p#r"	True
"aQa"	Like	"a[a-z]a"	False
"aba"	Like	"a[a-z]a"	True
"aba"	Like	"a[!a-z]a"	False
"aBa"	Like	"a[!a-z]a"	True

Sometimes a single expression in an `If…Then…Else` statement is not enough. You can use multiple expressions to create a single `True` or `False` value for an `If…Then…Else` statement. You can use the logical operators to create compound expressions that, as a whole, return a single Boolean value. Table 4.3 lists the logical operators.

Table 4.3   Logical Operators

LOGICAL OPERATOR	RESULT
And	Both expressions should be True to get a True result.
Not	Expression must evaluate to False for a True result.
Or	Either of the expressions must be True for a True result.
Xor	One expression can be True for a True result.

You may need to test multiple conditions in an `If…Then` statement. VB.NET provides this functionality as well. The following list details the available operators. You can combine them to create compound expressions. Let's take a look at some examples of compound expressions:

OPERATORS	RESULT
0=0 And 1=2	False
0=0 And 1<2	True
0<0 Or 1=2	False
0=0 Or 1=2	True

(continues)

OPERATORS	RESULT	*(CONTINUED)*
(0=0 And 1=2) Or 1=3	False	
(0=0 And 1=2) Or 1<3	True	
Not 1=1	False	
0=0 And Not 1=2	True	
0=0 Xor 1<2	False	
0=0 Xor 1<2	True	

Select Case

Another type of loop that's very useful is the Select Case statement, which is very similar in functionality to the If…Then statement. Select Case is most often used as a replacement for an If…Then statement that gets too long. As an If…Then statement grows in length, it gets much more difficult to read. The Select Case statement is much easier to read as you'll see in the following examples:

```
Select Case X
     X<= 5
            Y = 10
     X>5 And X<=10
            Y = 15
     X>10 And X<=15
            Y = 20
     X>15 And X<=20
            Y = 25
End Select
```

For Loops

The For loop is used when you want to execute a block of code a finite number of times. For loops are often used when you wish to read or write to or from an array. For loops use a counter to keep track of the number of iterations. A *start* value is the beginning value of the counter and an *end* value is used as the maximum value for the loop. There's also an optional *step* value with a default of 1. It instructs the loop how much to increment the counter during each pass of the loop. The step value can be a negative or positive number. For example, here's a simple loop:

```
Dim I As Integer
```

```
For I = 1 to 100
      Q = I * I
Next I
```

 Another variation of the form is the For...Each *loop. It's most often used with arrays to loop through every item in the array.*

While Loops and Do Until Loops

For loops work well if you know the exact number of times you'd like to execute a loop beforehand. There's another loop called the While loop that allows you to execute code blocks without knowing the values. It executes the loop until the condition that is being tested remains True. This loop is started with the Do While keywords.

A condition is checked to see if it's True prior to each execution of the loop.

A variation of the While Loop is the Do Until statement, which will execute until the condition is True. A third variety, know as While...Wend, is no longer available in Visual Basic .NET.

Here's a quick example of a Do While Loop in VB.NET :

```
Dim X As Integer = 0

Do While X < 1000
X = X + 100
Loop
```

This loop will execute until the X value is greater than or equal to 1000; it actually checks to see if X < 1000 and, if so, it continues. You don't always have to wait until the loop is finished before you exit it. You can use the Exit Do statement at any time. Here's an example:

```
Dim X As Integer = 5
Dim Y As Integer = 10

Do While X < 10
X = X+1
Y = Y + 1

If Y > 12 Then
Exit Do
End If
Loop
```

BASICS OF FUNCTIONS AND PROCEDURES

Functions and *procedures* are blocks of code that can be called at any time in an application. They typically perform a set type of function that's useful to the application. For example, you could have a function that calculates the square root of a number. You would then call this function whenever you needed to perform this calculation. We'll be using functions and procedures throughout the book, so we'll go over a few simple examples right now:

```
Function LessThan500(ByVal num as Integer) As Boolean
If num<500 Then
Return True
Else
Return False
End If
End Function
```

This function will return a Boolean value of True or False depending on whether the value of the number that's passed to the function is less than 500. You can call this function in your own program as you would any of the built-in varieties. For example, you could use a variable to pass it like this:

```
Dim LT500 As Boolean
Dim X As Integer

X = 10
LT500 = LessThan500(X)
```

This would pass the value of 10, and because it's less than 500, it would assign True to the value of LT500.

Another way to return a value from a function is to assign the function name itself to a value. Using the same preceding example, you'll notice the lack of the word, *Return*:

```
Function LessThan500(ByVal num as Integer) As Boolean
If num<500 Then
LessThan500 = True
Else
LessThan500 False
End If
End Function
```

You can use the method that's easier for you.

There's a big difference between how parameters are passed to functions compared to the earlier versions of VB. Formerly, parameters were passed by reference by default. In Visual Basic .NET, parameters are passed by value by default. At first, this might not seem like a big difference but it can be in your VB.NET applications. If a parameter is passed by *value*, any changes made to the value occur only within the function and the rest of the code in the application doesn't see them. On the other hand, when a parameter is passed by *reference*, if changes are made to the value, the change is seen by the rest of your program.

Sub procedures are similar to functions but they don't return any values. You call them exactly the same as you would a function such as the following:

```
somproc(10)
```

You can create a simple Sub procedure as you would a function:

```
Sub somproc(ByVal x as Integer)
If x > 5 then
      Temp = 5
Else
      Temp = 10
End Sub
```

You'll notice that this snippet looks almost identical to the previous example of a function with the exception of returning a value.

CHAPTER REVIEW

In this chapter, we covered a great deal of basic information about VB.NET. We began with variables and then moved on to constants, structures, and the CTS. We created several examples of declaring variables and constants. After these topics, we moved our attention to arrays and showed you how to use them. Lastly, we looked at several varieties of loops and then briefly touched on functions and procedures.

In the next chapter, we're going to look at the most important new feature of VB.NET: the object-oriented (OO) programming techniques.

5

OBJECT-ORIENTED PROGRAMMING WITH VB.NET

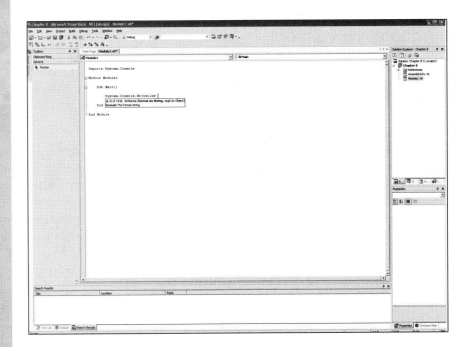

Since Version 4, Visual Basic has offered some object-oriented (OO) programming abilities although the implementation was less than perfect. VB.NET becomes the first truly OO version of VB with this release. There's now full inheritance, along with other features such as abstraction, encapsulation, and polymorphism. VB.NET now allows you to use classes written in other programming languages such as C# or C++.

It's important to understand how object orientation will change your programs and the process of creating applications in VB.NET. It's a big shift in the way you'll actually develop your applications. Because this is such a large topic, there are volumes of materials already written on object-oriented concepts and how they can be utilized effectively. We'll focus on the ideas that most often come into play with VB.NET and how they can be used.

In this chapter, we'll go over each of these ideas, which may be new to VB programmers.

ABSTRACTION

VB has supported *abstraction* since Version 4 and it's actually a simple concept. It's a view of an entity that includes only those aspects that are relevant for a particular situation. In other words, it's the ability of a language to create "black-box" code that takes a concept and creates an abstract representation of it within a program.

For instance, suppose that we want to create the code that provides services for keeping an employee information database. We'll need to store the following list of items:

- Name
- ID
- IncreaseSalary
- DecreaseSalary
- Salary

One of the most important ideas to keep in mind is that we included several items in this list for basic information such as Name and ID. However, we also have an action entity that will increase or decrease salary. These actions are referred to as *methods* in VB.NET. In pseudocode, the object would look like the following:

```
Employee Object
Name
```

```
    ID
    IncreaseSalary()
DecreaseSalary()
    Salary
    End Employee Object
```

ENCAPSULATION

Encapsulation is the process of taking the abstract representation that we create and encapsulating the methods and properties, exposing only those that are totally necessary from a programmer's standpoint. The properties and methods of the abstraction are known as *members* of the abstraction. The entire set of the members is known as the *interface*. Simply put, encapsulation allows a developer to control the methods and properties that are available outside the object.

INHERITANCE

VB.NET is the first version of VB that supports *inheritance*, which is based on the idea that a class can gain the preexisting interface and behaviors of an existing class. In other words, a class can inherit these behaviors from the existing class through a process known as *subclassing*.

When an object is inherited, all of its properties and methods are included automatically in the new object. For example, suppose we revisit the employee pseudocode object that we've been looking at in this chapter. Now, let's create a new object that tracks managers instead of employees:

```
    Manager Object
      Inherits Employee Object
      ManagerPosition
    End Manager Object
```

This new manager object will now have the same properties as the employee object (an ID, Name, and so on) but it also includes a property to detail the position that the manager holds. This is a very powerful way to share the code that you've already written instead of creating the code over again.

POLYMORPHISM

Polymorphism was introduced with VB 4. Polymorphism simply means having or passing through many different forms. That is, it's the ability to write one routine that can operate on objects from more than one class while treating different objects from different classes in exactly the same way. An easy example would be to create several classes that inherit the Name property from the Employee class we've been looking at. Basically, this would mean that the Name property would be available in many different forms.

Polymorphism allows an inherited method to be overridden. Again, looking at the Employee object, we could create a new object that inherited the Employee object but with a new method with the same name as the IncreaseSalary method we used earlier in this chapter. Although the new object would then have the methods and properties of the original one, because the new method exists, it will execute it.

CLASSES

A *class* is used to define an object. It's a sort of template that you can use to define the properties and methods of your objects and it is the structure that can contain events, constants, and variables.

To create a class, you begin with the Class keyword and assign a name to create instances of the class. Any time we need to create a class in VB.NET, we simply put all the code for the class within the Class…End Class block. This is similar in many ways to the loops we looked at in the previous chapter.

Statements within the class comprise its methods, properties, and events. Members declared as Private are available only within the class. Public members, on the other hand, are available outside the class and are the default declaration if neither is specified.

Methods in VB.NET are created using the Sub or Function keywords. A method created with Sub doesn't return a value, while a Function must return a value as a result. We've already looked at the concepts of a Function or Sub earlier in this chapter, so we won't spend any additional time on them. You can declare methods as follows:

- Private: Only visible within the class.
- Friend: Visible by code within the project.
- Public: Visible by code outside the class.
- Protected: Available to subclasses.
- Protected Friend: Visible to the project and by code in subclasses.

Properties store information in an object and can be specified by either `Public` variables or as `Property` methods. When properties are declared using a `Public` variable, they're also referred to as *fields*. This method doesn't provide the ability to control (validate) reading and writing a property. `Property` methods allow you to control read and write operations of properties in a class using the `ReadOnly` keyword.

For example, let's look again at the `Employee` object that we've talked about in pseudocode throughout this chapter. We'll create a simple class:

```
Class Employee
Public ID As Integer = 1

    Public Property Salary() As Integer ' This is a Property.
    Get
        Return Salary
    End Get

    Set(ByVal Value As Integer)
        NumWheelsValue = Value
    End Set
    End Property
End Class
```

This doesn't take into account everything we'd need to include in a real `Employee` object such as `Name`, and so on, but the concepts for creating them are exactly the same as the preceding code. We begin by creating a `Public` property called `Salary` and then use `Get`/`Set` to retrieve or set the property value in our code. Like their names imply, `Get` will retrieve a property and `Set` will assign a property. For example, after the class is available in the project, you can create a new `Employee` object as follows:

```
Dim clsEmployee As New Employee()
```

Then, you could assign a salary to an employee as follows:

```
clsEmployee.Salary = 500
```

We could also add methods to the example class:

```
Class Employee
Public ID As Integer = 1

    Public Property Salary() As Integer ' This is a Property.
```

```
        Get
            Return Salary
        End Get

        Set(ByVal Value As Integer)
            NumWheelsValue = Value
        End Set
        End Property

        Public Sub IncreaseSalary()
            'We need code for increasing salary
        End Sub

    End Class
```

Again, these are very simple examples. Don't worry if all of this doesn't click at this time. We'll go over these types of ideas as we use them in the book in real examples.

CONSTRUCTORS

Constructors are methods of a class that are executed when a class is instantiated.

They're very often used to initialize the class. To create a constructor, you simply add a `Public` procedure called `New()` to your class. You can also use a *parameterized constructor*. This allows you to create a class that can have parameters passed to it when it's called.

Back to our `Employee` class concept, we could create a constructor as follows:

```
Public Sub New()
    Salary = 500
End Sub
```

Using this example, when the class is initialized, we set the salary to a value of 500. This doesn't mean that it cannot be changed, but instead of assigning every employee a salary, they would begin with a salary of 500 that could be added to, subtracted from, or just changed completely. We could also allow the user of the object to the constructor to pass in the initial value instead of assigning it to 500. We could use a parameterized constructor to do this. We'll add a parameter for the `InitialSalary` as follows:

```
Public Sub New(ByVal InitialSalary As Integer)
    Salary = InitialSalary
End Sub
```

The user of the class could then create an object as follows:

```
Dim clsEmployee as New Employee (500)
```

This would work well, but suppose we wanted to offer a third option for the user of the class. Instead of assigning the salary by default to a value of 500, or using a constructor that requires the user to assign it, let's use the Optional keyword to create an optional constructor:

```
Public Sub New(Optional ByVal InitialSalary As Integer = 500)
    Salary = InitialSalary
End Sub
```

Now, if the user assigns a value, it'll override the default 500 value. If a value isn't passed, the value is the default of 500.

Although these have been very simple examples, you can see how constructors can be utilized in your applications.

OVERLOADING

Overloading is one of the more appealing aspects of polymorphism. It allows you to create multiple methods or properties with the same name but with different parameter lists. You can change the parameters to completely different types. For example, look at the following example Sub:

```
Public Sub MyMethod(X As Integer, Y As Integer)
```

To overload this method, you can come up with an entirely different list of parameters. For example, you can use Integer and Double:

```
Public Overloads Function MyFunction(X As Integer, Y As Double)
```
or Double and Integer:

```
Public Overloads Function MyFunction (X As Double, Y As Integer)
```

To put this into an example, let's suppose we wanted to create a class that multiplied numbers together. We could use the Overloads keyword to create the methods and then perform the appropriate action as necessary. Although it really doesn't make any difference in our simple example, we're going to create options for passing two integers or two reals. We could have made a single function that would have taken either of these, but for example purposes, we'll ignore this obvious fact:

```
Public Overloads Function Multiply(ByVal x As Integer, ByVal y
As Integer)
        Return x + y
    End Function
    Public Overloads Function Multiply(ByVal x As Double, ByVal y
As Double)
        Return x + y
    End Function
```

Then use these:

```
clsName.Multiply(1,5)
clsName.Multiply(1.5, 5.5)
```

Now, when the function is utilized, if two integers are passed (such as in the first preceding example), the first function is executed. Interestingly, if one of the two parameters is a real number, the second Multiply function is executed. This is because VB implicitly converts the integer parameter to a Double data type in this instance. Similarly, if both values that are passed are real values, the second function is executed.

OVERRIDING

When you inherit a class, it allows you to use all of the methods and properties available in the class. While this is obviously very useful, there might be times when you want to alter the inherited properties or methods. Instead of creating a new method or property with a new name, you can simply *override* the existing member, which is another feature of polymorphism.

To do this, you use the Overridable keyword in the original base class and then the Override keyword in the class derived from the original. For example, we'll use our original Employee class:

```
Class Employee
    Public Overridable Function IncreaseSalary(byVal amt as
Integer) As Integer
        Return amt+Salary
    End Function
End Class
```

Now, let's take a look at a new class derived from this one:

```
Class Employee2
Inherits Employee
    Public Overrides Function IncreaseSalary(ByVal amt As
Integer) As Integer
        Return amt*2
    End Function
End Class
```

Although you'll notice that the IncreaseSalary function that we created doesn't have any real program values, it's easy to use as an example. In the original class, we take the amount passed to the function and then add it to Salary. In the inherited class, we take the same amount and double it. You'll notice that the Overridable and Overrides keywords in the previous code were the only additional requirements.

There are a few other keywords that you can use when dealing with overriding members of a class. In addition to the two we already looked at (Overrides and Overridable), we can use the NotOverridable keyword to specify a method or property that cannot be overridden. You don't actually have to use NotOverridable as it's the default, so unless you specifically use Overridable, it can't be overridden. You can choose to use NotOverridable or simply leave it blank—both are acceptable.

Another keyword is MustOverride. Like its name indicates, if you use MustOverride, classes that are derived from a base class are required to override the property or method. For example, suppose we were to create a class that did mathematical calculations, but at the time of its creation, we didn't really know what type of math was going to be used. We could simply create a MustOverride method in our class and then the classes that were derived from the original would be forced to override the method and use the appropriate math.

SHARED MEMBERS

There's one final area we'll look at that's related to classes in VB.NET: shared members. If you were to create multiple instances of a class and then change the value of a property in one of them, it would not alter the value of the other. If you have a need to alter members of multiple classes simultaneously, you can create a shared member, which allows you to create members that are shared among all instances of a class.

NAMESPACES AND ORGANIZING CLASSES

As we've been working our way through the basics of VB.NET, you may have been wondering how the classes would be organized. After all, if you have methods from many different classes, it's likely that you would have some names that are identical. You wouldn't want to browse through hundreds of method names just to make sure that you didn't use the same names in your classes, not to mention the classes that you'll ultimately use that others have created.

For example, let's look at a very common method name such as Open. You might have a method named Open for many different classes that all have unique code written for it. Keeping this in mind, we need a way to organize the many classes and methods that are part of .NET so that they don't conflict with one another. This is where the .NET *namespace* comes into play.

Understanding the concept of the namespace is very simple as you've been using similar ideas in everyday life. For example, almost every town has a single or multiple McDonald's restaurant. You distinguish between the restaurants by their locations. These addresses are similar to the way the namespace works in VB.NET as classes and methods in your application can be separated by locating them accordingly in a namespace.

Here's an example. Suppose we have a custom class with an Open method. The class is myclasses.clayton.fill. The built-in class System.IO has an Open method as well that is related to handling the file input and output (I/O) features in VB.NET. So, if we were writing an application and wanted to include the System.IO features, we could do so as follows:

```
Imports System.IO
```

We could then use the class as follows:

```
Dim oFile As FileStream = New FileStream ("C:\text.txt",
FileMode.Open, FileAccess.Read)


Dim oStream As StreamReader = New StreamReader(oFile)

MsgBox(oStream.ReadLine)
oFile.Close()
oStream.Close()
```

You'll notice that in the preceding code, we begin with the Imports keyword. We could have typed the entire System.IO.FileStream out every time we wanted to use it, but instead we can use the Imports keyword to allow us to shorten it up to just FileStream. Similarly, we use StreamReader instead of System.IO.StreamReader. This makes your code much easier to read and follow while saving you time during typing. We're not really interested at this time in what the preceding code does, but we're using it as an example of how classes are organized and how the Imports keyword can be used in your future applications.

CHAPTER REVIEW

In this chapter, we covered the basics of object-oriented (OO) programming in VB.NET. We touched on abstraction, encapsulation, inheritance, polymorphism, classes, constructors, overloading, overriding, shared members and namespaces, and organizing classes.

In the next chapter, we'll look at strings, GDI + (graphics device interface), and error handling.

6

STRINGS, GDI+, AND ERROR HANDLING IN VB.NET

A s you've seen in the previous chapters leading up to this point, there are many changes that have taken place in this version of VB. There are completely new approaches to development, and although some of the old functions are still in place, it's recommended that you focus on learning the new items in VB.NET rather than functions that may or may not exist down the road.

In this chapter, we'll continue to look at some of these new items, and will specifically deal with the changes to strings, math, and error handling in VB.NET.

.NET Strings

If you've been using previous versions of VB, you'll have undoubtedly utilized the many powerful string functions it has always offered. Like other areas of VB.NET, the string functions are still there but they are implemented in a different manner. Now, if you remember that everything in VB.NET is considered an object (although this has been repeated many times, it's an important point to remember), you'll realize that as you `Dim` a `String` variable, you're actually creating an instance of the `String` class.

If you refer back to Chapter 4 where we looked at some of the basics of the .NET language, you'll see that we did a little work with how strings are used. We'll expand on that information in this chapter beginning with the list of the common methods built into the string class, as shown in Table 6.1.

Table 6.1   Common Methods of the String Class

CLASS METHODS	DESCRIPTION
Compare	Compares two strings.
Concat	Concatenates strings.
Copy	Creates a new instance with the same value.
Equals	Determines if two strings are equal.
Format	Formats a string.
Equality Operator	Allows strings to be compared.
Chars	Returns the character at a specified position in the string.
Length	Returns the number of characters in a string.
EndsWith	Checks the string to see if it ends with a specified string.
IndexOf	Returns the index of the first character of the first occurrence of a substring within this string.

(continues)

Table 6.1   *(continued)*

CLASS METHODS	DESCRIPTION
IndexOfAny	Returns the index of the first occurrence of any character in a specified array of characters.
Insert	Inserts a string in this string.
LastIndexOf	Returns the index of the first character of the last occurrence of a substring within this string.
LastIndexOfAny	Returns the index of the last occurrence of any character in a specified array of characters.
PadLeft	Pads the string on the left.
PadRight	Pads the string on the right.
Remove	Deletes characters at a specified point.
Replace	Replaces a substring with another substring.
Split	Splits a string up into a string array.
StartsWith	Checks if a string starts with the specified string.
SubString	Returns a substring within the string.
ToLower	Converts a string to all lowercase letters.
ToUpper	Converts a string to all uppercase letters.
Trim	Removes all specified characters from string.
TrimEnd	Removes all specified characters from the end of a string.
TrimStart	Removes all specified characters from the beginning of a string.

A quick glance at Table 6.1 is all that it takes to see some of the ways that you can use the various methods that are available in .NET. Before we look at a specific example, you should be aware that the index of the first character in a VB.NET string is a 0 rather than a 1. In previous versions of VB, strings were one-based instead of zero-based. Although simple, it's something that you'll have to keep in mind as you're upgrading projects or using VB.NET to build new ones as the old habits will occasionally creep into the picture.

Here's a simple example using the String methods:

```
Dim strTest as String = "ABCDEFG"
Dim strlength as Integer

strlength =  strTest.Length()
```

This example simply takes the string variable strTest and assigns the length of it to strlength. We can test other features simply as well:

```
strTest = strTest + "HIJKLMNOP"
```

Now, the string that is stored in strTest will actually be "ABCDE-FGHIKLMNOP".

Later, we'll use strings in many of the sample applications. Now, we're going to focus on the new and exciting graphics capabilities offered in VB.NET.

GRAPHICS WITH GDI+

In VB.NET, we have a completely new way of drawing graphics. It's based on drawing to a GDI (graphical device interface) surface rather than using the old Line, Circle, and Print methods. If you have used C++ in the past, you know the frustration that was involved in GDI development with MFC. Furthermore, if you're a VB developer, you'll know how limited you've been with the simple methods that were available in VB 6 and earlier.

In VB.NET, we now have access to GDI+. It's a superior implementation and is easier to use than traditional GDI. GDI+ provides a variety functions for you. For example, if you want to set the background or foreground color of a control, you can set the ForeGroundColor property of the control. GDI+ is easier to use, but there are also many new features that have been added including these:

- Antialiasing support
- Gradient brushes
- Splines
- Transformation and matrices
- Alpha blending

There are several namespaces that you'll need to become comfortable with in order to master GDI+ development. The GDI+ classes are grouped under the six following namespaces, which reside in the System.Drawing.dll assembly:

- System.Drawing
- System.Drawing.Design
- System.Drawing.Printing
- System.Drawing.Imaging
- System.Drawing.Drawing2D
- System.Drawing.Text

We'll take a quick look at a few of these namesapaces.

System.Drawing Namespace

The System.Drawing namespace provides the basic GDI+ functionality. It contains the definition of basic classes such as Brush, Pen, Graphics, Bitmap, Font and so on. The Graphics class plays a major role in GDI+ and contains methods for drawing to the display device. Tables 6.2 and 6.3 detail some of the System.Drawing namespace classes, structures, and their definitions.

Table 6.2   System.Drawing Classes

CLASS	DESCRIPTION
Bitmap	Indicates the Bitmap class.
Image	Indicates the Image class
Brush (Brushes)	Defines objects to fill GDI objects such as rectangles, ellipses, polygons, and paths.
Font (FontFamily)	Defines a particular format for text, including font face, size, and style attributes .
Graphics	Encapsulates a GDI+ drawing surface.
Pen	Defines an object to draw lines and curves
SolidBrush (Texture Brush)	Fills graphics shapes.

Table 6.3   System.Drawing Structures

STRUCTURE	DESCRIPTION
Color	Indicates RGB color.
Point (PointF)	Represents 2D x and y coordinates. Takes x, y values as a number. If you need to use floating-point numbers, you can use PointF.
Rectangle (RectangleF)	Represents a rectangle with integer values for Top, Left, Bottom, and Right. RectangleF allows you to use floating-point values.
Size	Indicates the size of a rectangular region given in width and height. SizeF takes floating-point numbers.

System.Drawing.Drawing2D Namespace

This namespace contains 2D and vector graphics functionality. It contains classes for gradient brushes, matrix and transformation, and graphics path. Tables 6.4 and 6.5 list some of the common classes and enumerations.

Table 6.4   System.Drawing.Drawing2D Classes

CLASS	DESCRIPTION
Blend (ColorBlend)	Defines the blend for gradient brushes.
GraphicsPath	Represents a set of connected lines and curves.
HatchBrush	Indicates a brush with hatch style, a foreground color, and a background color.
LinearGradientBrush	Provides functionality for linear gradient.
Matrix	3 x 3 Represents geometric transformation.

Table 6.5   System.Drawing.Drawing2D Enumerations

ENUMERATION	DESCRIPTION
DashStyle	Indicates the style of dashed lines drawn with a Pen.
HatchStyle	Represents different patterns available for HatchBrush.
QualityMode	Specifies the quality of GDI+ objects.
SmoothingMode	Indicates quality (smoothing) of GDI+ objects.

GRAPHICS CLASS

The Graphics class is a key component of GDI+ development. Before you draw an object such as a rectangle or line, you'll need a surface to draw it to. You have to use the Graphics class to create these surfaces before you can draw.

There are a few ways in which you can put a Graphics object to use in your application. First, you can get it in the form Paint event. Another option is to override the OnPaint() method of a form. Either way, you use the following:

```
System.Windows.Forms.PaintEventArgs.
```

Here's a simple example overriding the `OnPaint()` method:

```
protected overrides sub OnPaint(ByVal e As
System.Windows.Forms.PaintEventArgs)

    Dim g As Graphics = e.Graphics

    End Sub
```

This creates the `Graphics` object for us and we can now use any of the methods that are included with the `Graphics` class. For example, we can use any of the classes in Table 6.6.

Table 6.6   Classes Available in the Graphics Object

CLASS	DESCRIPTION
DrawArc	Draw an arc.
DrawBezier (DrawBeziers)	Draws Bézier curves.
DrawCurve	Draws a curve.
DrawEllipse	Draws an ellipse or circle.
DrawImage	Draws an image.
DrawLine	Draws a line.
DrawPath	Draws a path.
DrawPie	Draws an outline of a pie section.
DrawPolygon	Draws an outline of a polygon.
DrawRectangle	Draws an outline of a rectangle.
DrawString	Draws a string.
FillEllipse	Fills the interior of an ellipse.
FillPath	Fills the interior of a path.
FillPie	Fills the interior of a pie section.
FillPolygon	Fills the interior of a polygon defined by an array of points.
FillRectangle	Fills the interior of a rectangle.
FillRectangles	Fills the interiors of a series of rectangles.
FillRegion	Fills the interior of a region.

Now that we have a basic understanding of some of the things we can do, let's try a simple example to draw a line:

```
protected overrides sub OnPaint(ByVal e As
System.Windows.Forms.PaintEventArgs)

Dim g As Graphics = e.Graphics
Dim pn As Pen = New Pen(Color.Green, 5)
g.DrawLine(pn, 1, 50, 100, 500)

End Sub
```

OBJECTS

You have access to several types of objects when drawing items such as an ellipse and a line, to name a few. You can use the four following common GDI+ objects to fill GDI+ items:

- Brush: Fills enclosed surfaces with patterns, colors, or bitmaps.
- Pen: Draws lines and polygons, including rectangles, arcs, and so on.
- Font: Renders text.
- Color: Renders a particular object; in GDI+ color can be alpha blended.

We're going to look at a few examples of each of these.

The Pen Class

A pen, as you have already seen, draws a line of specified width and style. You can initialize a new instance of the Pen class with the specified color, a specified brush, a specified brush and width, or a specified color and width. Here's an example:

```
Dim pn as Pen = new Pen( Color.Blue )
```

The preceding code initialized the Pen with the color blue. The following example initializes it and also assigns a width of 10:

```
Dim pn as Pen = new Pen( Color.Blue, 10 )
```

Color Structure

A Color structure represents an ARGB color. ARGB properties are described as follows:

- A: Alpha component value for the color.
- R: Red component value for the color.

- G: Green component value for the color.
- B: Blue component value for the color. You use the `Color` structure to change the color of an object and you can call any of its members. For example, you can change the color of a `Pen` like this

```
Dim pn as Pen = new Pen( Color.Red )
```

or like this:

```
Dim pn as Pen = new Pen(Color.Green)
```

Font Class

The `Font` class defines a particular format for text such as font type, size, and style attributes. You can create a new instance of the `Font` class as follows:

```
Public Sub New(Font, FontStyle)
```

Here's an example:

```
Dim myFnt as Font = new Font ("Times New Roman",12)
```

There are many variations and possibilities of what you can do with the `Font` class, and we'll look at them more closely as we use them in the examples in the book.

ERROR HANDLING

In earlier versions of VB, we used the `On Error GoTo` statement to handle errors. This traditional error checking in VB has involved reviewing the result of a function and then responding appropriately to whatever value is returned. While checking errors in this manner has worked, it's often-times a gamble on how effective it will be. For example, you could check the value using an incorrect value or even forget one of the values that will cause an error. This leaves this type of error checking open to many more problems. There are times when you'll be forced to do this, but for many errors in VB.NET, we can use exception error handling.

To do this type of error handling at execution, we check for run-time errors that are called *exceptions*. When an error is encountered, the program takes the appropriate steps to continue executing. The code that's executed will only be executed when an error has occurred. We use the `Try` and `Catch` keywords in this form of error handling, which typically works as follows:

```
Try
      Code
Catch
      Error
End TryTry
```

A simple way of dissecting this approach is looking at the keywords. For starters, realize that the `Try` keyword is used to begin the exception handler. You place code after `Try` that you believe could cause some problems.

The next section, `Catch`, is the code that's executed, which will try to help your program overcome the errors. You can use multiple `Catch` blocks of code if you need different code for different errors. For example, suppose that you have some code that's written to save a file of some type. The error handling could be present for several types of errors:

1. The user didn't enter a filename.
2. An invalid character was entered for the filename such as an asterisk (*).
3. A network drive that existed previously is no longer available.

These are just a few examples.

You could create multiple `Catch` blocks that would handle these errors appropriately as you probably wouldn't want your application responding to an invalid filename in the same way that it responds to a network drive being unavailable.

Here's an actual example that causes a Division by Zero error:

```
Dim a as Integer = 10
Dim b as Integer = 0
Dim c as Integer = 0

Try
b = a / c
Catch
      MessageBox.Show(err.ToString)
b=0
End Try
```

In the preceding code, we begin with the three integer variables a, b, and c. The variable b is going to hold the value of a divided by c. Because we initialize c with a value of 0, the attempted division is met with an error. The line is inside the Try block of code, so it'll then move on to the Catch block for handling the error. We display a MessageBox that details the error and then sets the variable b equal to 0 so that the program can continue execution.

At this time, the code will set b equal to 0 regardless of the program error. We can further enhance this example by checking for the specific Division by Zero error as follows:

```
Dim a as Integer = 10
Dim b as Integer = 0
Dim c as Integer = 0

Try
    b = a / c
Catch As DivideByZeroException
    MessageBox.Show("You tried to divide by zero.")
    b=0
Catch err As Exception
    MessageBoxShow(err.ToString)
End Try
```

This example checks the DivideByZeroException. If the code encounters it, the appropriate code will execute. Otherwise, the code will continue on and the next Catch will find any other errors that are generated.

CHAPTER REVIEW

Like previous chapters, we covered a great deal of information beginning with .NET strings. From strings, we ventured into graphics with GDI +, the Graphics class, objects, and touched upon some of the error-handling capabilities of VB.NET.

In the next chapter, we're going to cover .NET math.

CHAPTER

7

MATH AND RANDOM NUMBER FUNCTIONS IN VB.NET

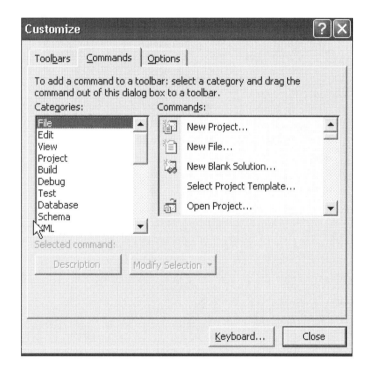

I n previous versions of VB, there were a multitude of functions that aided a developer in the creation of complex mathematical development. The functions also exist in VB.NET, but like everything else, they're implemented a little differently and reside in the `System.Math` class.

SYSTEM.MATH

The `System.Math` class contains a variety of methods that you can use for mathematical calculations. There are functions such as square root, Pi, absolute value, rounding, and trigonometry to name a few. We'll look at each of them in a little detail here. Later in the book, we'll use them to build a fully functional calculator.

Raising to a Power

We'll begin our discussion of the `System.Math` class by looking at the `Pow` method. The `Pow` method is used to raise a number to a power. For example, you can raise a number to a power of 2 with the following code:

```
Dim X As Integer
X = Math.Pow(2, 2)
```

The preceding code is assuming that we imported the `System.Math` class. We then assign the integer variable X equal to 2 to a power of 2. We could also rewrite the code as follows:

```
Dim X As Integer
X = 2 ^ 2
```

Now, let's use the `Pow` method to do a useful calculation. For example, suppose we are interested in calculating the area of a circle (it is equal to Pi * radius squared). We could do it as follows:

```
Dim X as Double
Dim dblRadius as Double

dblRadius = 50
X = Math.PI * Math.Pow(radius,2)
```

The preceding code assigns a value of 50 to the radius and then calculates the area and assigns it to X. You'll notice that we used `Math.PI` for the value of Pi. It's another built-in method available to us in VB.NET.

Square Root

The square root method (`Sqrt`) resides in the `System.Math` class as do the other VB.NET math functions. You can use it to calculate the square root of a value. The following example demonstrates its use:

```
Dim X as Double
X = Sqrt (100)
```

Absolute Value

We can use the absolute value (`Abs`) method to return an absolute value of a number. If you're unfamiliar with the absolute value, it's simply the value of a number without regard to its sign. In other words, it's a positive number. Here's an example:

```
Dim X as Double
X = Abs( -10.5)
```

This will return a value of `10.5`. Similarly, the following example will return the same value:

```
Dim X as Double
X = Abs(10.5)
```

Likewise, if you'd like to return the sign of a number, you can use the `Sign` method. If the number is negative, `Sign` returns -1; if it's positive, `Sign` returns 1; and if the number is equal to 0, `Sign` returns 0.

Here's an example:

```
Dim X1, X2, X3 As Double
Dim X4 As Integer
X1 = 5
X2 = -5
X3 = 0
X4 = Sign(X1)
```

This returns a value of 1:

```
Dim X1, X2, X3 As Double
Dim X4 As Integer
X1 = 5
X2 = -5
X3 = 0
X4 = Sign(X2)
```

This returns a value of −1:

```
Dim X1, X2, X3 As Double
Dim X4 As Integer
X1 = 5
X2 = -5
X3 = 0
X4 = Sign(X3)
```

This returns a value of 0:

Rounding Numbers

If you need to round values to the nearest Integer value, you can use the Round method. As an example, suppose you have a value of 5.12345 and need to round it:

```
Dim X as Double
X = Math.Round(5.12345)
```

This will round it to 5.

There are a few things to remember when using the Round method. If you have a number that's between two numbers (such as 5.5 or 6.5), the method may not return what you would at first believe. Most people would round these values up to the next highest value. However, if you created the following code, something interesting would happen:

```
Dim X1, X2 As Double
X1 = Math.Round(5.5)
X2 = Math.Round(6.5)
```

The values of X1 and X2 both return values of 6. The reason for this is that the Round method will actually return the even number closest to the two.

To truncate a number in VB.NET, you can use the `Floor` method. It returns the largest whole number smaller than the original number. So, the following code will return 5:

```
Dim X as Double
X = Math.Floor(5.6)
```

Negative values can behave unexpectedly, so you have to pay special attention to them. For example, if you were to create a similar project with a negative value, it would return a -6:

```
Dim X as Double
X = Math.Floor(-5.6)
```

Trigonometry

The `Math` class also contains a number of methods for making trigonometric and logarithmic calculations. These include methods for `Sin`, `Cos`, `Tan`, and `Atn`. They work like the other methods we've been looking at throughout the chapter:

```
Dim X as Double
X = Sin(1.1)
```

This will return a value in radians. If you'd like to convert from radians to degrees, you multiply by 180/Pi:

```
Dim X As Double
X = 180 / Math.PI * Sin(1.1)
Debug.WriteLine(X)
```

 If you have a degree value, you can convert it to radians by multiplying by Pi/180.

Logarithms

The `System.Math` class also provides functionality for logs and natural logs. You can use the `Exp` method of the class to return e raised to a power:

```
Dim X as Double
X = Math.Exp(2)
```

You can also use the `Log` method of the `Math` class to return the natural logarithm of a number:

```
Dim X as Double
X = Math.Log(5)
```

CREATING YOUR OWN MATH FUNCTIONS

There are obviously many great methods related to math built into the `System.Math` class. However, there are going to be times when you need to create your own. We can take a simple example for conversions to see how and why you'll do so. For example, let's suppose you're trying to convert Celsius to Fahrenheit. The formula for conversion is as follows: Celsius to Farhenheit:

```
Value * 1.8 + 32
```

Farhenheit to Celsuis:

```
(Value–32)/1.8
```

The functions can then be created as follows:

```
Function CToF(ByVal value as Single) as Single
    CToF = value * 1.8  +32
End Function

Function FToC(ByVal value as Single) as Single
    FToC=(value-32)/1.8
End Function
```

We can use the functions in a program as follows:

```
Dim X As Single
X = CToF(25)
```

Here's another example. Let's suppose we need to return the decimal part of a number. We can calculate this simply by subtracting the number from the decimal portion:

```
Function Decm(Value as Double) As Double
    Decm = value–fix(value)
```

```
End Function
```

We could then use this as follows:

```
Dim X as Double
X = Decm(10.5)
```

This would return a value of 0.5.

GENERATING RANDOM NUMBERS

The `System.Random` class is used to draw a random number, and unlike the VB 6 `Rnd` function, `System.Random` can return both decimal and whole random numbers. Additionally, unlike `Rnd`, `System.Random` automatically seeds its random number generator with a random value derived from the current date and time.

You can use the `NextDouble` method of `System.Random` to return a `Double` random number between 0 and 1. You can use the `Next` method to return an `Integer` random number between two `Integer` values. The following example returns the random number:

```
Dim X As Double
Dim rnd As System.Random = New System.Random()
Dim i As Integer

For i = 1 To 10
    X = Round(rnd.NextDouble() * 10)
    Debug.WriteLine(X)
Next
```

This code will display a series of random numbers between 0 and 10. You can also use the `Next` method as follows:

```
Dim X As Double
Dim rnd As System.Random = New System.Random()
Dim i As Integer

For i = 1 To 10
    X = rnd.Next(0, 10)
    Debug.WriteLine(X)
Next
```

CHAPTER REVIEW

In this chapter, we worked on several topics that were related to the math functions available to us in VB.NET. This is the final chapter that will consist of only text information. In all of the remaining chapters, we're going to build applications. In doing so, we'll put some of the information that we have used to good use and we'll learn about many new topics as well.

In the next chapter, we're going to create our first VB.NET application.

8

YOUR FIRST PROGRAM

```
C:\Documents and Settings\Clayton\My Documents\VB.NET Book\Chapter 8\Project\Chapter...
Hello World!
Press any key to continue
```

N
ow that we've walked through some of the changes in VB.NET, we're going to take some of what we've learned and put it into a simple Hello World! application. We're going to create a Console application that will simply open and display the Hello World! text on the screen. This is by far the easiest application we'll create in the book. Nevertheless, it's still a good way to become acquainted with the integrated development environment (IDE) and learn how to build a VB.NET program.

TUTORIAL   USING THE IDE

At this time, it's assumed that you have a version of Visual Basic.NET installed on your PC and that you have set the profile information as directed in Chapter 1. Although it's not a requirement, the profile settings in the first chapter will allow your display and the figures in this chapter to be very similar.

You can follow these steps to create the simple application and use the basic settings of the VB.NET IDE:

1. Open the Visual Studio.NET IDE which can be seen in Figure 8.1.

FIGURE 8.1   The Visual Studio.NET IDE.

2. At this time, the IDE should be at the Start Page where you can select New Project. Alternately, you can choose File | New Project. Either way, the New Project window will be displayed (see Figure 8.2).

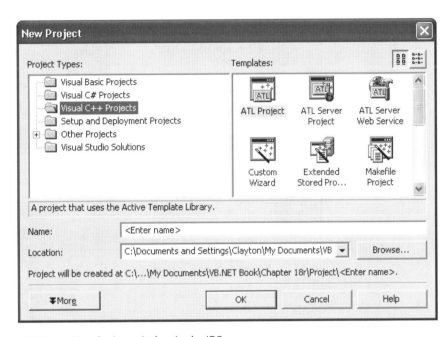

FIGURE 8.2   New Project window in the IDE.

3. Assign a location for the file to be stored along with a name for your project. These items can be set as you'd like but something like the following would work well:

```
Name: Chapter8
Location: C:\VBNET\Projects\
```

4. You'll notice a variety of application templates that can be used in VB.NET. At the left of the window, you'll see the Project Types list. Make sure that Visual Basic Projects is selected from the list as it is in Figure 8.3.
    The following list details the various templates:

- Windows Application: Traditional standalone Windows application.
- Class Library: A windowless project that's a reusable class or component that can be shared with other projects.
- Windows Control Library: Custom control to use on Windows Forms.
- ASP.NET Web Application: Creation of an ASP.NET Web application.

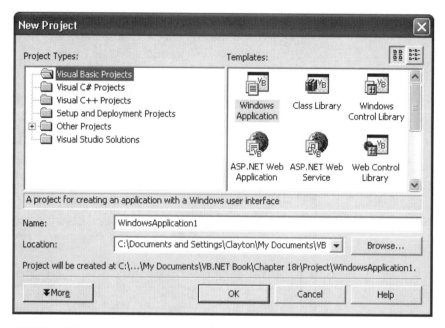

FIGURE 8.3 VB needs to be selected as the Project Type.

- ASP.NET Web Service: XML Web services authored with ASP.NET that can be published and called by an external application.
- Web Control Library: Custom control that can be used on Web Forms pages (similar to ActiveX-control creation in VB 6).
- Console Application: Command-line application; we're using this in our program.
- Windows Service: Applications that don't have a user interface. Formerly called NT services, these applications are used to do things such as monitor files or check performance of the machine.
- Empty Project: Empty project with the necessary file structure to store application information but all references, files, or components must be added manually.
- Empty Web Project: Empty environment for server-based application.
- New Project in Existing Folder: Blank project within an existing application folder for using files from a preexisting project.

For our application, we're going to choose Console Application. Once you have your file location and name settings and have clicked Console Application, click the OK button. Your screen should change to look like Figure 8.4.

FIGURE 8.4   The application has been created.

We're now in Module1.VB. You'll notice the Toolbox on the left side of the IDE and the Solution Explorer on the right. Because this is such a simple application, we don't really have a need for either of these at this time, but you can see where they're located. We'll use them in later chapters.

WRITING CODE

We're now in good position to write some code for our application. This will consist of a single line of output to the Console window that displays the characters, *Hello World!*. We'll first do this in a single line, then we'll do this using a variable. Lastly, we'll do this by using the Imports keyword. All of them are equally effective for this application, but it's useful to compare how you can do various things in VB.NET.

Single Line

Our first attempt at this application is to write a single line of code to output to the Console window. You'll see that the current VB created code is similar to the following:

```
Module Module1

    Sub Main()

    End Sub

End Module
```

`Sub Main()` is the entry point for our application. We'll need to write our output line between `Sub Main ()` and `End Sub`. We're going to use the `Systems.Console` class to display information to the window. First, click in the code editor so that your cursor is positioned between the `Sub Main()` and `End Sub` code. Next, add the following text:

```
System.
```

You'll notice that as soon as you add the period, Visual Studio will help you with the names of classes and functions (see Figure 8.5) because the .NET Framework publishes the type information.

You can continue adding characters to the line such as these:

```
System.Cons
```

At this time, you'll see `System.Console` selected. You can continue typing the rest of the word *Console* or simply hit the Tab key on your keyboard to move to the next item.

Continue adding the following code:

```
System.Console.writeline
```

Again, you can type out the entire line or let Visual Studio fill it in for you and then hit the Tab key. Either way, when you've finished typing the line, you need to hit the space bar, which brings up the parameter list for the class (see Figure 8.6).

You can scroll through the list using the arrow keys. Figures 8.7, 8.8, and 8.9 show a few of the options.

FIGURE 8.5   Visual Studio helps you with available classes and functions.

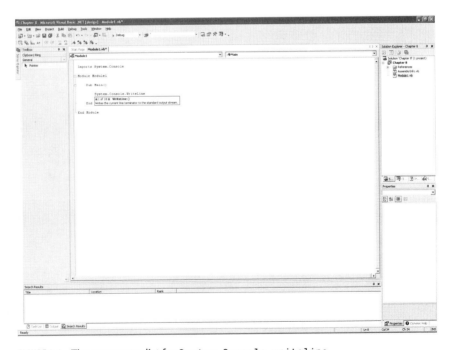

FIGURE 8.6   The parameter list for `System.Console.writeline`.

FIGURE 8.7 The first parameter list.

FIGURE 8.8 A second type of parameter.

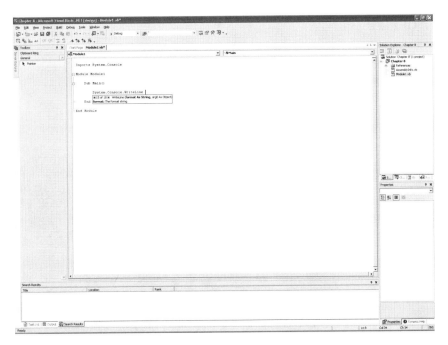

FIGURE 8.9 Third parameter.

The list continues on, and in this case, there are 18 parameters. You don't have to scroll through each of the items unless you choose to do so. It's a great feature if you don't know or remember the various parameters for a class or function.

We simply need to complete the line as follows:

```
System.Console.WriteLine("Hello World!")
```

Our complete code listing should look like this:

```
Module Module1

  Sub Main()
    System.Console.WriteLine("Hello World")
  End Sub

End Module
```

EXECUTING THE PROGRAM

We're now ready to execute the program in the IDE to see if it works. You can choose Debug | Start Without Debugging or press Ctrl +F5 as a shortcut. This will start the program and you'll see a window similar to Figure 8.10 displayed on your screen.

FIGURE 8.10 The Hello World! application.

That's all there is to this first application. If you hit any key on your keyboard, you'll return to the IDE. We're now going to implement the program in a slightly different way to use a simple variable so that you can get used to a few features in VB.NET.

USING A VARIABLE

We've discussed variables and declaring them in previous chapters so we don't have to spend a great deal of time on the concepts in this chapter. We're going to create a variable of type `String` and then assign the variable a value. We'll then use the `System.Console` class to display this information as we did in the first example.

Begin by removing the `System.Console.WriteLine("Hello World")` line from the code window.

```
Module Module1

    Sub Main()
```

```
       End Sub

End Module
```

We're now back to our original code listing. If you'd prefer, you can start a new project instead of removing the code, but because it's only a single line, it's probably unnecessary.

We'll begin by adding the following variable declaration to the code:

```
Dim str as String
```

This code will be placed after `Sub Main()` so that the listing looks like this:

```
Module Module1

  Sub Main()
      Dim str As String

  End Sub

End Module
```

The next step is to assign a value to the `str` variable:

```
str = "Hello World"
```

The code should now look as follows:

```
Module Module1

  Sub Main()
      Dim str As String
      str = "Hello World"

  End Sub

End Module
```

Lastly, we use the same `WriteLine` method of the `System.Console` class to output the variable information:

```
System.Console.WriteLine(str)
```

The final listing is as follows:

```
Module Module1

  Sub Main()
    Dim str As String
      str = "Hello World"
      System.Console.WriteLine(str)
  End Sub

  End Module
```

 Although every effort is made to ensure the code looks exactly as it does in your pro-ject, some of the code might wrap differently in the book. You can refer to the actual source code on the CD-ROM if you have questions about the code.

TESTING THE PROGRAM

Again, you can test the functionality of the program by choosing Debug | Start without Debugging (Ctrl+F5 is the shortcut to this function).

Your output should look like Figure 8.11.

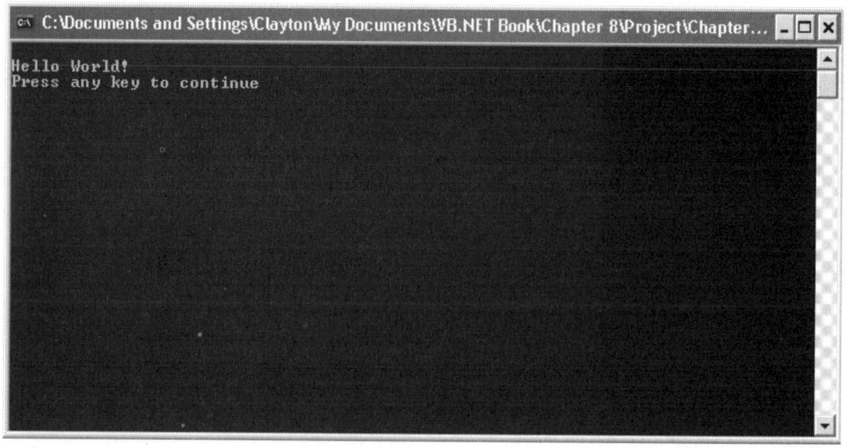

FIGURE 8.11   The output of the second program.

IMPORTS KEYWORD

Both of the options have worked and we're now going to look at a third one. This time, we're going to use the `Imports` keyword to import the `System.Console` class into our application. This will import all of the members of the `System.Console` namespace into our application. Although we have only one line that uses it in this example, you can see how this will very effectively save time when you're using much longer examples.

You can add the following `Imports` line above `Module Module1` in the code:

```
Imports System.Console
```

The code then looks as follows:

```
Imports System.Console

Module Module1

  Sub Main()
      Dim str As String
      str = "Hello World"
      System.Console.WriteLine(str)
  End Sub

End Module
```

We can then shorten the `System.Console.WriteLine(str)` line of code:

```
System.Console.WriteLine(str)
```

To

```
WriteLine(str)
```

The final code should now read:

```
Imports System.Console

Module Module1

  Sub Main()
      Dim str As String
      str = "Hello World"
```

```
            WriteLine(str)
        End Sub

    End Module
```

If you run the application again, your output will look like Figure 8.12.

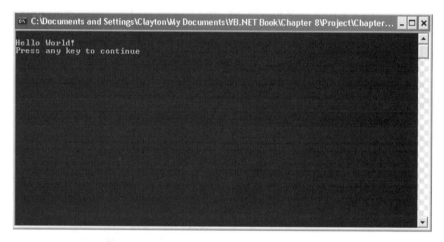

FIGURE 8.12   The final example.

FINAL CODE LISTING

The following code listings are the final listings for the three examples in this chapter:

Example 1:

```
Module Module1

    Sub Main()
        System.Console.WriteLine("Hello World")
    End Sub

End Module
```

Example 2:

```
Module Module1
```

```
Sub Main()
    Dim str As String
    str = "Hello World"
    System.Console.WriteLine(str)
End Sub

End Module
```

Example 3:

```
Imports System.Console

Module Module1

Sub Main()
    Dim str As String
    str = "Hello World"
    WriteLine(str)
End Sub

End Module
```

CHAPTER REVIEW

In this chapter, we built our first VB.NET application. While it was a simple example, it's a good basis for what we're going to do in the next chapter, which is to design a console application that takes user input and provides output. It will take the input of two numbers, calculate the third number, and then output it to the Console window.

CONSOLE APPLICATION INPUT/OUTPUT

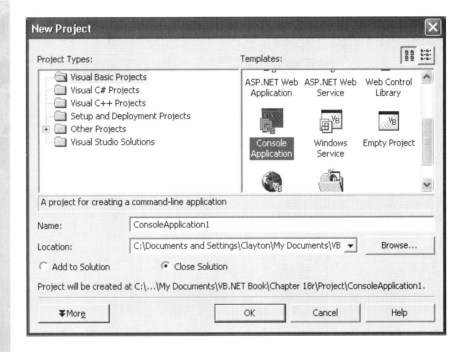

n the previous chapter, we spent some time putting together a very simple Console application that displayed Hello World! when executed. We're going to take what we learned in the example, and apply it to a new application that will add together numbers after they're input by the user. We'll then add the ability to calculate the Sine of a number to show the basics of the Trig functions being used in VB.NET.

GETTING STARTED

To start, we open Visual Basic and then choose Console Application from the Templates Library (see Figure 9.1).

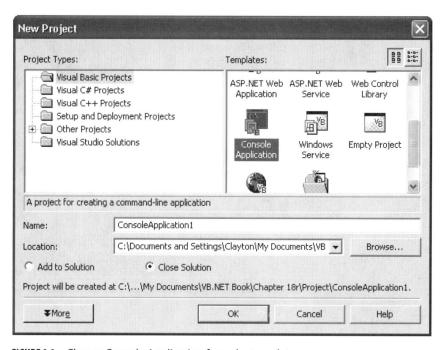

FIGURE 9.1   Choose Console Application from the templates.

Next, we're going to add some code to the project.

Writing Some Code

The first line of code to be added to the application will be Imports System.Console. This line must be present before Module Module1 and your code should look like the following listing after you enter it:

```
Imports System.Console
Module Module1

Sub Main()

End Sub

End Module
```

Next, we need to declare a couple of variables for the application:

```
Dim X,Y As Double
```

These variables are going to be used to store the values that are being input by the user and should be placed after the `Sub Main()` line in the code window. The code should look like the following list:

```
Imports System.Console
Module Module1

Sub Main()
Dim X, Y As Double
End Sub

End Module
```

Now, we're at a point to begin handling the input, but first, we need to let the user know that we're requesting information from them. We'll begin by using a `Write()` method to output text information such as "Please Enter First Number:". Instead of `WriteLine()`, which actually creates an entire line with a carriage return, we'll use `Write()` so that we can leave our cursor immediately beyond the end of the line for the user input.

Here's the code with the `Write()` method added:

```
Imports System.Console
Module Module1

Sub Main()
    Dim X, Y As Double
    Write("Please Enter First Number: ")
End Sub

End Module
```

Next, we're ready to handle the input from the user and store it in variable X. We can use the `ReadLine()` method to handle this input:

```
Imports System.Console
Module Module1

Sub Main()
    Dim X, Y As Double
    Write("Please Enter First Number: ")
    X = ReadLine()
End Module
```

We can repeat this same approach for output and input for variable Y:

```
Imports System.Console
Module Module1

Sub Main()
    Dim X, Y As Double
    Write("Please Enter First Number: ")
    X = ReadLine()
    Write("Please Enter Second Number: ")
    Y = ReadLine()
End Sub

End Module
```

The final step for this section of the code is to add together the numbers and then display the output using a `Write()` and `WriteLine()` method. We're using both methods as we'll use `Write()` to display text such as "Your final answer is:" and then we'll use `WriteLine()` to actually display the answer:

```
Imports System.Console
Module Module1

Sub Main()
    Dim X, Y As Double
    Write("Please Enter First Number: ")
    X = ReadLine()
    Write("Please Enter Second Number: ")
    Y = ReadLine()
    Write("Your final answer is: ")
    WriteLine(X + Y)
```

```
End Sub

End Module
```

If you run the application using Debug | Start without Debugging, you'll see output similar to Figure 9.2.

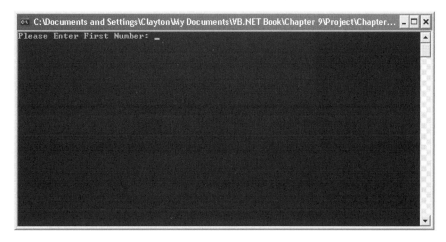

FIGURE 9.2   The code being executed.

We can check the input and output by entering values as prompted. Give a value of 10 and then hit the Enter key on the keyboard. Your window should now look like Figure 9.3.

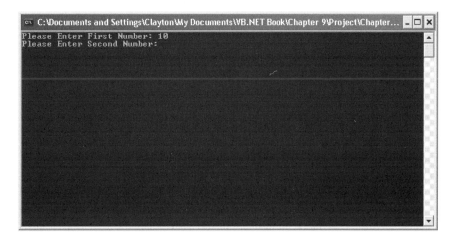

FIGURE 9.3   The program is asking for additional input.

Enter a value of 20 and then hit the enter key. This will move the program through the input and then it'll display the final answer of 30 as seen in Figure 9.4.

FIGURE 9.4   The answer is displayed.

Because we used a `Double` as the type of variable, you can also use decimal point values in the program. Try the following combinations:

```
X: -1.5
Y: 1.5

X: 1.2345
Y: -55.3433

X: 3.75
Y: 4.25
```

The values should all work equally and they aren't dependent on positive or negative values.

TRIG CALCULATIONS

The final step we're going to take in this program is to add one additional calculation. This time, we'll leave the addition operation as is but we're going to add input and output capabilities to calculate the `Sine` of a number.

This will require the same `ReadLine()`, `Write()` and `WriteLine()` methods that we used before:

```
Imports System.Console
Module Module1

Sub Main()
    Dim X, Y As Double
    Write("Please Enter First Number: ")
    X = ReadLine()
    Write("Please Enter Second Number: ")
    Y = ReadLine()
    Write("Your final answer is: ")
    WriteLine(X + Y)

    WriteLine()
    Write("Calculate Sine of what number: ")
    X = ReadLine()
End Sub

End Module
```

You'll notice that we're utilizing the same variable of X for reading the number. The next step is to then take the value stored in X and assign X equal to the Sine of the value using the Sin method:

```
Imports System.Console
Module Module1

Sub Main()
    Dim X, Y As Double
    Write("Please Enter First Number: ")
    X = ReadLine()
    Write("Please Enter Second Number: ")
    Y = ReadLine()
    Write("Your final answer is: ")
    WriteLine(X + Y)

    WriteLine()
    Write("Calculate Sine of what number: ")
    X = ReadLine()
    X = System.Math.Sin(X)
End Sub

End Module
```

Lastly, we'll use the `Write()` and `WriteLine()` methods to display the output:

```
Imports System.Console
Module Module1

Sub Main()
    Dim X, Y As Double
    Write("Please Enter First Number: ")
    X = ReadLine()
    Write("Please Enter Second Number: ")
    Y = ReadLine()
    Write("Your final answer is: ")
    WriteLine(X + Y)

    WriteLine()
    Write("Calculate Sine of what number: ")
    X = ReadLine()
    X = System.Math.Sin(X)
    Write("The Sine is: ")
    WriteLine(X)
End Sub

End Module
```

If you were to run the program at this time, it would prompt you for the first two values and then it would display the result after they have been added together. Then, after the calculation, the program would prompt you to enter another value. The program would then output the Sine of the value (see Figure 9.5).

FINAL CODE LISTING

This is the final code listing for this chapter:

```
Imports System.Console
Module Module1

Sub Main()
    Dim X, Y As Double
    Write("Please Enter First Number: ")
    X = ReadLine()
    Write("Please Enter Second Number: ")
```

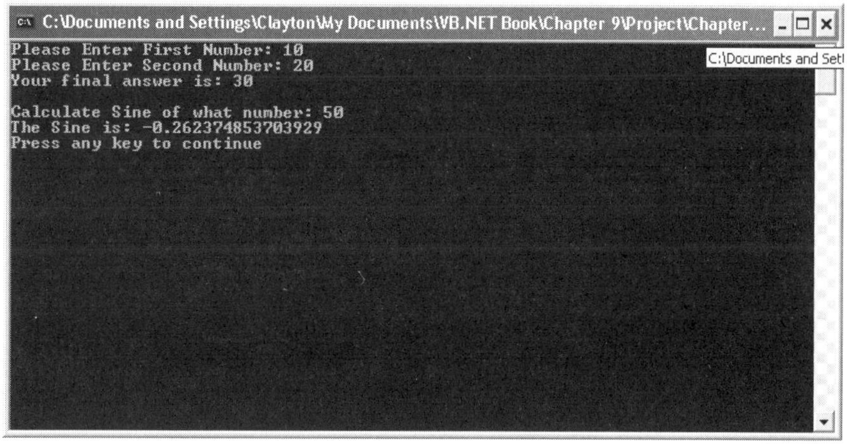

FIGURE 9.5   The final program is being executed.

```
        Y = ReadLine()
        Write("Your final answer is: ")
        WriteLine(X + Y)

        WriteLine()
        Write("Calculate Sine of what number: ")
        X = ReadLine()
        X = System.Math.Sin(X)
        Write("The Sine is: ")
        WriteLine(X)
    End Sub

End Module
```

CHAPTER REVIEW

In this chapter, we created another Console application, but unlike the previous chapter, we responded to user input and then made a few simple calculations based on the values that were entered. We used the Read-Line() method of the System.Console class to capture the input values, and the Sin() method of the System.Math class to calculate the Sine of the number that was being entered.

In the next chapter, we're going to build our last Console application, this time using the Sort() method that's included in the System.Console class.

SORTING IN VB.NET

```
C:\Documents and Settings\Clayton\My Documents\VB.NET Book\Chapter 10\Project\Chapte...
How many names would you like to sort : 5
Please Enter Name # 1 : John
Please Enter Name # 2 : Bob
Please Enter Name # 3 : Bill
Please Enter Name # 4 : Fred
Please Enter Name # 5 : Sally
Sort 0 : Bill
Sort 1 : Bob
Sort 2 : Fred
Sort 3 : John
Sort 4 : Sally
Reverse 0 : Sally
Reverse 1 : John
Reverse 2 : Fred
Reverse 3 : Bob
Reverse 4 : Bill
Press any key to continue
```

I n the previous two chapters, we built Console applications so we won't spend a great deal of time in the setup of this one. We're building an application that will take user input in the form of string values and then sort them alphabetically. We'll also then sort them in reverse order (see Figure 10.1)

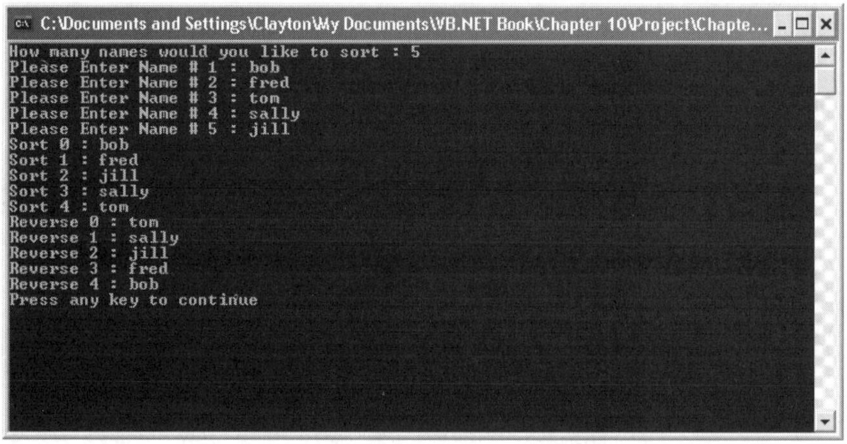

FIGURE 10.1 The application we're going to build in this chapter sorts and reverses names.

GETTING STARTED

Like the earlier applications, the first step is to start Visual Basic and select Console Application from the templates. This will open display Module 1 where we can begin to add the code for our application. Our first line of code will be to import the System.Console class into the application:

```
Imports System.Console
```

Remember that this line needs to be placed above any other lines of code in the application.

The next step is to create the variables for our application. We'll need a variable to store the text information that will be entered by the user at runtime along with variables for a loop that we'll use.

The first variable we'll create is ArrayList. It'll be used to store the information that the users will enter when the program is being run. The following code is all that's required to create it:

```
Dim X As New ArrayList()
```

It should be entered immediately after the `Module Module1` line of code:

```
Imports System.Console

Module Module1
    Dim X As New ArrayList()

    Sub Main()

    End Sub

End Module
```

The next two variables will be of type `Integer`. They are listed as follows:

```
Dim I,Temp As Integer
```

This line of code should be placed directly beneath the previous line. The code should now look like the following list:

```
Imports System.Console

Module Module1
    Dim X As New ArrayList()
    Dim I, Temp As Integer

    Sub Main()

    End Sub

End Module
```

INPUT

The next step is to capture the input from the user. We begin by displaying the text information "How many names would you like to sort :". We then store the input from the user in the `Temp` value. Here's the code:

```
Imports System.Console

Module Module1
    Dim X As New ArrayList()
    Dim I, Temp As Integer
```

```
Sub Main()
    Write("How many names would you like to sort : ")
    Temp = ReadLine()

End Sub

End Module
```

The next step is to create a loop that will count through all of the values from 1 to the value stored in `Temp`. Inside this `For…Next` loop, we'll display text information that will prompt the user to enter a name. It'll also track which number we've currently entered. Next, we'll store the user input in the `ArrayList` variable X.

Here's the code:

```
Imports System.Console

Module Module1
    Dim X As New ArrayList()
    Dim I, Temp As Integer

    Sub Main()
Write("How many names would you like to sort : ")
Temp = ReadLine()

For I = 1 To Temp
Write("Please Enter Name # " & I & " : ")
X.Add(ReadLine())
Next

    End Sub

End Module
```

SUB PROCEDURES

Now, we have the information stored in the array. The next step is to create a procedure that will sort, reverse sort, and display the items. We can use the `Sort()` method of the `ArrayList` along with the `Reverse()` method. To display the items, we can create a `Sub` procedure that will count from 0 to Temp −1.

Let's begin by creating the procedure for sorting and reverse sorting the `ArrayList`. We'll use the `Sort()` method for the `ArrayList` and also the `Reverse` method. We can create two procedures for these methods:

```
Public Sub Sort()
    X.Sort()
End Sub

Public Sub Reverse()
    X.Reverse()
End Sub
```

Once the `ArrayList` has been sorted and reversed, we need a way to display it. We can create a procedure that will be passed a string value of either "Sort" or "Reverse", depending on which one we're displaying. The next step will be to count from 0 to `Temp`—1 and then step through the various elements in the `ArrayList`.

Here's the code:

```
Public Sub DisplayItems(ByVal str As String)
    For I = 0 To Temp - 1
Write(str & " " & I & " : ")
WriteLine(X(I))
    Next
End Sub
```

Now, we need to add the calls to the `DisplayItems` `Sub` procedure that we just created. The calls can be made in the `Sort` and `Reverse` procedures that we created:

```
Public Sub Sort()
    X.Sort()
    DisplayItems("Sort")
End Sub

Public Sub Reverse()
    X.Reverse()
    DisplayItems("Reverse")
End Sub
```

The last code we need to write consists of the calls to the `Sort` and `Re-verse` `Sub` procedures. These lines can be added to the bottom of the code immediately above the `End Sub` and `End Module` lines.

Here's the code listing without the `Sub` procedures showing the calls to `Sort` and `Reverse`:

```
Imports System.Console

Module Module1
    Dim X As New ArrayList()
    Dim I, Temp As Integer

    Sub Main()
Write("How many names would you like to sort : ")
Temp = ReadLine()

For I = 1 To Temp
    Write("Please Enter Name # " & I & " : ")
    X.Add(ReadLine())
Next

Sort()

Reverse()

    End Sub

End Module
```

TESTING THE APPLICATION

If you were to run the application (Ctrl-F5), you would see a screen like Figure 10.2.

Enter a 5 and then hit Enter. This will display a screen like Figure 10.3.

The next step is to enter five names, one at a time, hitting Enter between them. You can use the following list:

John
Bob
Bill
Fred
Sally

Once you've entered all five names, the program will sort them alphabetically and then in reverse order (see Figure 10.4).

FIGURE 10.2   You need to enter a number before moving on.

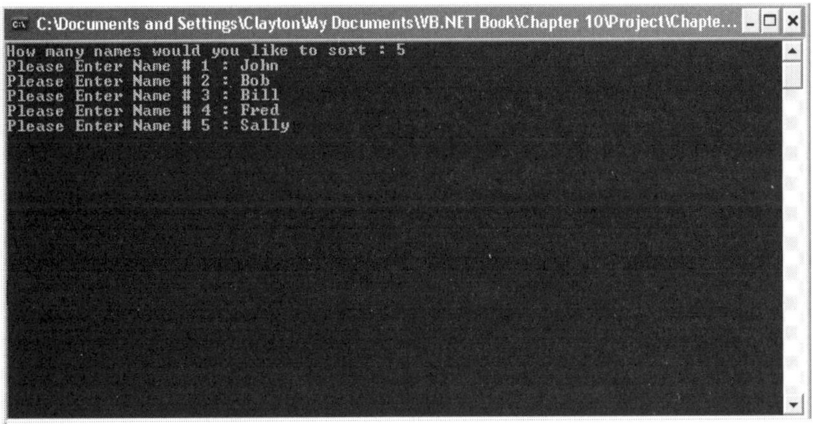

FIGURE 10.3   The application waits for you to enter the five names.

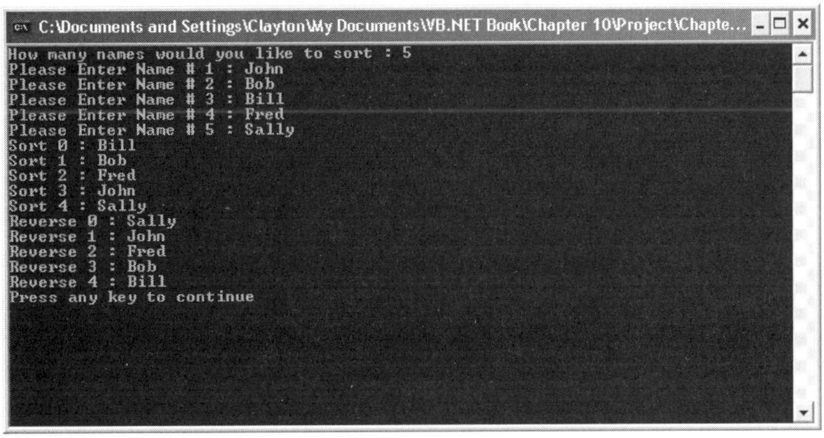

FIGURE 10.4   The names sorted and reversed.

FINAL CODE LISTING

Here's the final code listing for this chapter:

```
Imports System.Console

Module Module1
    Dim X As New ArrayList()
    Dim I, Temp As Integer

    Public Sub DisplayItems(ByVal str As String)
For I = 0 To Temp - 1
    Write(str & " " & I & " : ")
    WriteLine(X(I))
Next
    End Sub

    Public Sub Sort()
X.Sort()
DisplayItems("Sort")
    End Sub

    Public Sub Reverse()
X.Reverse()
DisplayItems("Reverse")
    End Sub

    Sub Main()
Write("How many names would you like to sort : ")
Temp = ReadLine()

For I = 1 To Temp
    Write("Please Enter Name # " & I & " : ")
    X.Add(ReadLine())
Next

Sort()

Reverse()

    End Sub

End Module
```

CHAPTER REVIEW

In this chapter, we built our third and final Console application. We created our first `Sub` procedures in this application and also used various methods of the `ArrayList` along with the `ReadLine()`, `Write()` and `Write-Line()` methods of the `System.Console` class.

In the next chapter, we're going to build our first VB.NET Windows Form Application.

11

YOUR FIRST WINDOWS
FORM APPLICATION

I n the previous three chapters, we built console applications in VB.NET.
In this chapter, we'll look at building a Windows Form application,
which is a much more common type of program for VB developers
(see Figure 11.1).

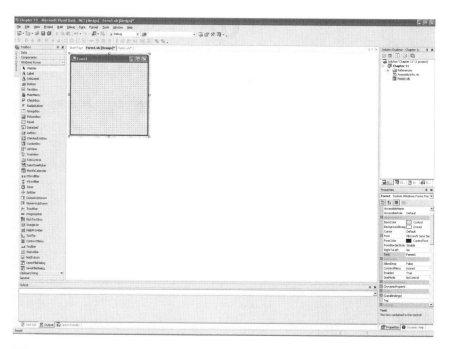

FIGURE 11.1   A Windows Form application.

TUTORIAL

PROJECT OVERVIEW

We'll begin this chapter by creating a user interface for our application. The
user interface is probably the first step you'll take when developing most typical VB.NET applications. Follow these steps to create the user interface:

1. Start the Visual Basic IDE and select Windows Form Application from the
   templates that appear.
2. Place controls on the default form that appears. There are two separate
   approaches you can use to do this. You can double-click on one of the intrinsic Visual Basic controls that appear in the toolbar, which will place a
   single instance of the control on the Form. Alternatively, you can click the
   tool in the Toolbox.

3. Move the mouse pointer to the Form window where the cursor changes to a crosshair.
4. Place the crosshair at the upper-left corner of where you want to position the control.
5. Press the left mouse button and hold it down while dragging the cursor toward the lower-right corner. As you can see in Figure 11.2, when you release the mouse button, the control is drawn.

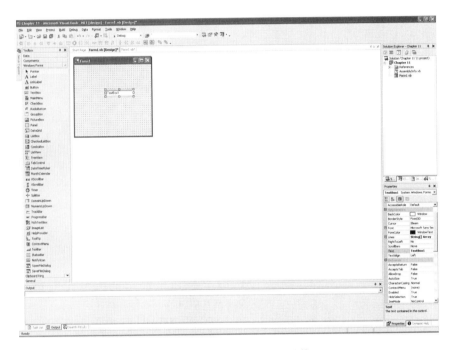

FIGURE 11.2   You can place controls on a form in several different ways.

You don't have to place controls precisely where you want them as you can move them. Visual Basic provides the necessary tool to reposition them at any time during the development process. To move a control you've created with either process, click the object in the Form window and drag it, releasing the mouse button when you have it in the correct location. You can resize a control very easily as well by clicking the object so that it's in focus and the sizing handles appear (see Figure 11.3). These handles can then be clicked and dragged to resize the object.

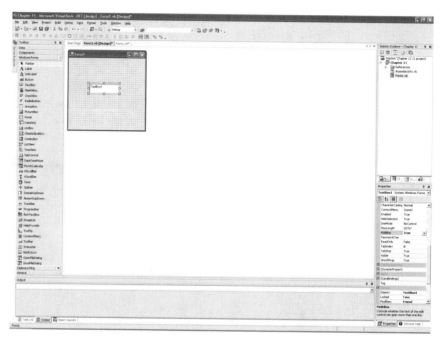

FIGURE 11.3   Handles are useful for positioning and resizing objects.

Follow these steps to create your first project:

1. Place a text box and a Command button on the form and position them so that they look something like Figure 11.4.

   The Command button will need to have its Text property changed in the Properties window. It can be changed to *Click* (see Figure 11.5).
2. Double-click the Command button, which will bring up the code window and leave you something that looks similar to Figure 11.6.
3. Your cursor should be flashing beneath the Private Sub Command1_Click() line. Type the following lines into your application:

```
Private Sub Button1_Click(ByVal sender As System.Object, ByVal
e As System.EventArgs) Handles Button1.Click
    Dim strInfo As String
    strInfo = "My First Windows Application"
    MessageBox.Show("Hello World")
    End Sub
```

4. Click on the tab at the top of the screen that says Form1.vb [Design].
5. Double-click on the form to open the Form_Load event.

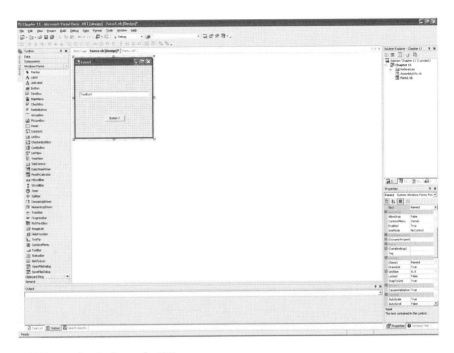

FIGURE 11.4   Beginnings of a GUI.

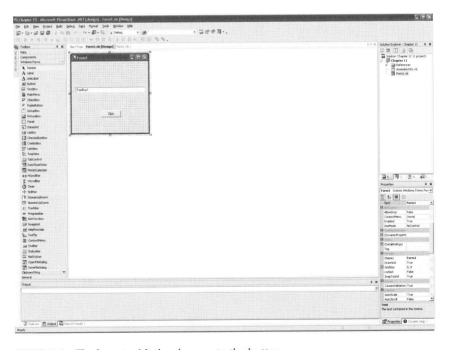

FIGURE 11.5   The layout with the changes to the button.

FIGURE 11.6   When you double-click an object on a Visual Basic form, it opens an event in the code window.

6. Enter the following code and continue reading for an explanation:

```
Private Sub Form1_Load(ByVal sender As System.Object, ByVal e
As System.EventArgs) Handles MyBase.Load

    TextBox1.Text = "Form Load"

End Sub
```

ON THE CD

The CD-ROM that's included with this book contains all of the sample code for each of the projects that we'll create. This saves you time and programming mistakes, which will allow you to focus only on the task at hand—learning VB.NET. It also contains several additional applications. Please see the CD-ROM for a complete list of projects and applications.

THE CODE EXPLANATION

That's all we need for this application. Although this project is very simple, we did use variables for storing text information. Now is the time to point out several features of VB.NET. First, there are a few simple rules that you should keep in mind when using variables:

- Make them less than 255 characters
- Include letters, numbers, and underscores (_)
- Avoid using one of the Visual Basic reserved words—for example, you cannot name a variable `Text`
- Begin them with a letter

Now, let's look carefully at what the code does. The line that begins with `Private Sub Button1_Click` tells Visual Basic to run the procedure when someone clicks on the Command button that you created called Button1. When they do, the lines of code you typed in are executed. Interestingly, it isn't the beginning part of the line that really matters in this case. Instead, the end of the line which reads `Handles Button1_Click` instructs Visual Basic to handle the clicking of the button. Visual Basic assigns the name to the beginning part of this line for us automatically so that it is easier for programmers to follow along, especially those with prior Visual Basic experience.

The `End Sub` simply informs Visual Basic that it's time to stop running the code. This event and subsequent code was created automatically for you when you double-clicked on Button1 in a previous step. The `Form_Load` event was created automatically for you when you double-clicked the form. Inside the event, you added a line that set the text box equal to Hello World.

Similar to the `Button1_Click` event, the code is run only as the form is loaded when the program runs. The first line of code that you entered creates the variable `strInfo` as a string. The next line assigns the text string `Form   Load` to the variable and the final line uses the `MessageBox.Show` method to display the message box.

You may have noticed some additional code in your code editor that we haven't looked at or mentioned in this example. Specifically, you'll see something that says `Windows Form Designer Generate Code` that contains a plus (+) sign next to it. If you click the plus sign, you'll see an enormous amount of code that was created for you automatically. This code is the underlying code that is created when you make a form. We'll ignore this section of code for the examples in this book. Because the code will be created by VB.NET automatically, we don't really have a need to list it.

RUNNING THE PROGRAM

You can execute the program from within Visual Basic by pressing Ctrl-F5. You should see a window that appears something like Figure 11.7.

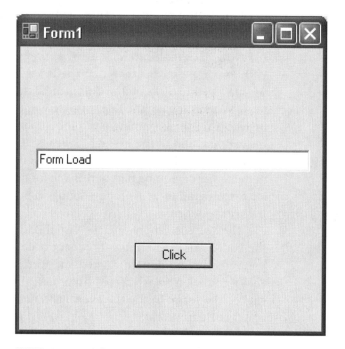

FIGURE 11.7   Your first program is running inside the IDE.

You can close it like any Windows program or select the Stop button from within the Visual Basic IDE.

You've created your first Windows Forms program. You can save your changes, if you would like, by choosing File | Save. When saving a project, it's best to create a new directory in which you can store all the files necessary for the project. In this way, you keep the files in one easy-to-manage area without the risk of another project corrupting the source code or data.

COMPLETE CODE LISTING

The following code is the complete listing for this chapter:

```
Public Class Form1
    Inherits System.Windows.Forms.Form

    Private Sub Button1_Click(ByVal sender As System.Object,
ByVal e As System.EventArgs) Handles Button1.Click
    Dim strInfo As String
    strInfo = "My First Windows Application"
    TextBox1.Text = strInfo
    MessageBox.Show("Hello World")
    End Sub

    Private Sub Form1_Load(ByVal sender As System.Object, ByVal e
As System.EventArgs) Handles MyBase.Load
    TextBox1.Text = "Form Load"
    End Sub
End Class
```

CHAPTER REVIEW

In this chapter, we built our first Windows Form Application after dealing with Console Applications in the chapters leading up to this. The ability to develop both types are a big plus for VB.NET developers. In this first Windows Form Application, we developed a simple application by using a few intrinsic controls and some basic code, and then proceeded to run it inside the Visual Basic IDE.

Now that you have some of the basics out of the way, let's move to the next chapter where the real fun begins as we create a VB calculator.

12

VB CALCULATOR

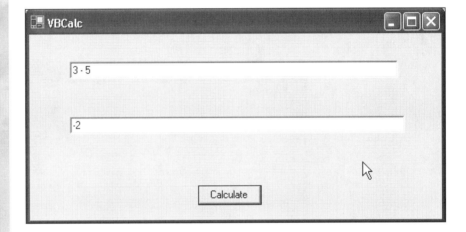

n the previous chapter we created our first Windows Forms application. In this chapter, we're going to build another Windows Forms project. But this time, we're going to create a calculator that can be used for adding, subtracting, multiplication, and division.

GETTING STARTED

Although this program is going to have functions similar to a standard calculator, we're not going to design the user interface in this manner. Instead, the program will look something like Figure 12.1 and will allow user input via a TextBox control.

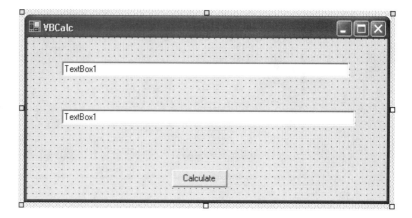

FIGURE 12.1   The user interface for the program.

The user will enter their information in the following manner:

1. Enter first #
2. An operator (*,-,+,/)
3. Enter second #

The result will then be calculated. You can see the calculation in Figure 12.2.

Start Visual Studio and then choose a VB.NET Windows Forms application template. This will create an empty form on which we can place controls. We'll need to change a couple of properties on the form as follows:

```
Text: VBCalc
Size: 500,250
```

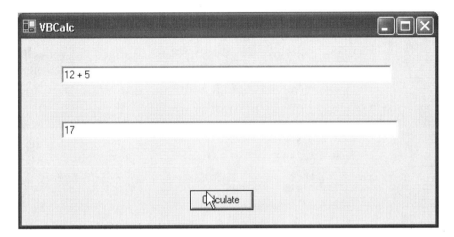

FIGURE 12.2 The result is calculated after user input.

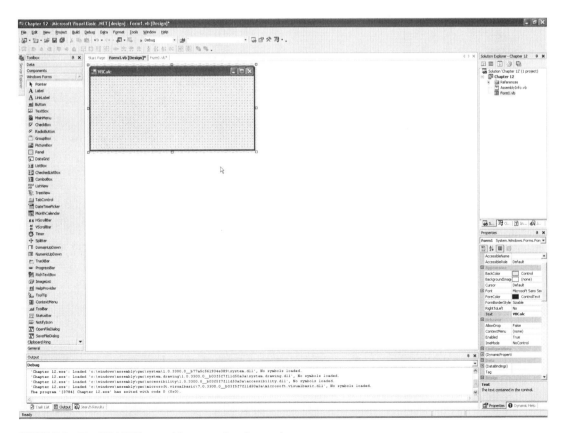

FIGURE 12.3 The VB.NET form with properties changed.

The form should now look something like Figure 12.3 as the changes are made instantly in the IDE.

We're going to use polymorphism, or function overloading, in this example. This affects the way we design the application, but you don't need to worry much about it at this time. It's sufficient to know that we need the following controls placed on the form:

```
Control Type: TextBox
Name : txtEquation

Control Type: TextBox
Name : txtResult
Control Type: Button
Name: btnCalculate
```

You can position and resize these controls so that they are similar in appearance to Figure 12.4.

WRITING SOME CODE

Now that the interface is out of the way, we'll focus on writing some code. Double-click the form to take us to the code editor. This will place the cursor inside the Form_Load event, which will fire when the application is first executed.

We're going to use this event to assign properties programmatically to the TextBox controls that we added to the form in an earlier step. We could have assigned them in the properties editor in the IDE, but we're going to assign them equal to empty strings ("") so that you see how you can do the same thing programmatically.

The code consists of the following two lines:

```
txtResult.Text = ""
txtEquation.Text = ""
```

The actual Form_Load event should look like the following:

```
Private Sub Form1_Load(ByVal sender As System.Object, ByVal e
As System.EventArgs) Handles MyBase.Load
   txtResult.Text = ""
   txtEquation.Text = ""

End Sub
```

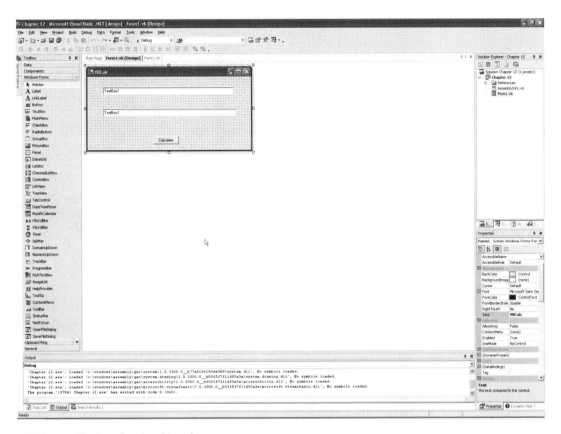

FIGURE 12.4 The interface is taking shape.

Calculate Function

The next step is to create a function that will handle the actual calculation. If you remember, we're going to enter information in the `txtEquation` TextBox that will contain a number that's separated by a space, then an operator (+,-,/,*), and lastly, another number.

We're not going to concern ourselves with how we're handling those individual elements but it's necessary to understand what the individual elements are going to comprise of. First, we'll have a number of type `Double`, an operator of type `String`, and a number of type `Double`. We'll use these types in the creation of the function:

```
Private Function Calculate(ByVal FirstNumber As Double, ByVal
Operator As String, ByVal SecondNumber As Double) As Double

End Function
```

You'll notice that the parameter list contains the `Double`, `String`, and `Double` data types that we were just going over.

The next step is to create a variable for the function. The variable will hold the result of the calculation and will be returned as a value. The declaration is a single line of code:

```
Dim Result As Double = 0
```

The line should have been placed beneath the `Private` function line as follows:

```
Private Function Calculate(ByVal FirstNumber As Double, ByVal
Operator As String, ByVal SecondNumber As Double) As Double
    Dim Result As Double = 0

End Function
```

Now, we're at a point where we can turn our attention to the calculations. We'll first take a look at the operator to see what has been passed into the function. Depending on the operator, we need to perform different calculations. For instance, if a "+" is passed, we need to perform an addition. We'll use a `Select...Case` statement to test the operator to see what calculation we need to perform.

Here's the code:

```
Select Case Operator
Case "+"
  Result = FirstNumber + SecondNumber
Case "-"
  Result = FirstNumber - SecondNumber
Case "*"
  Result = FirstNumber * SecondNumber
Case "/"
  ' Cannot divide by zero
  If SecondNumber <> 0 Then Result = FirstNumber / SecondNumber
```

Next, we need to return the value of the result variable. This is a single line of code:

```
Return Result
```

The entire function, with everything in place, appears here:

```
    Private Function Calculate(ByVal FirstNumber As Double, ByVal
Operator As String, ByVal SecondNumber As Double) As Double
    Dim Result As Double = 0
    Select Case Operator
    Case "+"
      Result = FirstNumber + SecondNumber
    Case "-"
      Result = FirstNumber - SecondNumber
    Case "*"
      Result = FirstNumber * SecondNumber
    Case "/"
      ' Cannot divide by zero
      If SecondNumber <> 0 Then Result = FirstNumber / SecondNumber
    End Select

    Return Result

    End Function
```

Before moving on, you should pay particular attention to the line that begins with a single quotation (') mark. The entire line reads `'Cannot divide zero`. This line doesn't actually perform a function in the application. The single quotation instructs the compiler to ignore anything after it. You can use these types of comment lines to give yourself and others who might use your code at a later date some idea of what you're doing. Also, by leaving yourself comments throughout a project, when you go back to them in the future, it's much easier to see what you were doing in a particular code block. Oftentimes, it's very difficult to remember when you refer back to code that you haven't seen in some time.

There are multiple ways that you can leave comments in code. First, you can use the `REM`, which stands for *remark*, statement. It's used as follows:

```
REM This is a comment
```

You can also use it at the end of a line of code:

```
Dim Result As Double = 0 REM This stores the value for the
function.
```

You can also use the single quotation for the comments:

```
' This is a comment
```

Likewise, you can also use it at the end of a line:

```
Dim Result As Double = 0 ' This stores the value for the
function.
```

The second style of comment that occurs at the end of a line is known as an *inline comment*. Inline comments are useful for giving details about what a particular variable is going to do in your application while the other varieties are most often used to describe what a particular procedure or code block accomplishes.

The last line of the function is an If…Then statement that checks to see if the value of the second number isn't equal to 0. If it happened to be 0, we could not perform a division as it would cause a Division by Zero error.

CALLING THE CALCULATE FUNCTION

The final piece of the puzzle is to create the code that will call the Calculate function that we've just finished. Click on the Form1.vb tab in the IDE to display your form. Double-click the btnCalculate button to create the btnCalculate_Click event. This will set up the necessary code to handle the click of the button. Your cursor should be in the created procedure that should look like the following code:

```
Private Sub btnCalculate_Click(ByVal sender As System.Object,
ByVal e As System.EventArgs) Handles btnCalculate.Click

    End Sub
```

The first step is to set up the variables that we'll need for this procedure. We need two variables (x and y) as Doubles that will be used to pass the values to the Calculate function. We'll also need to create a variable of type String (z) that will store the operand that will also be passed to the Calculate function.

Here are the declarations:

```
Private Sub btnCalculate_Click(ByVal sender As System.Object,
ByVal e As System.EventArgs) Handles btnCalculate.Click
    Dim X, Y As Double
    Dim Z As String
    End Sub
```

The next step is to declare an array that will be used to store the various elements of the string data that is entered into txtEquation. This information will be split into a beginning number, operand, and last number by using the Split function. The information will be stored in a(0), a(1) and a(2), respectively.

Here's the code:

```
Private Sub btnCalculate_Click(ByVal sender As System.Object,
ByVal e As System.EventArgs) Handles btnCalculate.Click
    Dim X, Y As Double
    Dim Z As String
    Dim a(2) As String
    a = txtEquation.Text.Split(" ")
End Sub
```

Now, we have an array that contains the three elements of the equation but the information is still in string format. You'll remember our Calculate function needs to have the values in type Double before they can be passed.

Keeping this in mind, our next step is to convert the a(0) and a(2) values into Doubles. We'll use the X and Y variables to store these values and will also set Z to (a1). This isn't a requirement but it makes the call to Calculate easier to follow:

```
Private Sub btnCalculate_Click(ByVal sender As System.Object,
ByVal e As System.EventArgs) Handles btnCalculate.Click
    Dim X, Y As Double
    Dim Z As String
    Dim a(2) As String

    a = txtEquation.Text.Split(" ")

    X = CDbl(a(0))
    Y = CDbl(a(2))
    Z = a(1)
End Sub
```

The final steps are to make the actual call to Calculate. We'll create a variable called temp, of type Double, that will be used to store the value that is returned by Calculate. We'll then take the temp value and convert it to a string. Finally, we'll set the Text property of txtResult equal to the string value.

Here's the code:

```
Private Sub btnCalculate_Click(ByVal sender As System.Object,
ByVal e As System.EventArgs) Handles btnCalculate.Click
    Dim X, Y As Double
    Dim Z As String
    Dim a(2) As String
    Dim temp As Double

    a = txtEquation.Text.Split(" ")

    X = CDbl(a(0))
    Y = CDbl(a(2))
    Z = a(1)

    temp = Calculate(X, Z, Y)
    txtResult.Text = temp.ToString
End Sub
```

TESTING THE PROGRAM

If you save and run your program in the IDE (Ctrl-F5), the calculator form will appear (see Figure 12.5).

Next, try some examples to see if it's working correctly. Figures 12.6 through 12.11 display various examples with final values.

FINAL CODE LISTING

Here's the complete code listing for the application:

```
Public Class Form1
Inherits System.Windows.Forms.Form

Private Function Calculate(ByVal FirstNumber As Double, ByVal
Operator As String, ByVal SecondNumber As Double) As Double
    Dim Result As Double = 0
    Select Case Operator
    Case "+"
      Result = FirstNumber + SecondNumber
    Case "-"
      Result = FirstNumber - SecondNumber
    Case "*"
```

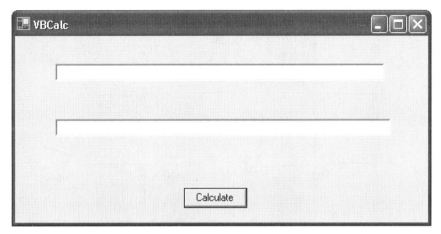

FIGURE 12.5   The calculator appears at open.

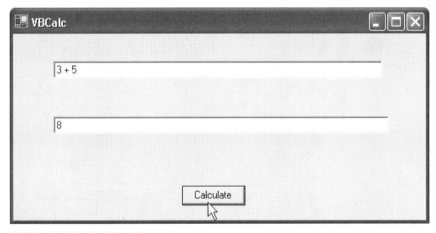

FIGURE 12.6   Testing "3 + 5".

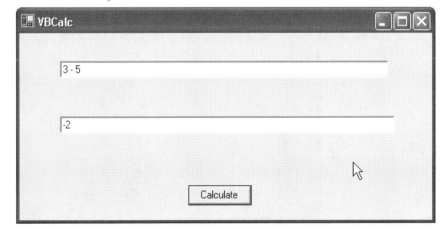

FIGURE 12.7   Testing "3 – 5".

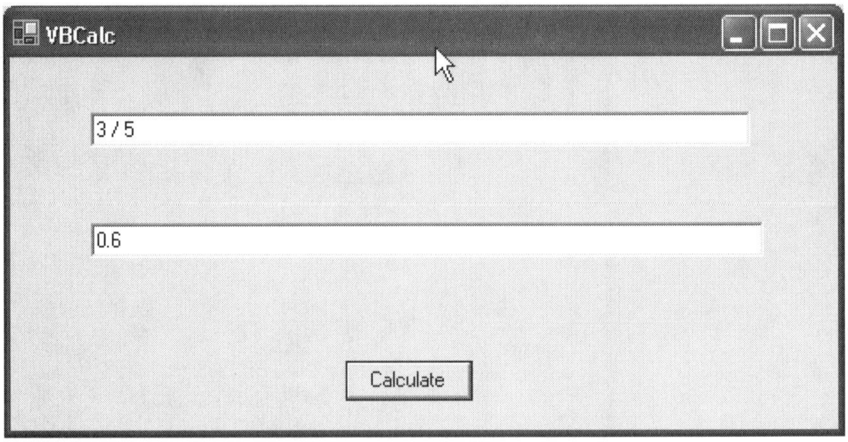

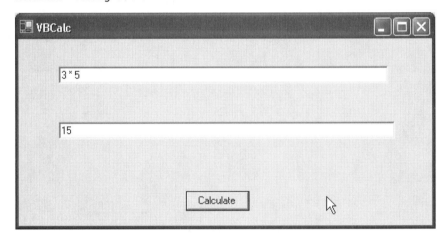

FIGURE 12.8   Testing "3 / 5".

FIGURE 12.9   Testing "3 * 5".

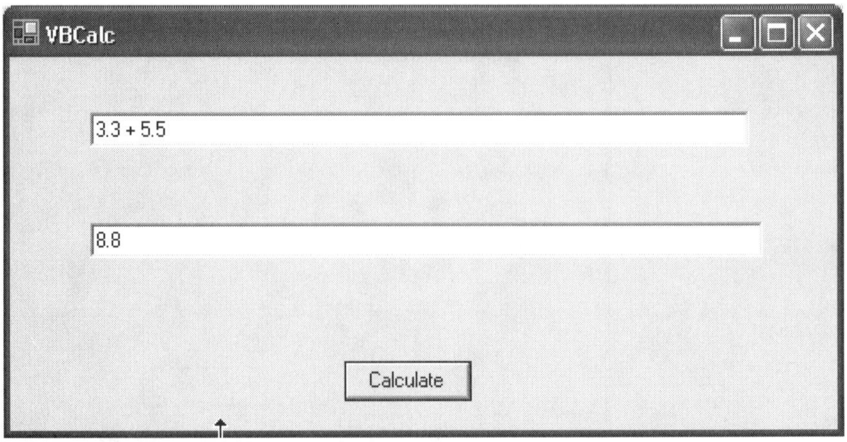

FIGURE 12.10   Testing "3.3 + 5.5".

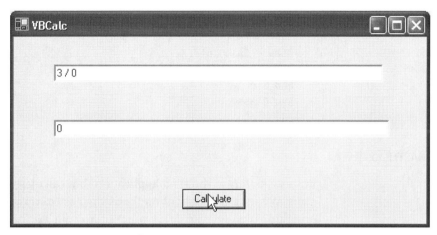

FIGURE 12.11　Testing "3 / 0".

```
    Result = FirstNumber * SecondNumber
Case "/"
  ' Cannot divide by zero
If SecondNumber <> 0 Then Result = FirstNumber / SecondNumber
End Select

Return Result

End Function

Private Sub Form1_Load(ByVal sender As System.Object, ByVal e
As System.EventArgs) Handles MyBase.Load
    txtResult.Text = ""
    txtEquation.Text = ""
End Sub

Private Sub btnCalculate_Click(ByVal sender As System.Object,
ByVal e As System.EventArgs) Handles btnCalculate.Click
    Dim X, Y As Double
    Dim Z As String
    Dim a(2) As String
    Dim temp As Double

    a = txtEquation.Text.Split(" ")

    X = CDbl(a(0))
    Y = CDbl(a(2))
```

```
        Z = a(1)

        temp = Calculate(X, Z, Y)
        txtResult.Text = temp.ToString
        End Sub
        End Class
```

CHAPTER REVIEW

In this chapter, we built an application that calculates various math functions. We used a variety of methods such as `ToString` in constructing this program. We used the `Split` function to split up the string value, which consists of a three-part equation with a number, operand, and a final number. We also used a `Select…Case` statement to sort through the various operands. Finally, we performed the appropriate math function and returned the resulting value.

In the next chapter, we'll deal with files and folders in VB.NET.

13

USING WMI TO RETRIEVE INFORMATION ABOUT YOUR PC

I n the previous chapter, we designed a calculator and learned about several features that are available to VB.NET programmers. In this chapter, we're going to develop an entirely different type of application and one that would be much more difficult in VB 6. The program will be based on the Windows Management Instrumentation (WMI) class. WMI is an industry initiative to develop a standardized technology for accessing management information in enterprise environments. This information includes the state of system memory, inventories of currently installed client applications, and various other pieces of data (see Figure 13.1).

FIGURE 13.1   The final application with information displayed.

PROJECT OVERVIEW

In this project, we're going to take advantage of the WMI classes that are included in VB.NET to build an application that lists the various components and information about your PC. Our application is going to include the following information, but as you'll see, there's much more that can be included by making a few simple changes to this program:

Network Card
MAC Address of Network Card
Network Card Description

BIOS Information
Name
Serial Number
Manufacturer
Release Date
SMBIOS Version
SMBIOS Major Version
SMBIOS Minor Version
Software Element ID
Software Element State
Version
Current Language

Computer System Information
Caption
Primary Owner Name
Domain
Domain Role
Manufacturer
Number of Processors
System Type
System Startup Display
Total Physical Memory

You can see that this program would be quite useful for troubleshooting information or simply for retrieving information from a system. This information could be used for copy protection code by retrieving a serial number and then writing a key generation program to produce a single valid key based on this number. You could also use this in an About Box to give the user details about their system. Suffice it to say, there are many ways that you could put this information to good use.

TUTORIAL   ## GETTING STARTED

This application will be in the area of a user interface. We could have just as easily used a Console Application template for this project, but we're going to use a Windows Forms template. This will allow us much more flexibility if we want to add the ability to email this information to someone, or if we wish to expand this program at a later date to include more information. Additionally, we could simply use this in another application as an About Box or a troubleshooting screen.

The following steps will get us started in creating our program:

1. Create a Windows Forms application by starting VB.NET and then choosing the Windows Forms template. This will display the default form like the one seen in Figure 13.2.
2. The next step is to change the properties of the form as follows:

```
Size: 500,500
Text: System Information
```

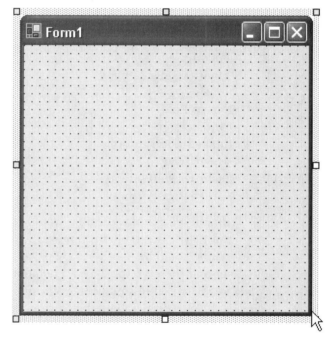

FIGURE 13.2   The default form in VB.NET.

You should see these changes instantly in the IDE (see Figure 13.3).

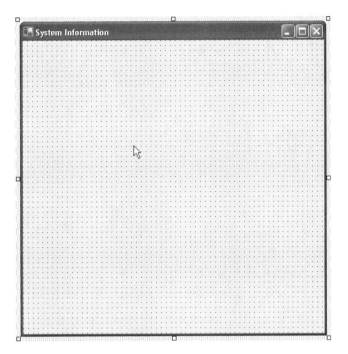

FIGURE 13.3   The form is changed instantly in the IDE.

3. Add a ListBox control to the form. This control will be utilized to store all of the information about the PC including the Basic Input Output System (BIOS), network, and system. You can add it to the form and then make these changes to it:

```
Size: 450,450
Location: 10,10
```

Your form should now look like Figure 13.4.

 You'll notice that we left the Form1 and ListBox1 names intact. If we'd been creating an application that contained more items in its user interface, we probably would have changed these names to reflect their purposes. However, because this example only contained a single form and a single control, it wasn't really necessary.

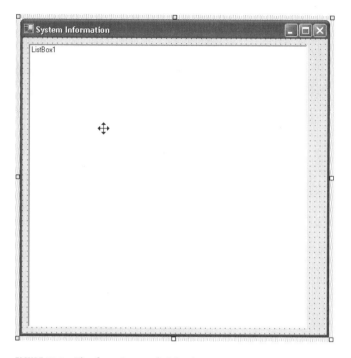

FIGURE 13.4   The form is now finished.

WRITING SOME CODE

The next step is to begin writing some code for the application. You can double-click on the form to display the code editor. This will place you in the `Form_Load` event although you'll need to move to the top of the code editor and add an `Imports` statement.

The `Imports` statements will be the first line of code in the application and it should appear before any other code. The line will import `System.Management` into the application.

Here's the code:

```
Imports System.Management
```

You can add them to the code editor, which should contain something like the following code when you're finished:

```
Imports System.Management

Public Class Form1
```

```
    Inherits System.Windows.Forms.Form

    Private Sub Form1_Load(ByVal sender As System.Object, ByVal e
As System.EventArgs) Handles MyBase.Load

    End Sub

End Class
```

WMI REFERENCES

Before we move on, let's take a look at some of the things that we can accomplish with WMI and VB.NET. The following list gives you an idea of the various classes that are exposed:

Class Name
Win32_X Management classes
Win32_ComputerSystem
Win32_DiskDrive
Win32_LogicalDisk
Win32_NetworkAdapter
Win32_NetworkAdapterConfiguration
Win32_NetworkLoginProfile
Win32_OperatingSystem
Win32_Printer
Win32_Process
Win32_Processor
Win32_Service
Win32_VideoController

A thorough list of the classes follows.

Win32_ComputerSystem Class

This class allows access to information about windows PCs. Tables 13.1 through 13.3 list the domain roles, properties, and methods of this class, respectively.

Table 13.1 Domain Roles for the Win32_ComputerSystem Class

DOMAIN ROLE	DESCRIPTION
0	Standalone Workstation
1	Member Workstation
2	Standalone Server
3	Member Server
4	Backup Domain Controller
5	Primary Domain Controller

Table 13.2 Properties for the Win32_ComputerSystem Class

PROPERTY	DESCRIPTION
Caption	Name of the Windows PC.
PrimaryOwnerName	Windows 2000-only owner of the PC.
Domain	Name of the domain that the PC is a part of.
DomainRole	Role that the PC has in the domain.
Manufacturer	Manufacturer of the PC.
Model	Model of the PC.
NumberofProcessors	Number of processors in the PC.
SystemType	Processor class of the PC.
SystemStartupDelay	Amount of time in seconds for the user to choose an OS on startup.
TotalPhysicalMemory	Amount of installed RAM in the system.

Table 13.3 Methods for the Win32_ComputerSystem Class

METHOD	DESCRIPTION
Put_()	Saves changes made to the class.

Win32_DiskDrive Class

This class allows access to disk drive information. Table 13.4 lists the properties of this class.

Table 13.4   Properties of the Win32_DiskDrive Class

PROPERTY	CLASS
Caption	Description of the drive.
Description	Brand name of the drive.
InterfaceType	Type of the drive.
Manufacturer	Manufacturer of the drive.
Partitions	Number of partitions on the drive.
Sectors	Sectors of the drive.
ScsiBus	SCSI bus number.
ScsiTargetID	SCSI ID.
Size	Size of the drive in bytes.

Win32_LogicalDisk Class

This class allows access to logical drives. Table 13.5 lists the properties of this class.

Table 13.5   Properties of the Win32_LogicalDisk Class

PROPERTY	DESCRIPTION
DriveType	Type of drive (1: removable; 2: floppy; 3: HD; 4: network; 5: CD-ROM).
FileSystem	File system of the drive.
Freespace	Amount of free space on disk drive in bytes.
Name	Disk drive letter.
Size	Size of the drive in bytes.
VolumeName	Volume name of the logical disk drive.
VolumeSerialNumber	Serial number of the disk drive.

Win32_NetworkAdapter Class

This class allows access to Windows network adapter properties. Table 13.6 lists the properties of this class.

Table 13.6   Properties of the Win32_NetworkAdapter Class

PROPERTY	DESCRIPTION
Description	Name of the network adapter .
MACAddress	MACaddress of the network adapter.

Win32_NetworkAdapterConfiguration Class

This class allows access to Windows network adapters (NIC) configuration. Tables 13.7 and 13.8 list the collections and properties of this class, respectively.

Table 13.7   Collections of the Win32_NetworkAdapterConfiguration Class

COLLECTION	DESCRIPTION
DefaultIPGateway	Collection of all default Internet Protocol (IP) gateways.
DNSServerSearchOrder	Collection of all domain name server (DNS) server IPs.
Ipaddress	Collection of all IP addresses for the adapter.
IPsubnet	Collection of all subnet masks.
WinsPrimaryServer	Collection of all Windows Internet Naming Service (WINS) server IPs.

Table 13.8   Properties of the Win32_NetworkAdapterConfiguration Class

PROPERTY	DESCRIPTION
Description	Name of the network adapter.
DHCPenabled	(-1: if DHCP isn't enabled; 0: not enabled; 1: DHCP enabled).
DHCPLeaseObtained	Number representing the date and time that the DHCP lease was obtained.
DHCPLeaseExpires	Number representing date and time DHCP lease expires.
DHCPServer	IP address of the Dynamic Host Configuration Protocol (DHCP) server.
DNSHostname	Name of the host.
DNSDomain	Name of the DNS domain.
Ipenabled	Is True if the adapter has an enabled IP address.
MACAddress	MAC address of the network adapter.

Win32_NetworkLoginProfile Class

This class allows access to network login profile information. Table 13.9 lists the properties of this class.

Table 13.9   Properties of the Win32_NetworkLoginProfile Class

PROPERTY	DESCRIPTION
LastLogin	Last login of the user.
Name	Username of the user

Win32_OperatingSystem Class

This class allows access to Windows functions. Tables 13.10 and 13.11 list the properties and methods of this class, respectively.

Table 13.10   Properties of the Win32_OperatingSystem Class

PROPERTY	DESCRIPTION
BootDevice	Drive that boots the operating system (OS).
BuildNumber	Build version of the OS.
BuildType	Build type.
Caption	Name of the OS.
CSName	Name of the system.
CsdVersion	Service Pack version.
CurrentTimeZone	Time zone.
FreePhysicalMemory	Amount of free memory in RAM in KB.
FreeVirtualMemory	Amount of free virtual memory in KB.
InstallDate	Date the OS was installed.
LastBootUpTime	Number representing date and time since PC was last booted up.
NumberofProcesses	Number of processes running currently.
Organization	Organization that was set when installed.
OsLanguage	Number representing the language of the OS.
Primary	Is True if OS is in use.
RegisteredUser	User of the OS.
SerialNumber	Serial number of the OS.
SystemDevice	Drive that has the OS files.
SystemDirectory	Path to the system directory.

(continues)

Table 13.10 *(continued)*

PROPERTY	DESCRIPTION
TotalVirtualMemorySize	Total size of virtual memory in KB.
Version	Version of the OS.
WindowsDirectory	Path to the Windows directory.

Table 13.11   Methods of the Win32_OperatingSystem Class

METHOD	DESCRIPTION
Reboot()	Reboots the PC.
Shutdown()	Shuts down the PC.

Win32_Printer Class

This class allows access to Windows printers. Table 13.12 lists the property of this class.

Table 13.12   Property of the Win32_Printer Class

PROPERTY	DESCRIPTION
Description	Name of the printer.

Win32_Process Class

This class allows access to Windows processes. Tables 13.13 and 13.14 list the properties and methods of this class, respectively.

Table 13.13   Properties of the Win32_Process Class

PROPERTY	DESCRIPTION
Caption	Name of the Windows process.
CreationDate	String representing date and time that the process was started.
Name	Name of the Windows process.
Priority	Priority level of the process.
ProcessID	ID of the Windows process.
ThreadCount	Number of process threads.
WorkingSetSize	Amount of memory dedicated to the process in Kb.

Table 13.14   Methods of the Win32_Process Class

METHOD	DESCRIPTION
Create(strProcess)	Creates a new process.
Terminate()	Terminates the process.

Win32_Processor Class

This class allows information about the processor. Tables 13.15 and 13.16 list the CPU interfaces and properties of this class, respectively.

Table 13.15   CPU Interfaces of the Win32_Processor Class

CPU INTERFACE	DESCRIPTION
1	Other
2	Unknown
3	Daughterboard
4	ZIF Socket
5	Replacement
6	None
7	LIF Socket
8	Slot1
9	Slot2
10	370 Pin
11	SlotA
12	SlotM

Table 13.16   Properties of the Win32_Processor Class

PROPERTY	DESCRIPTION
AddressWidth	Processor data width in bits.
CurrentClockSpeed	Clock speed of the processor.
Extclock	External clock speed of the processor.
DeviceID	CPU ID of the processor.
Description	CPU class, family, model, and stepping of the processor.
L2CacheSize	Size of the L2cache on the processor in Kb.
L2CacheSpeed	Speed of the L2 cache on the processor.

(continues)

Table 13.16 *(continued)*

PROPERTY	DESCRIPTION
Name	Brand name of the processor.
UpgradeMethod	CPU interface.

Win32_Service Class

This class allows access to Windows services. Tables 13.17 and 13.18 list the properties and methods of this class, respectively.

Table 13.17   Properties of the Win32_Service Class

PROPERTY	DESCRIPTION
Description	Name of the service.
DisplayName	Same as description.
ServiceType	Type of service, "ShareProcess" or "Own Process".
State	Current state of the service, "Running" or "Stopped".
Status	Current status of the service, "OK".
StartMode	Current star mode of the service, "Auto", "Manual", or "Disabled".
StartName	Start name of the service, "LocalSystem".

Table 13.18   Methods of the Win32_Service Class

METHOD	DESCRIPTION
StopService()	Stops the service.
ChangeStartMode(strMode)	Changes the start mode of the service; Mode("Automatic", "Manual").

Win32_VideoController Class

This class allows access to video properties. Table 13.19 lists the properties of this class.

Table 13.19　Properties of the Win32_VideoController Class

PROPERTY	DESCRIPTION
Caption	Name of the video card.
CurrentHorizontalResolution	Horizontal resolution of the screen.
CurrentVerticalResolution	Vertical resolution of the screen.
CurrentNumberOfColors	Color depth of the screen.

USING THE CLASSES

Now that you have an idea of the classes that we can utilize, we're going to put them to use in this application. Specifically, we're going to use `NetworkAdapterConfiguration`, `BIOS`, and `ComputerSystem`.

Let's begin with a simple property of the `ListBox` control. We're going to be placing a great deal of information in it, so we'll need to have scroll bars. Let's use the `ScrollAlwaysVisible` property:

```
ListBox1.ScrollAlwaysVisible = True
```

You can add this line to the `Form_Load` event, which should now look like the following code:

```
Private Sub Form1_Load(ByVal sender As System.Object, ByVal e
As System.EventArgs) Handles MyBase.Load

        ListBox1.ScrollAlwaysVisible = True

End Sub
```

The next step is to create some variables for the `ManagementClass` and `ManagementObject`. These are both part of the `System.Management` namespace that we imported in the first line of code for this project. Here's the code:

```
Dim mc As Management Class
Dim mo As ManagementObject
```

Next, we'll assign mc equal to a new `ManagementClass`. The `ManagementClass` in this case will be the Network Adapter Configuration ("Win32_NetworkAdapterConfiguration"). We can also set moc equal to a `ManagementObjectCollection`.

Here's the code for those lines:

```
mc = New ManagementClass("Win32_NetworkAdapterConfiguration")
Dim moc As ManagementObjectCollection = mc.GetInstances()
```

Now, it's time to begin sending information to the ListBox. We'll begin with a couple of lines that will be used to send some basic text information to the ListBox. We'll use its Add method as follows:

```
ListBox1.Items.Add("Network Information")
ListBox1.Items.Add("—————————")
```

This information will be used so that the user can quickly look through the ListBox to see the information they're looking for.

The next step is to use a For Each loop to repeat a group of statements for each element in an array or, for our particular needs, a collection. We'll then check to see if IPEnabled is True. If so, we'll then output the MAC Address and Description properties of the network adapter.

Here's the code:

```
For Each mo In moc
   If mo.Item("IPEnabled") = True Then
     ListBox1.Items.Add("MAC address : " &
mo.Item("MacAddress").ToString())
     ListBox1.Items.Add("Description : " &
mo.Item("Description").ToString())
    End If
  Next
```

At this point, we would have the network card information so we'll add a couple of blank lines to the ListBox to help separate the areas. Here's the code for those lines:

```
ListBox1.Items.Add("")
ListBox1.Items.Add("")
```

Now we're going to turn our attention to the BIOS. This information is obtained through the "Win32_BIOS" management class. We'll set mc and moc similarly to the earlier step:

```
mc = New ManagementClass("Win32_BIOS")
moc = mc.GetInstances()
```

Again, we'll use a `For Each` loop to repeat the code necessary to add the information to the `ListBox`. This time, we're going to use a `With` statement so that we don't have to type `ListBox1.Items` for every line in this code. Instead, we can use a `With` statement to shorten this up.

Here's the code:

```
For Each mo In moc
    With ListBox1.Items
    .Add("BIOS Information")
    .Add("—————————————————-")
    .Add("Name : " & mo.Item("Name").ToString())
    .Add("Serial Number : " & mo.Item("SerialNumber").ToString())
    .Add("Manufacturer : " & mo.Item("Manufacturer").ToString())
    .Add("Status : " & mo.Item("Status").ToString())
    .Add("Release Date : " & mo.Item("ReleaseDate").ToString())
    .Add("SMBIOS Version : " &
mo.Item("SMBIOSBIOSVersion").ToString())
    .Add("SMBIOS Major Version : " &
mo.Item("SMBIOSMajorVersion").ToString())
    .Add("SMBIOS Minor Version : " &
mo.Item("SMBIOSMinorVersion").ToString())
    .Add("SMBIOS Present : " &
mo.Item("SMBIOSPresent").ToString())
    .Add("Software Element ID : " &
mo.Item("SoftwareElementID").ToString())
    .Add("Software Element State : " &
mo.Item("SoftwareElementState").ToString())
    .Add("Version : " & mo.Item("Version").ToString())
    .Add("Current Lang. : " &
mo.Item("CurrentLanguage").ToString())
    .Add("")
    .Add("")
    End With
    Next
```

We'll now repeat the same process with the `ComputerSystem` management class. Here's the code:

```
mc = New ManagementClass("Win32_ComputerSystem")
moc = mc.GetInstances()

For Each mo In moc
```

```
With ListBox1.Items
  .Add("Computer System")
  .Add("————————————-")
  .Add("Caption : " & mo.Item("Caption").ToString())
  .Add("Primary Owner Name : " &
mo.Item("PrimaryOwnerName").ToString())
  .Add("Domain : " & mo.Item("Domain").ToString())
  .Add("Domain Role : " &  mo.Item("DomainRole").ToString())
  .Add("Manufacturer : " &  mo.Item("Manufacturer").ToString())
  .Add("Model : " & mo.Item("Model").ToString())
  .Add("Number Processors : " &
mo.Item("NumberofProcessors").ToString())
  .Add("System Types : " &  mo.Item("SystemType").ToString())
  .Add("System Startup Delay : " &
mo.Item("SystemStartupDelay").ToString())
  .Add("Physical Memory : " &
mo.Item("TotalPhysicalMemory").ToString())
End With

Next
```

TESTING THE APPLICATION

At this time, you can test the application by pressing F5, choosing
Debug | Start, or clicking on the Start button in the IDE. Regardless of
your choice, your application will open and should look similar to Figure 13.5.

FINAL CODE LISTING

This is the final code listing for the application:

```
Imports System.Management


Public Class Form1
  Inherits System.Windows.Forms.Form

  Private Sub Form1_Load(ByVal sender As System.Object, ByVal e
As System.EventArgs) Handles MyBase.Load

    ListBox1.ScrollAlwaysVisible = True
```

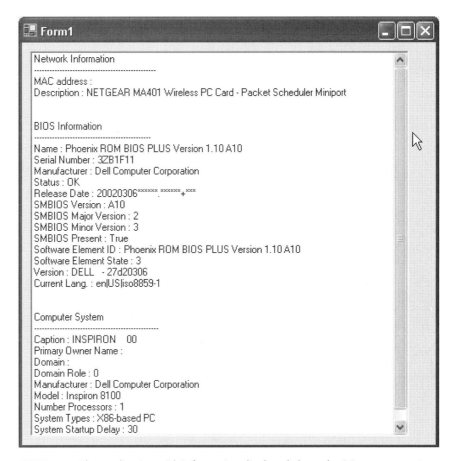

FIGURE 13.5   The application with information displayed about the PC.

```
'System.Management
Dim mc As ManagementClass

Dim mo As ManagementObject

'Network Info
mc = New ManagementClass("Win32_NetworkAdapterConfiguration")
Dim moc As ManagementObjectCollection = mc.GetInstances()

ListBox1.Items.Add("Network Information")
ListBox1.Items.Add("————————————————")

For Each mo In moc
```

```
            If mo.Item("IPEnabled") = True Then
                ListBox1.Items.Add("MAC address : " &
mo.Item("MacAddress").ToString())
                ListBox1.Items.Add("Description : " &
mo.Item("Description").ToString())
            End If
    Next

    ListBox1.Items.Add("")
    ListBox1.Items.Add("")

        'BIOS Info
        mc = New ManagementClass("Win32_BIOS")
        moc = mc.GetInstances()

        For Each mo In moc

          With ListBox1.Items
            .Add("BIOS Information")
             .Add("———————————————")
             .Add("Name : " & mo.Item("Name").ToString())
             .Add("Serial Number : " &
mo.Item("SerialNumber").ToString())
             .Add("Manufacturer : " &
mo.Item("Manufacturer").ToString())
             .Add("Status : " & mo.Item("Status").ToString())
             .Add("Release Date : " &
mo.Item("ReleaseDate").ToString())
             .Add("SMBIOS Version : " &
mo.Item("SMBIOSBIOSVersion").ToString())
             .Add("SMBIOS Major Version : " &
mo.Item("SMBIOSMajorVersion").ToString())
             .Add("SMBIOS Minor Version : " &
mo.Item("SMBIOSMinorVersion").ToString())
             .Add("SMBIOS Present : " &
mo.Item("SMBIOSPresent").ToString())
             .Add("Software Element ID : " &
mo.Item("SoftwareElementID").ToString())
             .Add("Software Element State : " &
mo.Item("SoftwareElementState").ToString())
             .Add("Version : " & mo.Item("Version").ToString())
             .Add("Current Lang. : " &
mo.Item("CurrentLanguage").ToString())
             .Add("")
```

```
                    .Add("")
         End With



    Next



              'Computer Info
              mc = New ManagementClass("Win32_ComputerSystem")
              moc = mc.GetInstances()

              For Each mo In moc

                  With ListBox1.Items
                          .Add("Computer System")
                          .Add("-----------------------------------
--------------")
                          .Add("Caption : " &
mo.Item("Caption").ToString())
                          .Add("Primary Owner Name : " &
mo.Item("PrimaryOwnerName").ToString())
                          .Add("Domain : " &
mo.Item("Domain").ToString())
                          .Add("Domain Role : " &
mo.Item("DomainRole").ToString())
                          .Add("Manufacturer : " &
mo.Item("Manufacturer").ToString())
                          .Add("Model : " &
mo.Item("Model").ToString())
                          .Add("Number Processors : " &
mo.Item("NumberofProcessors").ToString())
                          .Add("System Types : " &
mo.Item("SystemType").ToString())
                          .Add("System Startup Delay : " &
mo.Item("SystemStartupDelay").ToString())
                          .Add("Physical Memory : " &
mo.Item("TotalPhysicalMemory").ToString())
                      End With
                Next

           End Sub
       End Class
```

CHAPTER REVIEW

In this chapter, we built a very useful application that can be customized for your particular needs. It would be excellent to include with another project for an About Box or a troubleshooting mode. We touched on several new topics including a `ListBox` control, the `With` statement, a `For Each` loop, and obviously, the WMI.

In the next chapter, we'll build a directory browser using the `TreeView` control.

14 FILE AND FOLDER BROWSER

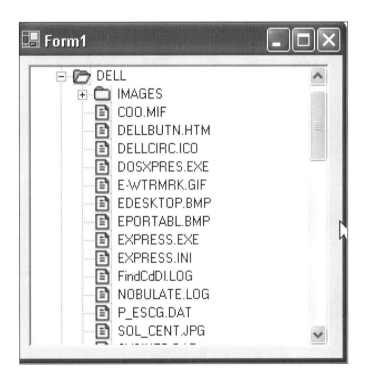

In the previous chapter, we built an application using WMI to retrieve information from the system, including the network card and BIOS. In this chapter, we're going to continue to look in the area of file utilities with the creation of a file and folder browser (see Figure 14.1). This will allow us to look at several topics and controls that we have yet to cover and also build an application that can be useful to you in future projects.

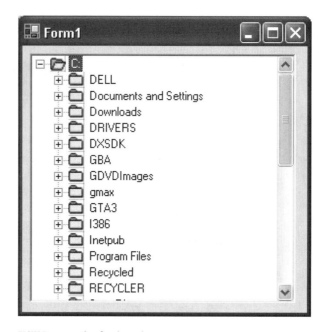

FIGURE 14.1   The final application.

PROGRAM OVERVIEW

The program we're working on in this chapter allows a user to browse their hard drive and see all the files and folders that are contained on it.

TUTORIAL   ## USER INTERFACE

We'll begin this application like most VB applications, with the user interface:

1. Start VB and create a Windows application.
2. Using the default form that's created, add a `TreeView` control to the form. It should look something like Figure 14.2.

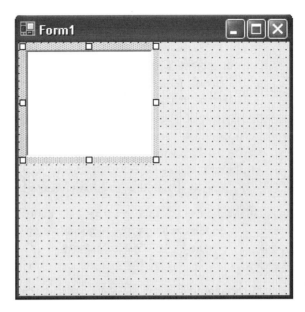

FIGURE 14.2   The only control that we need in this
application is TreeView.

3. Resize the TreeView so that it takes up most of the space in the form (see
Figure 14.3).

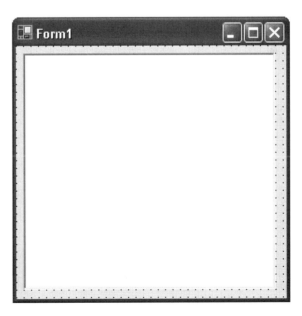

FIGURE 14.3   The control has been resized.

TREEVIEW CONTROL

The TreeView control uses image lists, so the next step is to add this control to your project. You'll notice that the control is placed beneath the form rather than inside it (see Figure 14.4). This control cannot be seen by the user. So it's nice to have it beneath the form where you can see it, manipulate it as necessary and, if your forms become cluttered with a great deal of controls, it's much easier to remember that this control exists at design time. This is one of the small, new features that can make a difference for VB 6 developers who upgrade.

Follow these steps to add images to the ImageList:

1. Single-click on the ImageList1 control, and then click on the Images button in the Properties window. As you see in Figure 14.5, you need to click on the button that contains the "…".

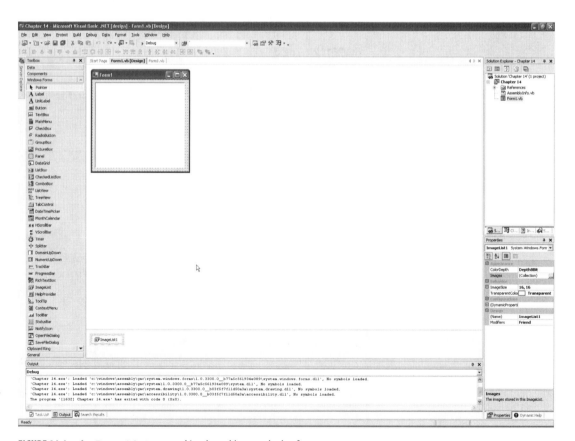

FIGURE 14.4   An ImageList control is placed beneath the form.

FIGURE 14.5   The Properties window.

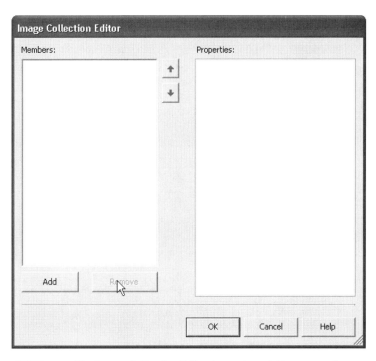

FIGURE 14.6   The Image Collection Editor is used to add images to the `ImageList` control.

This will open a window, similar in appearance to Figure 14.6. This window is the Image Collection Editor and is used to add images to the `ImageList`.

2. Click Add in the Image Collection Editor. This will open a dialog box like the one shown in Figure 14.7.

You can browse to the following directory: *C:\Program Files\Microsoft Visual Studio.Net\Common7\Graphics\Bitmaps\Outline* . The graphics directory contains hundreds of images that you can use in your application. We're using images in the *Bitmaps\Outline* directory as this contains the type of images we need for our `TreeView` control.

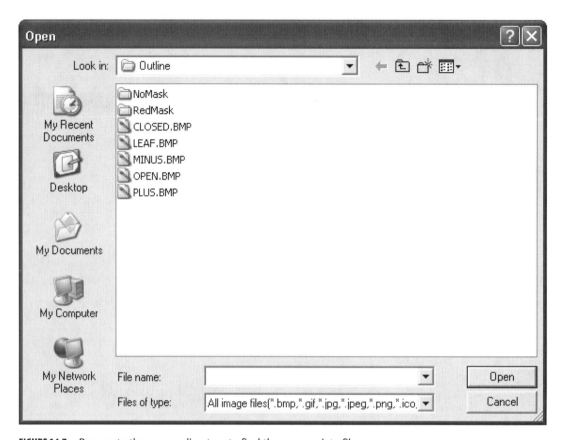

FIGURE 14.7   Browse to the proper directory to find the appropriate files.

3. One at a time, add the *Closed.bmp* file, *Open.bmp* file, and the *Leaf.bmp* file. Add them in that particular order as we'll use a number to access them programmatically, later. Your Image Collection Editor window will now look like Figure 14.8.

4. Click OK to close the dialog box. At this point, we have images in our application but the TreeView control doesn't have access to them.

5. Click on the TreeView control and then select ImageList1 in the ImageList property.

You can now use the images in the TreeView.

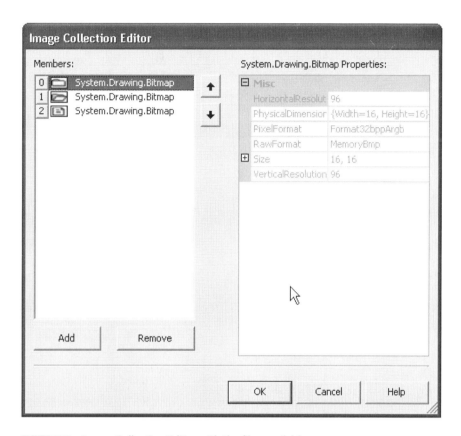

FIGURE 14.8   Image Collection Editor with the files available.

WRITING SOME CODE

For this example, we're going to use some of the objects in the System.IO namespace. Specifically, we're going to look at the FileInfo and DirectoryInfo classes.

FileInfo Class

The FileInfo class provides instance methods for creating, copying, deleting, moving, and opening files. Table 14.1 will give you more details on what's available in the FileInfo class.

Table 14.1   FileInfo Class

NAME	DESCRIPTION
Directory	Gets an instance of the parent directory.
DirectoryName	Gets a string representing the directory's full path.
Length	Gets the size of the current file or directory.
Name	Gets the name of the file.
Create	Creates a file.
CreateText	Creates a StreamWriter that writes a new text file.
Open	Opens a file.
OpenRead	Creates a read-only FileStream.
OpenText	Creates a StreamReader that reads from an existing text file.
OpenWrite	Creates a write-only FileStream.
AppendText	Creates a StreamWriter that appends text to a file.
CopyTo	Copies an existing file to a new file.
MoveTo	Renames an existing file.

DirectoryInfo Class

The `DirectoryInfo` class provides instance methods for creating, moving, and enumerating through directories and subdirectories (Table 14.2).

Table 14.2   DirectoryInfo Class

NAME	DESCRIPTION
Parent	Gets the parent directory of a specified subdirectory.
Root	Gets the root portion of a path.
Create	Creates a directory.
CreateSubDirectory	Creates a subdirectory or subdirectories on the specified path.
GetDirectories	Returns the subdirectories of the current directory.
GetFiles	Returns a file list from the current directory.
GetFileSystemInfos	Retrieves an array of strongly typed FileSystemInfo objects.
MoveTo	Moves a DirectoryInfo instance and its contents to a new path.

Double-click on the form to bring up the code editor. This will place your cursor in the `Form_Load` event. We plan to use several references from `System.IO`, so we can add an `Imports` statement before any other code to reduce the amount of code that we have to write:

```
Imports System.io
```

Go back to the `Form_Load` event because we're going to deal with this aspect of the program first. The only programming that needs to be completed in this event is to create a single node called `"C"` that represents drive C.

The first line that we need to write creates a new `Node` object as `System.Windows.Forms.TreeNode`. This is the necessary code:

```
Dim oNode As New System.Windows.Forms.TreeNode()
```

Next, we need to set the `SelectedImageIndex` = 0 so that the closed bitmap that we imported into the `ImageList` is displayed. We also need to set the text of the `Node` to `"C:"`. Finally, we need to add the node as follows:

```
oNode.ImageIndex = 0' Closed
    oNode.SelectedImageIndex = 0
    oNode.Text = "C:"
    TreeView1.Nodes.Add(oNode)
    oNode.Nodes.Add("")
```

Here's the complete `Sub`:

```
Private Sub Form1_Load(ByVal sender As System.Object, ByVal e
As System.EventArgs) Handles MyBase.Load
    Dim oNode As New System.Windows.Forms.TreeNode()

    oNode.ImageIndex = 0' Closed
    oNode.SelectedImageIndex = 0
    oNode.Text = "C:"
    TreeView1.Nodes.Add(oNode)

End Sub
```

If you were to execute the program at this time, it would only display simply a `"C:"` folder and nothing more. The next step is to add the code that responds to a user clicking on a node in the `TreeView` control.

TREEVIEW

The first item that we need to deal with in this section is the event that occurs when a user clicks a node to expand it in the TreeView. At the top of the code editor, you'll see two combo boxes. In the left combo box, you can select the TreeView1 control and in the right combo box you can select BeforeExpand. You'll see that this creates the BeforeExpand event for us automatically. This is another way to create these types of events. The following code should be displayed.

```
Private Sub TreeView1_BeforeExpand(ByVal sender As Object,
ByVal e As System.Windows.Forms.TreeViewCancelEventArgs) Handles
TreeView1.BeforeExpand

End Sub
```

If you look at this Sub procedure, you'll see a few interesting items. Most important for our project is the e object that's passed to this event handler. It contains the TreeNode object that's being expanded. If you remember, we used bitmap image 2 (*leaf.bmp*) to represent files. We can then test the object being passed to see if the ImageIndex is 2. If it is 2, then we need to exit the Sub procedure as we obviously would not want to expand a file. You can add this to the Sub procedure as the first line:

```
If e.Node.ImageIndex = 2 Then Exit Sub
```

Now, if the ImageIndex is anything besides a value of 2, we'll continue on to expand the node.

Here's the code that includes a call to ec (enumerate children) that we haven't yet created:

```
e.Node.Nodes(0).Remove()
EnumerateChildren(e.Node)
```

The last step is to set the ImageIndex to the open folder image if it has children; otherwise, we need to set it as a closed folder:

```
If e.Node.GetNodeCount(False) > 0 Then
        e.Node.ImageIndex = 1
        e.Node.SelectedImageIndex = 1
End If
```

Here's the complete listing for the Sub procedure:

```
    Private Sub TreeView1_BeforeExpand(ByVal sender As Object,
ByVal e As System.Windows.Forms.TreeViewCancelEventArgs) Handles
TreeView1.BeforeExpand
      If e.Node.ImageIndex = 2 Then Exit Sub

      e.Node.Nodes(0).Remove()
      ec(e.Node)

      If e.Node.GetNodeCount(False) > 0 Then
        e.Node.ImageIndex = 1
        e.Node.SelectedImageIndex = 1
    End If
  End Sub
```

In the code, we called a procedure ec. We have yet to create this sub-routine, so we'll turn our attention to it next.

EC SUB

We'll begin this Sub procedure by creating the following code:

```
    Private Sub ec(ByVal oParent As System.Windows.Forms.TreeNode)

    End Sub
```

The Sub procedure will be getting an object of type TreeNode. You'll have to type the upcoming lines of code into the code editor beneath the other code but above the Form End Class line. The next step is to create our variables using DirectoryInfo and FileInfo:

```
Dim oFS As New DirectoryInfo(oParent.FullPath & "\")
    Dim oDir As DirectoryInfo
    Dim oFile As FileInfo
```

The oFS object will be given a path name from the TreeNode that's being passed to it. This doesn't include a final "\", thus we added it to the first line.

The next step is to go through an array of DirectoryInfo objects that are available when we use the GetDirectories() method. We iterate through the objects and create a node for each directory:

```
For Each oDir In oFS.GetDirectories()
```

```
            Dim oNode As New System.Windows.Forms.TreeNode()
            oNode.Text = oDir.Name
            oNode.ImageIndex = 0
            oNode.SelectedImageIndex = 0
            oParent.Nodes.Add(oNode)
            oNode.Nodes.Add("")
        Next
```

Then, we do a similar thing with the `GetFiles()` method to create a node for each file:

```
For Each oFile In oFS.GetFiles()
    Dim oNode As New System.Windows.Forms.TreeNode()
    oNode.Text = oFile.Name
    oNode.ImageIndex = 2
    oNode.SelectedImageIndex = 2
    oParent.Nodes.Add(oNode)
Next
```

That's really all there is to adding the nodes for the `TreeView`. We could have added more detailed information in the `oNode.Text = oFileName` as there are several properties that we can access such as date, time, last access time, and so on. If you wanted, you could simply add it as follows:

```
oNode.Text = oFile.Name & " " & oFile.CreationTime
```

Here's the final code for this `Sub` procedure:

```
Private Sub ec(ByVal oParent As System.Windows.Forms.TreeNode)

    Dim oFS As New DirectoryInfo(oParent.FullPath & "\")
    Dim oDir As DirectoryInfo
    Dim oFile As FileInfo

    For Each oDir In oFS.GetDirectories()
      Dim oNode As New System.Windows.Forms.TreeNode()
      oNode.Text = oDir.Name
      oNode.ImageIndex = 0
      oNode.SelectedImageIndex = 0
      oParent.Nodes.Add(oNode)
      oNode.Nodes.Add("")
    Next

    For Each oFile In oFS.GetFiles()
```

```
        Dim oNode As New System.Windows.Forms.TreeNode()
        oNode.Text = oFile.Name
        oNode.ImageIndex = 2
        oNode.SelectedImageIndex = 2
        oParent.Nodes.Add(oNode)
    Next

    End Sub
```

We're almost finished with this project but we need to write the code that will handle the closing of the folder icon for a node. As we used the `BeforeExpand` event, it makes sense that we'll use the `BeforeCollapse` event here. It's as simple as taking the e object that's passed and assigning it to `ImageIndex = 0`.

Here's the code:

```
    Private Sub TreeView1_BeforeCollapse(ByVal sender As
Object, ByVal e As _
        System.Windows.Forms.TreeViewCancelEventArgs) Handles _
        TreeView1.BeforeCollapse

        e.Node.ImageIndex = 0
        e.Node.SelectedImageIndex = 0

    End Sub
```

FINISHING UP THE PROJECT

The code will work at this time, but there are a couple of things that we can add to clean it up. First, we can allow the `ListView` control to be re-sized when the form is resized. As you can see in Figures 14.9 and 14.10, the `ListView` control stays its same size regardless of the size of the form.

To change this, we can use the `Form Resize` event. You can click the Left combo box in the code editor and choose Base Class Events, and from the Right combo box you should choose Resize.

When the form is resized, we want the `TreeView` control to fill the entire client area. The following code in the `frmDirDemo Resize` event handler will do this. Because the form is now a class, you need to choose the third entry (Base Class), which gives you access to all the events of the base class. Next, select Resize from the right combo box to create the procedure as follows:

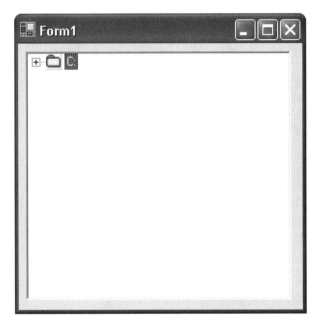

FIGURE 14.9   The form at startup.

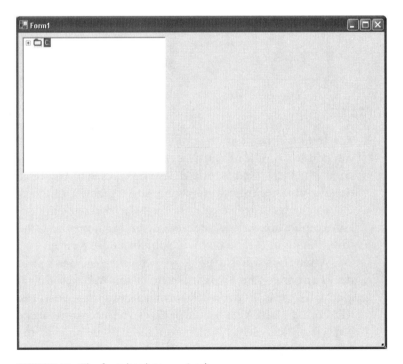

FIGURE 14.10   The form has been resized.

```
      Private Sub frmDirDemo_Resize(ByVal sender As Object, ByVal e
As System.EventArgs) Handles MyBase.Resize

         End Sub
```

We'll check to see if the form is being minimized. If it is, we'll exit the Sub procedure as we really don't need to resize if it cannot be seen. If it's being resized but not minimized, we set the `TreeView1` bounds property to a New Rectangle at 0,0 x and y values so that it starts in the top-left area of the form. We use the form Width and Height for the other two values:

```
      Private Sub frmDirDemo_Resize(ByVal sender As Object, ByVal e
As _
         System.EventArgs) Handles MyBase.Resize

         If Me.WindowState = FormWindowState.Minimized Then Exit Sub

         TreeView1.Bounds = New Rectangle(0, 0, Me.ClientSize.Width, _
             Me.ClientSize.Height)

      End Sub
```

TESTING THE PROGRAM

At this time, you can save your project and then execute it in the IDE. It will resemble Figure 14.11.

When you click on a node, you'll see that it can be opened and closed as you would expect. You can see these actions taking place in Figures 14.12 and 14.13.

FINAL CODE LISTING

This is the final code listing for the project:

```
      Imports System.IO

      Public Class Form1
      Inherits System.Windows.Forms.Form

      Private Sub Form1_Load(ByVal sender As System.Object, ByVal e
As System.EventArgs) Handles MyBase.Load
```

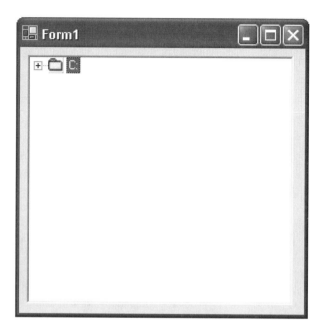

FIGURE 14.11 The final application is being executed.

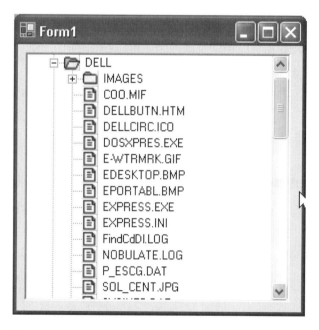

FIGURE 14.12 Opening a node.

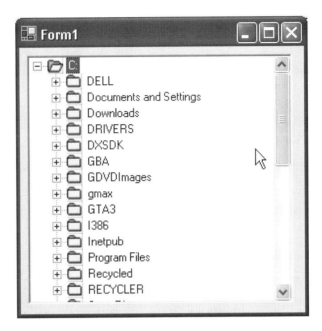

FIGURE 14.13   Closing a node.

```
Dim oNode As New System.Windows.Forms.TreeNode()

oNode.ImageIndex = 0' Closed
oNode.SelectedImageIndex = 0
oNode.Text = "C:"
TreeView1.Nodes.Add(oNode)
oNode.Nodes.Add("")

End Sub

Private Sub TreeView1_BeforeExpand(ByVal sender As Object,
ByVal e As System.Windows.Forms.TreeViewCancelEventArgs) Handles
TreeView1.BeforeExpand
    If e.Node.ImageIndex = 2 Then Exit Sub

    e.Node.Nodes(0).Remove()
    ec(e.Node)

    If e.Node.GetNodeCount(False) > 0 Then
      e.Node.ImageIndex = 1
      e.Node.SelectedImageIndex = 1
```

```
    End If
    End Sub

    Private Sub ec(ByVal oParent As System.Windows.Forms.TreeNode)

    Dim oFS As New DirectoryInfo(oParent.FullPath & "\")
    Dim oDir As DirectoryInfo
    Dim oFile As FileInfo

    For Each oDir In oFS.GetDirectories()
      Dim oNode As New System.Windows.Forms.TreeNode()
      oNode.Text = oDir.Name
      oNode.ImageIndex = 0
      oNode.SelectedImageIndex = 0
      oParent.Nodes.Add(oNode)
      oNode.Nodes.Add("")
    Next

    For Each oFile In oFS.GetFiles()
      Dim oNode As New System.Windows.Forms.TreeNode()
      oNode.Text = oFile.Name
      oNode.ImageIndex = 2
      oNode.SelectedImageIndex = 2
      oParent.Nodes.Add(oNode)
    Next

    End Sub

    Private Sub TreeView1_BeforeCollapse(ByVal sender As Object,
ByVal e As System.Windows.Forms.TreeViewCancelEventArgs) Handles
TreeView1.BeforeCollapse
        e.Node.ImageIndex = 0
        e.Node.SelectedImageIndex = 0
    End Sub

    Private Sub Form1_Resize(ByVal sender As Object, ByVal e As
System.EventArgs) Handles MyBase.Resize
        If Me.WindowState = FormWindowState.Minimized Then Exit Sub

    TreeView1.Bounds = New Rectangle(0, 0,Me.ClientSize.Width,
Me.ClientSize.Height)
    End Sub

    End Class
```

CHAPTER REVIEW

In this chapter, we built a directory browser application using the `Tree-View` control and the `System.IO` object. We used a variety of properties and methods in the construction of the application. It could be further expanded to open executable files by double-clicking on them or to add handlers for right-clicking.

In the next chapter, we're going to build an application that can watch files on the hard drive to see if they've been altered, created or deleted, displaying the results in a `ListBox`.

FILE WATCHER

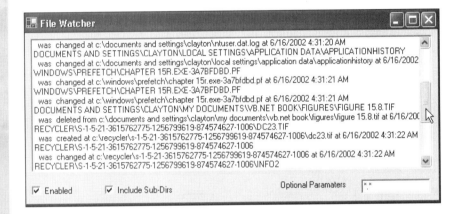

n the previous chapter, we created a file and folder browser using the TreeView control. We'll continue to deal with files in VB.NET as we create an application that watches all files and directories on your hard drive and responds when a file is created, deleted, or altered (see Figure 15.1).

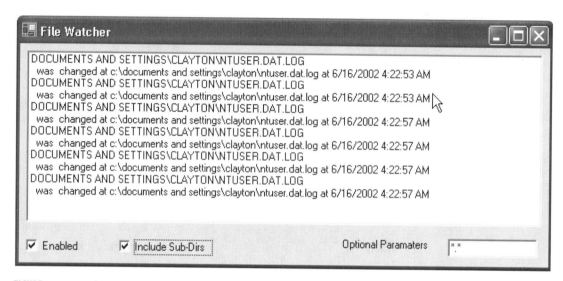

FIGURE 15.1   Final application responding to file events.

PROJECT OVERVIEW

This project is going to watch a user's hard drive to see if files or folders are altered in one of many ways. We can make use of several standard controls that we've already used in previous projects and we'll also use a few new ones.

TUTORIAL   CREATING A GUI

The first thing we'll do is create the simple graphical user interface (GUI) displayed in Figure 15.2:

1. Create a standard Windows application. This will produce the form seen in Figure 15.3.
2. Resize the form so that it's much wider than its height. The exact size is not really a concern, so you can use Figure 15.4 as a basis for this.

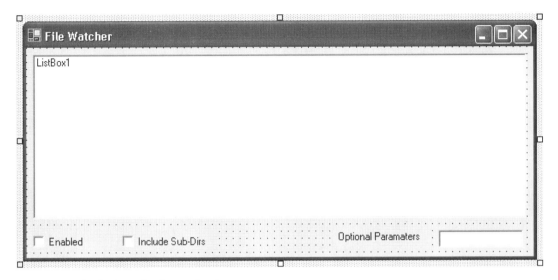

FIGURE 15.2   The final GUI for the application.

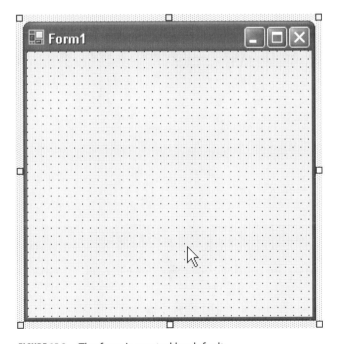

FIGURE 15.3   The form is created by default.

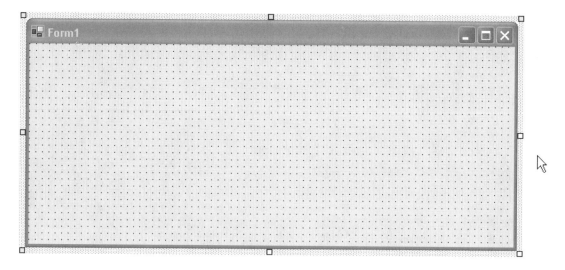

FIGURE 15.4   The form needs to be resized.

3. Add a ListBox control to the form and then position and resize it as shown in Figure 15.5.

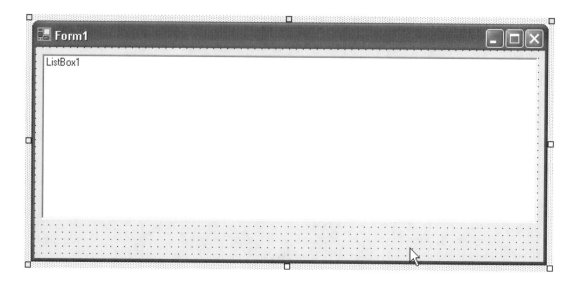

FIGURE 15.5   The ListBox control is resized to fill most of the form.

4. Add two CheckBox controls to the form and place them near the lower-left side of the form as is visible in Figure 15.6.

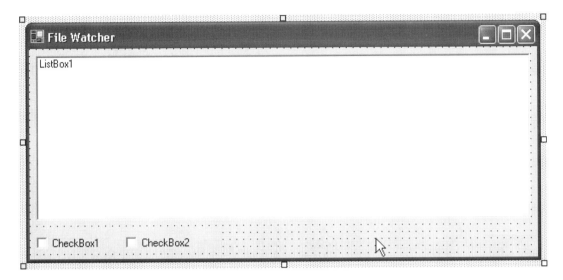

FIGURE 15.6   CheckBox controls in position.

5. Place a `Label` and TextBox control (see Figure 15.7).

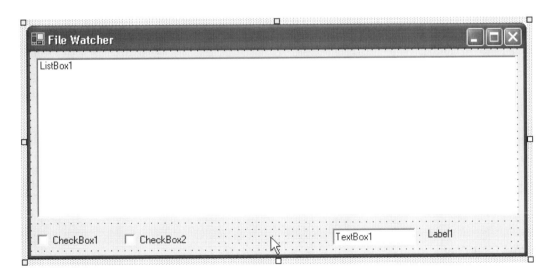

FIGURE 15.7   All of the controls are on the form.

We need to set the properties for the form, both `CheckBox` controls, the `Label` control, and the `TextBox` control as shown in Table 15.1.

Table 15.1 Correct Settings for the Controls

CONTROL	PROPERTY	VALUE
CheckBox1	Text	Enabled
CheckBox2	Text	Include Subdirectory
Label1	Text	Optional parameters:
TextBox1	Text	(leave blank)
Form1	Text	File Watcher

The form should look something like Figure 15.8.

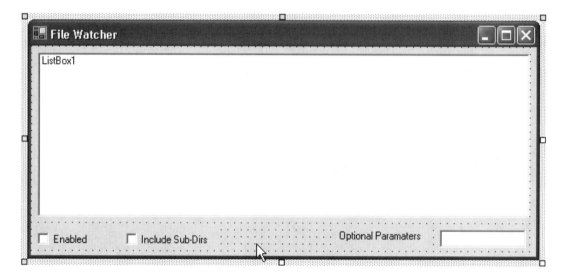

FIGURE 15.8 The final GUI looks like this.

WRITING SOME CODE

Follow these steps to write some code:

1. Add a `System.IO Imports` statement to the project.
2. Open the code editor and add the following line to the top:

```
Imports System.IO
```

3. Create a variable called fw. This will be the variable that we use throughout the program. We'll place it directly beneath the `Inherits` line in the code:

```
Dim fw As New FileSystemWatcher()
```

The code should now look like the following list:

```
Imports System.IO

Public Class Form1
    Inherits System.Windows.Forms.Form
    Dim fw As New FileSystemWatcher()

    End Sub
End Class
```

4. Set up the `Form_Load` event. Select Base Class Events from the drop-down list at the upper-left corner of the code editor and then from the right drop-down, you can choose Form_Load. This creates the following code:

```
    Private Sub Form1_Load(ByVal sender As System.Object, ByVal
e As System.EventArgs) Handles MyBase.Load

    End Sub
```

The only thing we're going to handle in the `Form_Load` event is assigning the `txtParams` equal to `"*.*"` so that the optional parameters include every possible file. The user can limit this to `"*.txt"` so that it only watches txt files; `"*.doc"`, so that it only watches doc ; or even `"c*.*"` so that it only watches files that begin with the letter *c*.

Here's the final `Form_Load` procedure:

```
    Private Sub Form1_Load(ByVal sender As System.Object, ByVal e
As System.EventArgs) Handles MyBase.Load
    txtParams.Text = "*.*"
    End Sub
```

Our next section of code is going to deal with making changes to the `CheckBox` controls. We can use the `CheckedChanged` event for both of the controls.

First, select `CheckBox1` from the upper-left drop-down list. From the right list, you can select `CheckedChanged` to create the following `Sub`:

```
Private Sub CheckBox1_CheckedChanged(ByVal sender As
System.Object, ByVal e As System.EventArgs) Handles
CheckBox1.CheckedChanged

End Sub
```

This `CheckBox` will be used to determine if we're watching for files being changed. So inside this event, we need to write the code that will change fw `EnabledRaisingEvent` to either `True` or `False` depending on the value of the `CheckBox` control. We can check the `CheckState` property of the `CheckBox`, and if it's equal to `CheckState.Checked`, then we'll set `fw.EnabledRaisingEvents` to `True`. Otherwise, we'll set this to `False`.

Here's the code:

```
Private Sub CheckBox1_CheckedChanged(ByVal sender As
System.Object, ByVal e As System.EventArgs) Handles
CheckBox1.CheckedChanged

    If CheckBox1.CheckState = CheckState.Checked Then
        fw.EnableRaisingEvents = True
    Else
        fw.EnableRaisingEvents = False
    End If

End Sub
```

We need to do a similar thing with `CheckBox2`, which determines if we're going to include subdirectories in our search. We can use the same `CheckState` property to see if the `CheckBox` is checked. If so, we set `fw.IncludeSubdirectories = True`. If not, we set it to `False`.

Here's the code:

```
Private Sub CheckBox2_CheckedChanged(ByVal sender As
System.Object, ByVal e As System.EventArgs) Handles
CheckBox2.CheckedChanged

    If CheckBox2.CheckState = CheckState.Checked Then
        fw.IncludeSubdirectories = True
    Else
        fw.IncludeSubdirectories = False
```

```
    End If

    End Sub
```

The next step is to create something to handle the file system events for files being created, deleted, and altered. We'll use two `Sub` procedures for this. First, the `txtParams TextChanged` event. We can create this event with the drop-down lists we've been using throughout this chapter. In this procedure, we'll need to set all of the properties for `fw`.

They are self-explanatory by looking at the comments that are in the following code listing:

```
    Private Sub txtParams_TextChanged(ByVal sender As
System.Object, ByVal e As System.EventArgs) Handles
txtParams.TextChanged
        fw.Path = "c:\" ' Entire Drive
        fw.IncludeSubdirectories = False ' Default is off
        fw.Filter = txtParams.Text   '"*.*" 'additional filtering
        fw.EnableRaisingEvents = False ' Default is off

        'Add the event handler for creation, altered or deleted

        AddHandler fw.Changed, New FileSystemEventHandler(AddressOf
OnFileEvent)
        AddHandler fw.Created, New FileSystemEventHandler(AddressOf
OnFileEvent)
          AddHandler fw.Deleted, New
FileSystemEventHandler(AddressOf OnFileEvent)
          End Sub
```

We're almost finished but have one `Sub` procedure left to create. You'll notice the `New FileSystemEventHandler (AddressOf OnFileEvent)` code from the previous listing. We need to create the corresponding `Sub` procedure, `OnFileEvent`.

This procedure will output the files being changed, deleted, or altered to the `ListBox` control. We use the `UCase` function to turn the filename to uppercase letters before we send it to the `ListBox` control. This is only to keep the files separated in the `ListBox`. We also add some additional information to the `ListBox` including what has happened ("`changed at,`" "`deleted at,`" or "`created at`") and what time it happens.

Here's the code:

```
          Private Sub OnFileEvent(ByVal source As Object, ByVal e As
FileSystemEventArgs)
          Dim str As String

          If e.ChangeType = WatcherChangeTypes.Changed Then
            str = " changed at "
          ElseIf e.ChangeType = WatcherChangeTypes.Created Then
            str = " created at "
          ElseIf e.ChangeType = WatcherChangeTypes.Deleted Then
            str = " deleted from "
          End If

          ListBox1.Items.Add(UCase(e.Name))
          ListBox1.Items.Add("  was " & str & e.FullPath & " at " &
Now())

          End Sub
```

TESTING THE APPLICATION

The next step is to save the project as we're now finished. You can test the application in the IDE and your output should be similar to Figure 15.9.

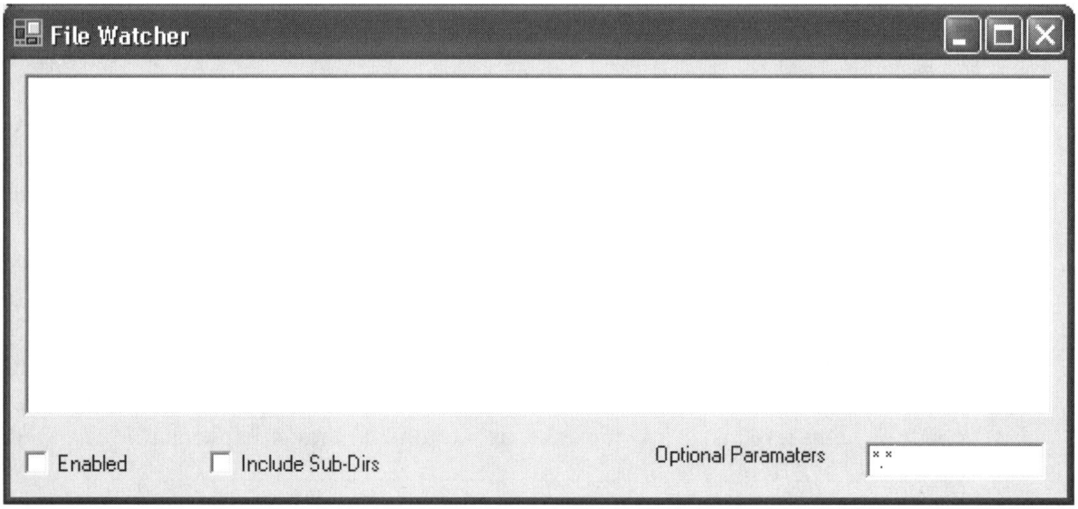

FIGURE 15.9   The final application.

You should try all of the options to see if they're working correctly. For instance, Figures 15.10 through 15.13 all have various options selected and you can see the output that occurs. For some of the options, you may have to create, delete, or alter the files manually so that the events occur.

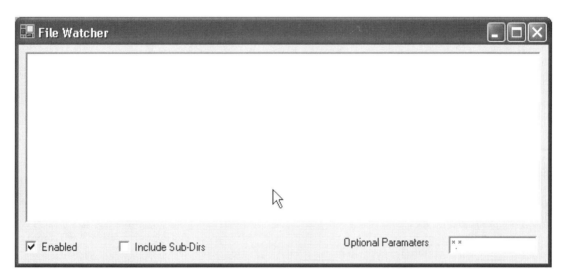

FIGURE 15.10   Default settings for the program with enabled selected.

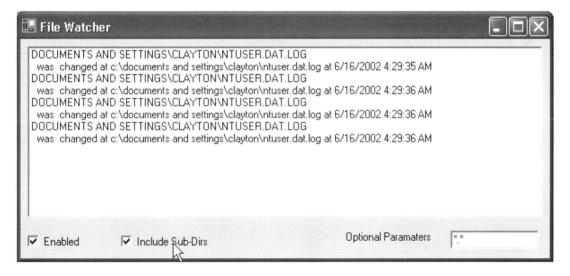

FIGURE 15.11   Including subdirectories.

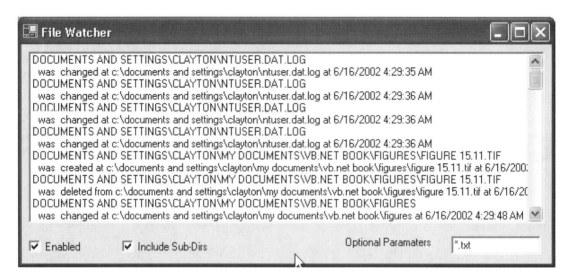

FIGURE 15.12   Watching only text files.

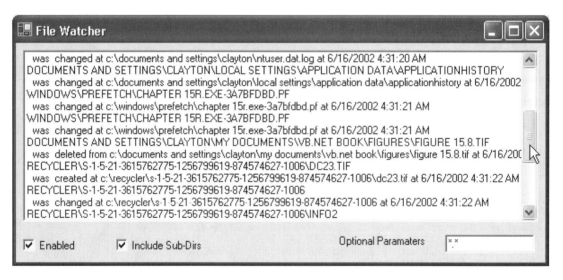

FIGURE 15.13   A file was deleted.

FINAL CODE LISTING

This is the final code listing for the application:

```
Imports System.IO

Public Class Form1
Inherits System.Windows.Forms.Form
Dim fw As New FileSystemWatcher()

Private Sub Form1_Load(ByVal sender As System.Object, ByVal
e As System.EventArgs) Handles MyBase.Load
    txtParams.Text = "*.*"
End Sub

Private Sub txtParams_TextChanged(ByVal sender As
System.Object, ByVal e As System.EventArgs) Handles
txtParams.TextChanged
    fw.Path = "c:\" ' Entire Drive
    fw.IncludeSubdirectories = False ' Default is off
    fw.Filter = txtParams.Text    '"*.*" 'additional filtering
    fw.EnableRaisingEvents = False ' Default is off

    'Add the event handler for creation, altered or deleted

    AddHandler fw.Changed, New
FileSystemEventHandler(AddressOf OnFileEvent)
    AddHandler fw.Created, New
FileSystemEventHandler(AddressOf OnFileEvent)
           AddHandler fw.Deleted, New
FileSystemEventHandler(AddressOf OnFileEvent)
End Sub

Private Sub CheckBox1_CheckedChanged(ByVal sender As
System.Object, ByVal e As System.EventArgs) Handles
CheckBox1.CheckedChanged
    If CheckBox1.CheckState = CheckState.Checked Then
      fw.EnableRaisingEvents = True
    Else
      fw.EnableRaisingEvents = False
    End If
End Sub
```

```
        Private Sub CheckBox2_CheckedChanged(ByVal sender As
System.Object, ByVal e As System.EventArgs) Handles
CheckBox2.CheckedChanged
                If CheckBox2.CheckState = CheckState.Checked Then
                        fw.IncludeSubdirectories = True
                Else
                        fw.IncludeSubdirectories = False
                End If
        End Sub

        Private Sub OnFileEvent(ByVal source As Object, ByVal e
As FileSystemEventArgs)
                Dim str As String

                If e.ChangeType = WatcherChangeTypes.Changed Then
                        str = " changed at "
                ElseIf e.ChangeType = WatcherChangeTypes.Created
Then
                        str = " created at "
                ElseIf e.ChangeType = WatcherChangeTypes.Deleted
Then
                        str = " deleted from "
                End If

                ListBox1.Items.Add(UCase(e.Name))
                ListBox1.Items.Add("  was " & str & e.FullPath & "
at " & Now())

        End Sub
    End Class
```

CHAPTER REVIEW

In this chapter, we created an application that watches the file activity on your local hard drive. We used `System.IO` and created an instance of the `FileSystemWatcher` class. We created two `CheckBoxes` and a `TextBox` to provide the ability to change parameters at runtime. Finally, we created an event handler to watch for the creation, deletion, or alteration of new files.

In the next chapter, we're going to build an application that can send an email message using only VB.NET.

16

SENDING EMAIL IN .NET

SMTP Mail

To:

From:

Subject:

Message:

Server:

Send

Attach

n the previous chapter, we created an application that was used to monitor the hard drive for any files that were altered. In these next few chapters, we're going to turn our attention to some of the communication capabilities built into .NET. In this particular chapter, we're going to begin by creating an application that can send email via Simple Mail Transfer Protocol (SMTP); see Figure 16.1.

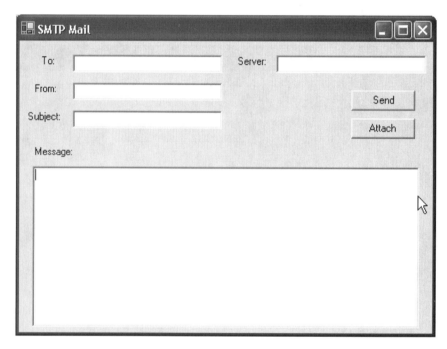

FIGURE 16.1 The final application can send email via SMTP.

PROJECT OVERVIEW

Like most VB.NET projects, we're going to build a user interface to get started. But before doing so, we'll spend a little time figuring out the general approach to this problem. First, we'll look at the classes that we're going to use. Doing so is actually quite simple for this project as .NET provides the `System.Web.Mail` namespace. This namespace is devoted to sending email and it offers everything we need for the development of this application with the following classes:

- System.Web.Mail.MailAttachment
- System.Web.Mail.MailEncoding
- System.Web.Mail.MailFormat
- System.Web.Mail.MailMessage
- System.Web.Mail.MailPriority
- System.Web.Mail.SmtpMail

Here's a little more detail on these classes:

- SmtpMail: Sends email via Windows 2000 SMTP services.
- MailMessage: Includes everything contained in an email message. An instance of it can be sent by the `SmtpMail` class.
- MailAttachment: Represents an attachment to an email.

Now that we have an understanding of the classes, we need to choose between two different methods of sending email. The quickest and easiest way is to just use the `Send` method as follows:

```
SmtpMail.Send(FromString, ToString, SubjectString,
MessageString)
```

While this works, it doesn't give us much control over the project. On the other hand, we can use the `MailMessage` object, which gives us several additional properties. The properties offer everything from the simple (To, From, and so on) to more advanced options, such as attachments that we would like to use in our example. Keeping that in mind, we're going to use the second method, which offers all of the properties listed in Table 16.1.

Table 16.1   MailMessage Properties

PROPERTY	DESCRIPTION
From	Email is from a user.
To	Email is to a user.
Cc	Email is copied to a user.
Bcc	Email is copied to a user without displaying the recipients.
Attachments	Collection of attachments to the email.
Subject	Subject of the email.
Body	Message body of the email.
BodyFormat	Format of the message body (text or HTML).
Priority	MailPriority of the message (High, Low, or Normal).

You can easily see how this method offers us many more abilities when creating an email application when compared with the Send method.

TUTORIAL

CREATING A GUI

Now that we know what we're going to use, it's time to create a new VB.NET application and produce the GUI:

1. Start VB.NET and create a new Windows application.
2. Add five `TextBox` controls to the form that's been resized to approximately 500 x 370 (see Figure 16.2). Its text property has been changed to "SMTP Mail."
3. You'll notice that the lowest `TextBox` is much larger than the others. To size it this large, change the `multiline` property to be equal to `True`.

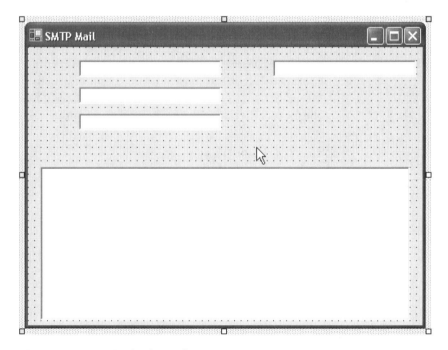

FIGURE 16.2   Start a GUI for the application.

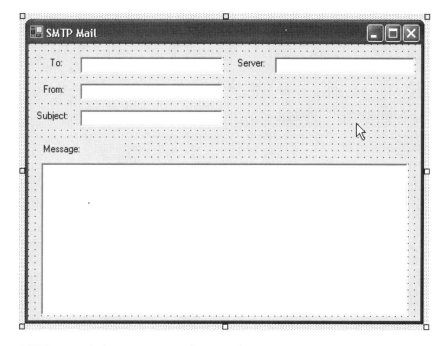

FIGURE 16.3   Labels appear next to the controls.

4. Add labels next to the TextBoxes so that an end user can determine what each TextBox is used for (see Figure 16.3).

5. Rename the TextBox controls according to the labels that are next to them. The names are as follows:

   - txtTo
   - txtFrom
   - txtSubject
   - txtServer
   - txtBody

6. Add two buttons named btnSend and btnAttach to the form (see Figure 16.4).

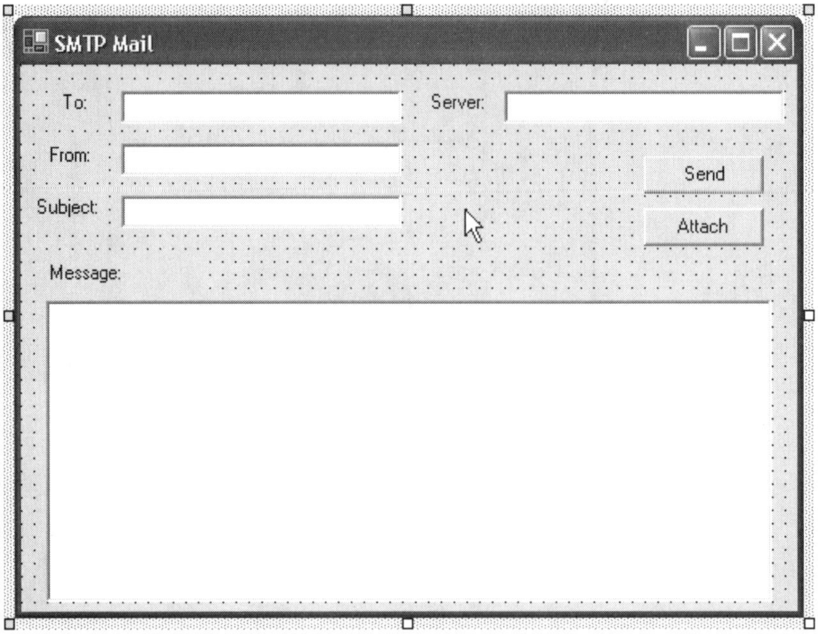

FIGURE 16.4 The final piece of the GUI.

ADDING SOME CODE

Now that the GUI is complete, we can begin writing the code for our application. We'll start by importing `System.Web.Mail` into our application:

```
Imports System.Web.Mail
```

This line should be placed above all others in the application.
Our next step is to create a variable called `msg` as follows:

```
Dim msg As New MailMessage()
```

You can place this directly beneath `Public Class` and `Inherits` form lines.

The `btnAttach` click event is a good place to begin writing code. It'll be used along with an `OpenFileDialog` (a standard file dialog you would find in any Windows application) to allow you to add files to the mail message. The procedure will begin by setting the initial directory of the `Open-FileDialog` control to `"c:\"`. You can add the control to the project before moving on. Once you've added the control to the form, you can include the following line in the `btnAttach` click event:

```
OpenFileDialog1.InitialDirectory = "c:\"
```

Next, we can set a few additional properties beginning with a filter that limits the dialog box to only certain types of files. For our application, we'll limit it to `*.txt` and `*.*`, which allow you to find only text files (`*.txt`) or all files (`*.*`). Here's the code:

```
OpenFileDialog1.Filter = "txt files (*.txt)|*.txt|All files
(*.*)|*.*"
```

We have two options for the user to choose from: txt files and all files. We can set the `Filter Index` property of the `OpenFileDialog` to 2 so that the all files selection is the default. Lastly, we'll set up a simple loop to check the result of the `OpenFileDialog`. If the appropriate result was given, we'll add a file as an attachment. Otherwise, we'll skip over it:

```
If OpenFileDialog1.ShowDialog() = DialogResult.OK Then
        Debug.WriteLine(OpenFileDialog1.FileName())
        msg.Attachments.Add(New
MailAttachment(OpenFileDialog1.FileName))
```

You may have noticed the `Debug.Writeline` line. This line outputs the filename to the Debug window in the IDE. The filenames will be displayed in the window as you add them. The debug lines can be removed for a final application, but is useful to make sure the code is working correctly. We could have done a similar thing by adding a message box that informs the user that they have added a file to a message.

Here's the complete procedure:

```
    Private Sub btnAttach_Click(ByVal sender As System.Object,
ByVal e As System.EventArgs) Handles btnAttach.Click
        OpenFileDialog1.InitialDirectory = "c:\"
        OpenFileDialog1.Filter = "txt files (*.txt)|*.txt|All
files (*.*)|*.*"
        OpenFileDialog1.FilterIndex = 2

        If OpenFileDialog1.ShowDialog() = DialogResult.OK Then
          Debug.WriteLine(OpenFileDialog1.FileName())
                    msg.Attachments.Add(New
MailAttachment(OpenFileDialog1.FileName))
```

```
        End If

    End Sub
```

The final code for this project will be the actual sending of the email. We'll start by adding the `btnSend` click event. To it, we'll include `With…End With`. This allows us to save time as we don't have to type `msg` a single time instead of every line.

Here are the first couple of lines:

```
Private Sub btnSend_Click(ByVal sender As System.Object, ByVal
e As System.EventArgs) Handles btnSend.Click

        With msg

        End With


    End Sub
```

We'll go through each of the various properties for `msg` (`From`, `To`, `Subject`, `BodyFormat`, `Body`, and `Priority`). Here's the code for the properties:

```
With msg
  .From = txtFrom.Text
  .To = txtTo.Text
  .Subject = txtSubject.Text
  .BodyFormat = MailFormat.Text
  .Body = txtBody.Text
  .Priority = MailPriority.Normal
End With
```

Now that those properties are set, we can move to the next step—checking the value in `txtServer`. We'll simply check to see if there's something in the `TextBox`. If so, we'll set the `SmtpMail.SmtpServer` equal to the value. If not, we'll display a message box to remind the user to enter some information. This is obviously not a very good check of this information. It could be improved by breaking apart the information in the `TextBox` to see if the format and so on were correct. Additionally, you could add checks for an email address for the `To` and `From` fields. However, the point of this application is to send an email, so we won't worry about it too much. If you would like, you can add these checks.

Here's the code for the server check:

```
If txtServer.Text <> "" Then
   SmtpMail.SmtpServer = txtServer.Text
Else
   MsgBox("Please enter a valid SMTP server",
MsgBoxStyle.Critical, "SMTP Server Error")
   Exit Sub
End If
```

The final step is to send the email:

```
SmtpMail.Send(msg)
```

Here's the entire procedure:

```
Private Sub btnSend_Click(ByVal sender As System.Object,
ByVal e As System.EventArgs) Handles btnSend.Click

   With msg
      .From = txtFrom.Text
      .To = txtTo.Text
      .Subject = txtSubject.Text
      .BodyFormat = MailFormat.Text
      .Body = txtBody.Text
      .Priority = MailPriority.Normal
   End With

   If txtServer.Text <> "" Then
      SmtpMail.SmtpServer = txtServer.Text
   Else
      MsgBox("Please enter a valid SMTP server",
MsgBoxStyle.Critical, "SMTP Server Error")
   Exit Sub
   End If

   SmtpMail.Send(msg)

   End Sub
```

If you were to execute the application at this time, it would display the user interface that we created earlier, which should look like Figure 16.5.

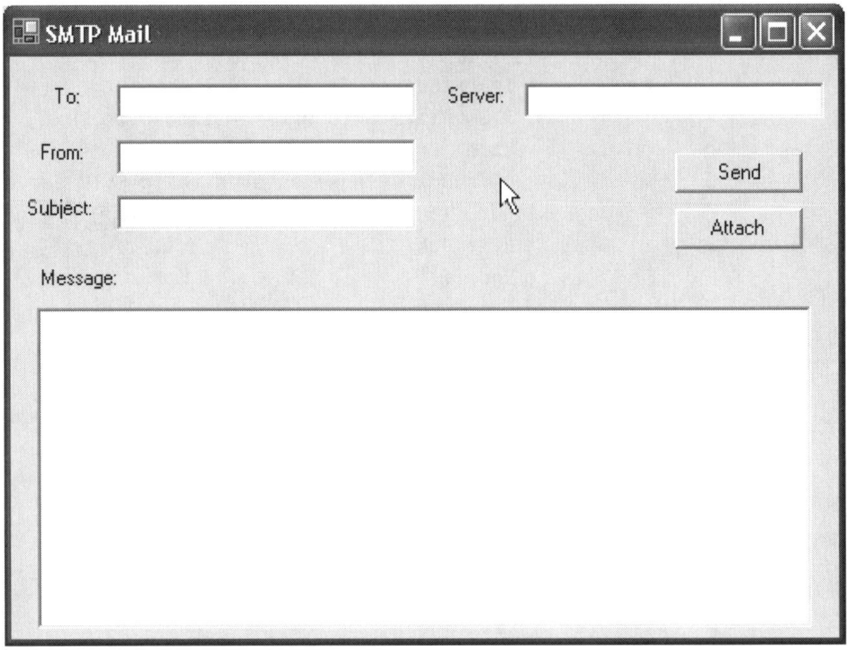

FIGURE 16.5   The final application.

If you click on the Attach button, you'll see an `OpenFileDialog` box like the one shown in Figure 16.6. You'll notice that All Files (`*.*`) was selected at startup and that we can change this to text (`*.txt`) files if needed.

At this time, you can attach a file and then click the OK button. Click the Send button and a message will pop up indicating that you need to enter information for a server (see Figure 16.7).

If you enter accurate information for your message and then click the Send button, the message will be sent.

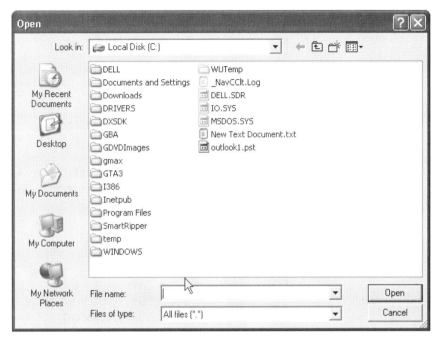

FIGURE 16.6   An OpenFileDialog box is displayed when the Attach button is clicked.

FIGURE 16.7   An error message is displayed
when information isn't entered for the server.

FINAL CODE LISTING

This is the final code listing for the application:

```
Imports System.Web.Mail

Public Class Form1
Inherits System.Windows.Forms.Form
Dim msg As New MailMessage()

Private Sub btnSend_Click(ByVal sender As System.Object,
ByVal e As System.EventArgs) Handles btnSend.Click

    With msg
      .From = txtFrom.Text
      .To = txtTo.Text
      .Subject = txtSubject.Text
      .BodyFormat = MailFormat.Text
      .Body = txtBody.Text
      .Priority = MailPriority.Normal
    End With

    If txtServer.Text <> "" Then
      SmtpMail.SmtpServer = txtServer.Text
    Else
      MsgBox("Please enter a valid SMTP server",
MsgBoxStyle.Critical, "SMTP Server Error")
      Exit Sub
    End If

    SmtpMail.Send(msg)

    End Sub


    Private Sub btnAttach_Click(ByVal sender As System.Object,
ByVal e As System.EventArgs) Handles btnAttach.Click
        OpenFileDialog1.InitialDirectory = "c:\"
        OpenFileDialog1.Filter = "txt files (*.txt)|*.txt|All
files (*.*)|*.*"
        OpenFileDialog1.FilterIndex = 2

        If OpenFileDialog1.ShowDialog() = DialogResult.OK Then
          Debug.WriteLine(OpenFileDialog1.FileName())
```

```
      msg.Attachments.Add(New
MailAttachment(OpenFileDialog1.FileName))
        End If

    End Sub

    End Class
```

CHAPTER REVIEW

In this chapter, we used the `System.Web.Mail` namespace to create an application that can send email messages. .NET provides several classes that make this task much easier than it would have been in earlier versions of VB.

In the next chapter, we're going to create a web browser with a multiple document interface (MDI).

17

MDI WEB BROWSER

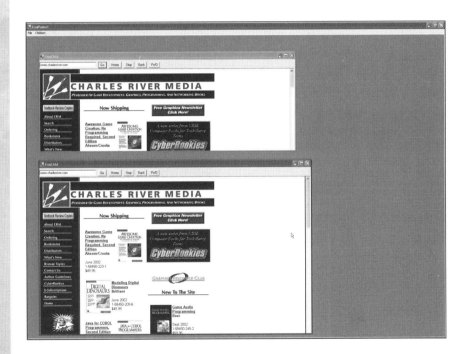

n this chapter, we'll create a Web browser based on the Microsoft Internet Control and will introduce you to the concept of a multiple document interface or MDI, which allows programmers to create applications that can have several documents open at once. Up to this point in the book, all of the applications have been single document interface (SDI); that is, they've been able to open one file at a given time.

MDI OVERVIEW

An MDI interface consists of any number of child windows and a single parent window. Although child windows can be minimized or maximized, they do so within the constraints of their parent window. To understand the differences between SDI and MDI, you can simply look at

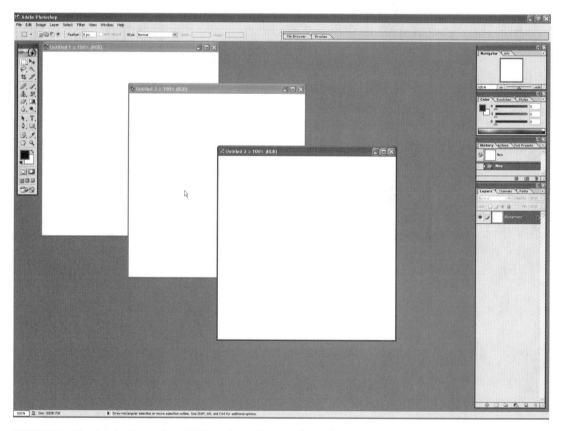

FIGURE 17.1   The Adobe Photoshop MDI interface allows multiple documents to be open at the same time.

Adobe Photoshop or Notepad, which are displayed in Figures 17.1 and 17.2, respectively. Notepad allows you to open a single text file at one instance while Word allows you to open several.

FIGURE 17.2 Notepad only allows access to a single document at any given time.

TUTORIAL BEGINNING THE PROJECT

We will begin this project by creating the forms we will need.

MDI PARENT AND CHILD FORMS

Creating an MDI project begins much like any VB program:

1. Start Visual Studio and create a Windows application named *WebBrowser*.
2. Rename the default form that's created with the project to *frmChld*. You can do this by right-clicking on the *Form1* name in the Solution Explorer and then renaming it to *frmChild*.
3. Right-click the *WebBrowser*, which is also in Solution Explorer. From the popup menu, select Add | Add Windows Form. A window will appear that asks you to name the form. You can use the name *frmParent*.

4. Use the Properties window to set the properties of the form to an MDI parent. Double-click on *frmParent* to open and display it in the IDE. You'll now have access to the properties.
5. From the *WindowStyle* section, change `IsMdiContainer` to `True`. This sets the form to an MDI parent.

Now that we have an MDI parent, we don't have to do anything to instruct the other form that it needs to be considered an MDI child.

The Web browser we're creating will be capable of displaying several windows at a time. We could create multiple forms and design them all with the controls necessary to be Web browsers. However, for our application, it'll be much easier to create new forms at runtime when we need them. We'll use `Dim form_name As New child_form`, which will create new instances of the child form dynamically at runtime.

The MDI child forms that will be created will be slightly different from their SDI counterparts. The following list details some of these differences:

- When a child form is maximized or minimized it does so within the confines of its parent window.
- When a child form is maximized, its form caption is combined with the form caption of its parent window.
- If you set the `Merge` property of all menu items located in child and parent forms, the menus items will be merged when the child is opened.

CREATING THE MENUS

We need to create a simple menu for both the child form and the MDI parent form. Add a `MenuItem` control to `frmParent` by dragging it onto the form. The control will be placed beneath the form as are all invisible controls. You'll notice a new entry at the top of the form where you can type your beginning entry. As you type into the areas, you'll see them immediately appear as you create the structure of the menu.

Here's the menu structure for the MDI parent:

```
&File
...&New
...&Close
```

You create a menu the same way for *frmChld* but with the following structure:

```
Child Forms
...&Close
```

Figure 17.3 displays the menu and how it should appear in *frmChild*.

FIGURE 17.3   The *frmChild* menu.

SOME CODE

While we can add forms to a project one at a time, we will use this opportunity to create forms dynamically. That is, we'll create a form programmatically when we need it.

Dynamic Creation of Child Forms

Let's begin writing code by creating the few lines that are needed to produce a new child form when the File | New menu is selected on the MDI parent. The menu will create a new child form and display it inside the MDI parent. The only other code that needs to be placed within the MDI parent is the closing code for the entire program that will occur when the File | Close menu is selected. You can get access to the menu events by double-clicking on them in Design view. The following code is all that's needed for both procedures:

```
    Private Sub mnuNew_Click(ByVal sender As System.Object, ByVal e
As System.EventArgs) Handles mnuNew.Click
        Dim frmChild As New frmChld() ' create child form
        frmChild.MdiParent = Me ' set this as parent form
        frmChild.Show() ' show form
    End Sub

    Private Sub mnuClose_Click(ByVal sender As System.Object, ByVal
e As System.EventArgs) Handles mnuClose.Click
        Me.Close()
    End Sub
```

At this point in time, if you run the application and click on the File | New menu, you'll create multiple child forms similar to Figure 17.4. You'll also notice that if you maximize a child form, the caption will become joined.

Child Form Menus

The next step is to add code to the child form along with its own menu that will contain only a single entry to close the child window. Add a menu control to the child form and create the following structure:

```
Children
...Close
```

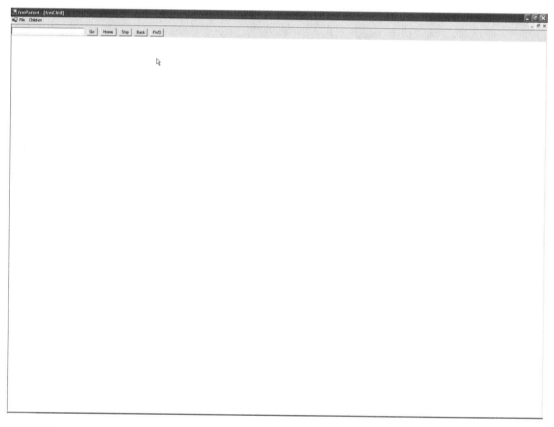

FIGURE 17.4 A maximized child form will change the caption of the parent form.

To close the form, we can use the click event for the close menu item. You will need to add a single line to this event (`me.close`). Here is the entire procedure:

```
Private Sub MenuItem2_Click(ByVal sender As System.Object,
ByVal e As System.EventArgs) Handles MenuItem2.Click
      Me.Close()
   End Sub
```

TUTORIAL

THE INTERNET CONTROL

Now, it's time to add the Microsoft Internet Control (MIC) to the form:

1. Right-click on the Toolbox window and select Customize Toolbox. In Component Object Model (COM) components, you'll see Microsoft Web Browser component; the dynamic linking library (DLL) is *Schdocvw.dll*.
2. Select the control and then click OK. It will now be present in the Toolbox and you can drag it onto the child form like any other control. You can resize it so that you can see at least a small portion of it is white. The white area will be the area that becomes the browsing window. You don't need to size it perfectly because we're going to add code that will size it to our exact needs.

The programming commands required to control the MIC are very intuitive. For example, to navigate to a Web site, you simply use the `Navigate` method of the Web browser control.

The following list gives you some basic ideas of the commands:

- WebBrowser1.Navigate www.website.com: Causes the Web site to be loaded into the control.
- WebBrowser1.GoBack: Instructs the control to go to the previous address.
- WebBrowser1.Stop: Stops a site if it's taking too long to load.
- WebBrowser1.Refresh: Refreshes the current Web site.

These are just a few of the basic methods that you can utilize to program the control. Next, we'll program our example.

PROGRAMMING THE BROWSER CONTROL

The code required for our project will encompass the basic functions that are associated with a web browser. The browser control makes this very easy for us to handle.

The GUI

A Web browser requires a few basic pieces of information before it can function, most notably the uniform resource locator (URL) of its destination and a way to input commands for instructions, such as Navigate and Stop. For this example, we'll use a text box to enter the destination and a series of command buttons that will enable the user to control the browser.

Table 17.1 lists the components that should be placed on the child form in an arrangement similar to Figure 17.5.

Table 17.1   The Components for our Project

COMPONENT	NAME	CAPTION
TextBox	txtURL	Blank
Button	LoadPage	GO
Button	Back	Back
Button	Forward	FWD
Button	Home	Home
Button	btnStop	Stop

The GUI is complete. So, it's time to code the browser control that will occur as the command buttons are clicked. The events that arise from the button clicks will be the locations of the necessary code.

CREATING THE BROWSER

Recall that the Web browser control used simple methods to control its functionality. This is noticeable in the following list of completed procedures for the command button navigation system that we've created:

```
    Private Sub LoadPage_Click_1(ByVal sender As System.Object,
ByVal e As System.EventArgs) Handles LoadPage.Click
        AxWebBrowser1.Navigate(txtURL.Text)
    End Sub

        Private Sub MenuItem2_Click(ByVal sender As System.Object,
ByVal e As System.EventArgs) Handles MenuItem2.Click
        Me.Close()
    End Sub
```

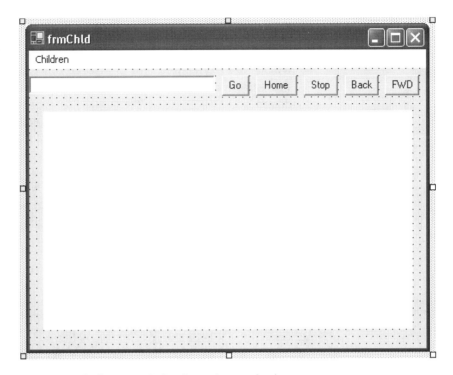

FIGURE 17.5   The browser window is starting to take shape.

```
        Private Sub Home_Click(ByVal sender As System.Object, ByVal
e As System.EventArgs) Handles Home.Click
            AxWebBrowser1.GoHome()
        End Sub


        Private Sub btnStop_Click(ByVal sender As System.Object,
ByVal e As System.EventArgs) Handles btnStop.Click
            AxWebBrowser1.Stop()
        End Sub


        Private Sub Back_Click(ByVal sender As System.Object, ByVal
e As System.EventArgs) Handles Back.Click
            AxWebBrowser1.GoBack()
        End Sub


        Private Sub Forward_Click(ByVal sender As System.Object,
ByVal e As System.EventArgs) Handles Forward.Click
            AxWebBrowser1.GoForward()
        End Sub
```

Resizing the Control

If you were to execute the program at this time, it would function as planned but you would notice the limitations that are currently visible. The Web browser control stays very small regardless of the size of the window or the Web page that's loaded. To handle this, we can simply use the Web-Browser StatusTextChange event to set the Width, Height, and Top positions of the Web browser. We need to take into account the height of the txtURL text box and subtract this from the values. Lastly, we need to subtract some additional space to allow some room for scroll boxes as necessary.

```
Private Sub Form1_Resize(ByVal sender As Object, ByVal e As
System.EventArgs) Handles MyBase.Resize
        AxWebBrowser1.Left = 0
        AxWebBrowser1.Top = txtURL.Top + 25
        AxWebBrowser1.Width = MyBase.Width - 10
```

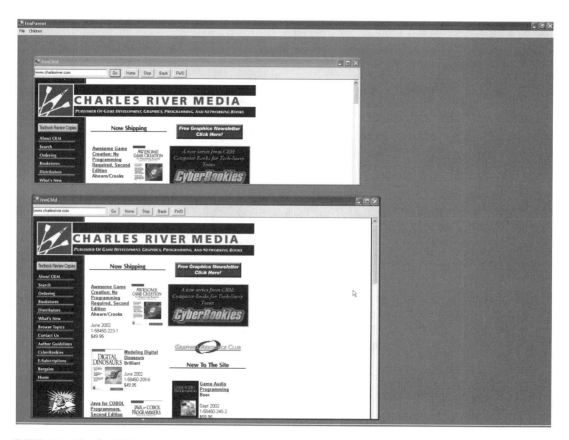

FIGURE 17.6   The final Web browser with multiple pages open.

```
        AxWebBrowser1.Height = MyBase.Height - 10
    End Sub
```

The final program, which looks similar to Figure 17.6, should now work whenever a child window is resized or a URL is loaded.

FINAL CODE LISTING

The following is the complete code listing for this chapter.

frmChild:

```
    Public Class frmChld
        Inherits System.Windows.Forms.Form


        Private Sub Form1_Resize(ByVal sender As Object, ByVal e As
    System.EventArgs) Handles MyBase.Resize
            AxWebBrowser1.Left = 0
            AxWebBrowser1.Top = txtURL.Top + 25
            AxWebBrowser1.Width = MyBase.Width - 10
            AxWebBrowser1.Height = MyBase.Height - 10
        End Sub

        Private Sub LoadPage_Click_1(ByVal sender As System.Object,
    ByVal e As System.EventArgs) HandlesLoadPage.Click
            AxWebBrowser1.Navigate(txtURL.Text)
        End Sub

        Private Sub MenuItem2_Click(ByVal sender As System.Object,
    ByVal e As System.EventArgs) Handles MenuItem2.Click
            Me.Close()
        End Sub

        Private Sub Home_Click(ByVal sender As System.Object, ByVal
    e As System.EventArgs) Handles Home.Click
            AxWebBrowser1.GoHome()
        End Sub

        Private Sub btnStop_Click(ByVal sender As System.Object,
    ByVal e As System.EventArgs) Handles btnStop.Click
            AxWebBrowser1.Stop()
        End Sub
```

```
        Private Sub Back_Click(ByVal sender As System.Object, ByVal
e As System.EventArgs) Handles Back.Click
            AxWebBrowser1.GoBack()
        End Sub

        Private Sub Forward_Click(ByVal sender As System.Object,
ByVal e As System.EventArgs) Handles Forward.Click
            AxWebBrowser1.GoForward()
        End Sub
    End Class
```

MDIForm1:

```
    Public Class frmParent
        Inherits System.Windows.Forms.Form


        Private Sub mnuNew_Click(ByVal sender As System.Object,
ByVal e As System.EventArgs) Handles mnuNew.Click
            Dim frmChild As New frmChld()
            frmChild.MdiParent = Me
            frmChild.Show()
        End Sub

        Private Sub mnuClose_Click(ByVal sender As System.Object,
ByVal e As System.EventArgs) Handles mnuClose.Click
            Me.Close()
        End Sub
```

CHAPTER REVIEW

This chapter introduced you to the Microsoft Internet Control, which immediately adds Internet browsing functionality to any form it's placed on by using very simple methods. You learned about several of the commands and how they worked. Lastly, you designed an MDI program and discovered the differences between the MDI and SDI.

In the next chapter, we're going to look at accessing the registry with VB.NET.

ACCESSING THE
REGISTRY IN VB.NET

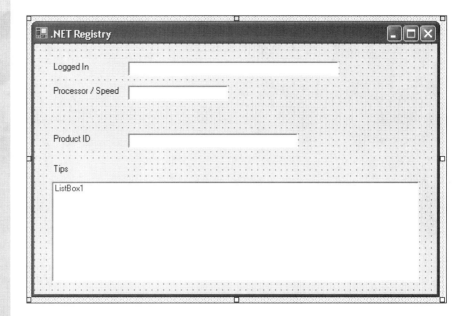

n the previous chapter, we built an MDI Web browser—the second consecutive chapter that dealt with communication issues in .NET. In this chapter, we're going to venture away from the communication area to create an application that can access the registry in VB (see Figure 18.1). In the following chapter, we'll return to the communication aspects of .NET to create an application that can retrieve the Hyper Text Markup Language (HTML) source of a Web page.

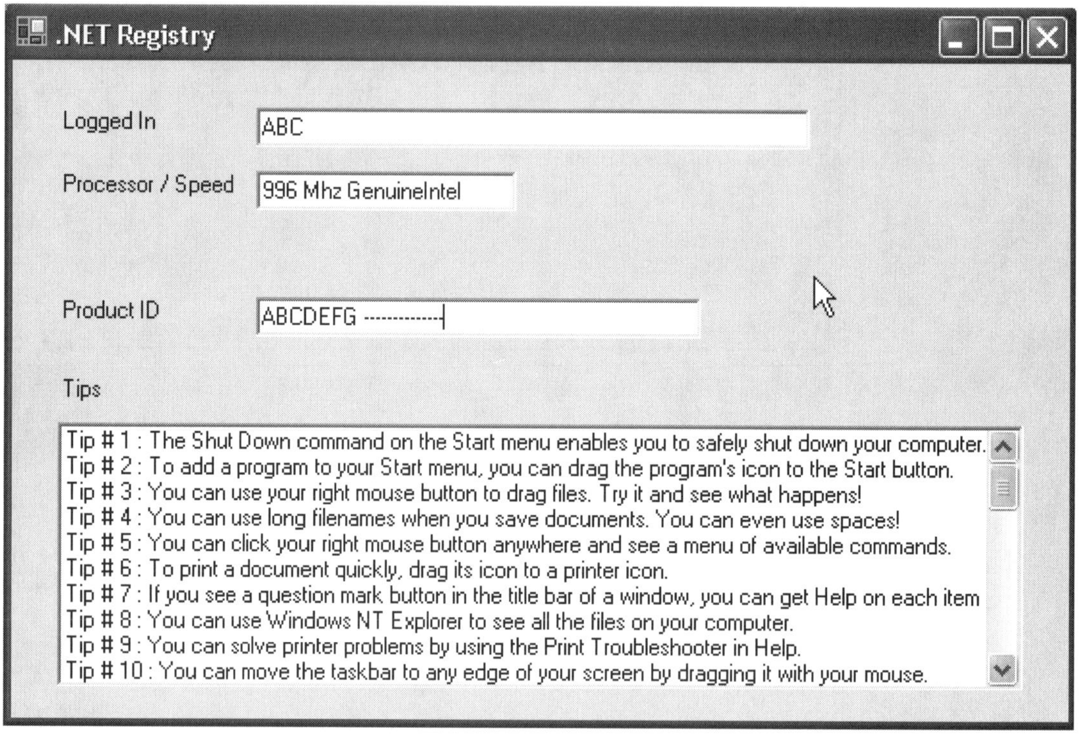

FIGURE 18.1   Accessing the registry in VB.NET.

TUTORIAL

Project Overview

This chapter will demonstrate how to use Visual Basic.NET to access the registry using the `Registry` and `RegistryKey` classes that are located in the `Win32` namespace. We'll retrieve various elements from the registry, including the currently logged-in user, and central processing unit (CPU) type and speed, to name a couple. The `Registry` class supplies the base registry keys to access values and subkeys in the registry.

If you're unfamiliar with it, the Windows registry is a central database for application configuration settings and other information that can be useful for applications, such as serial numbers. You can write to and read from the registry using a few classes in .NET. Before we start working on the program, we'll look at the registry in a little more detail:

1. Click the Start button and then choose Run from the popup menu. This displays the Run window (see Figure 18.2).

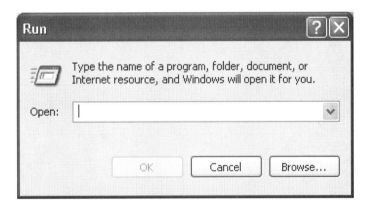

FIGURE 18.2   This window can be used to run applications.

2. In the Open box, enter regedit.exe and then click the OK button. This will open the Registry Editor that should look something like Figure 18.3.
3. As you can see from Figure 18.3, the registry serves as hierarchical data storage for various settings and includes five main keys under My Computer. You can click the + signs next to the folders to open them and browse the many settings that are in the registry.

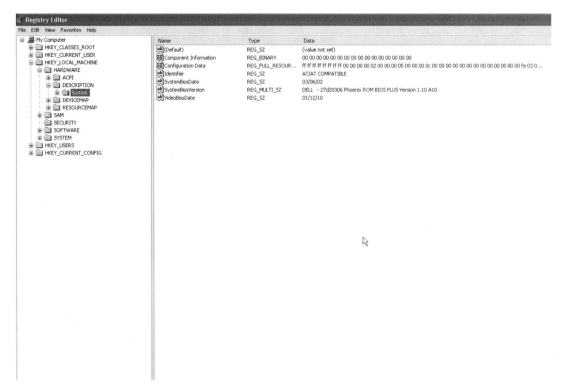

FIGURE 18.3   The Registry Editor is a built-in application for editing the registry.

.NET FRAMEWORK

The .NET Framework provides two classes that we can use to access the registry: `Registry` and `RegistryKey`. They are defined in Microsoft.Win32 namespace, so before using these classes, we need to add a reference to the namespace.

The Registry Class

The `Registry` class contains members that provide access to registry keys. We can define the following registry keys:

- CurrentUser: Stores user preference information.
- LocalMachine: Holds configuration information for the local machine.
- ClassesRoot: Stores information about types and their properties.
- Users: Contains information about the default user configuration.
- PerformanceData: Stores performance information for software components.
- CurrentConfig: Holds non-user-specific hardware information.
- DynData: Stores dynamic data.

The `Tegistry` class has a field corresponding to each of these key types:

- CurrentUser: Provides access to the HKEY_CURRENT_USER key.
- LocalMachine: Provides access to the HKEY_LOCAL_MACHINE key.
- Users: Returns a `RegistryKey` type that provides access to HKEY_USERS key.
- PerformanceData: Provides access to the HKEY_PERFORMANCE_DATA key.
- ClassesRoot: Provides access to the HKEY_CLASSES_ROOT key.
- CurrentConfig: Provides access to the HKEY_CURRENT_CONFIG key.
- DynData: Provides access to the HKEY_DYN_DATA key.

Keeping this in mind, it's easy to access information in the registry. For example, if you wanted to access HKEY_LOCAL_Machine, you could call `Registry.LocalMachine`.

RegistryKey Class

The `RegistryKey` class contains the members that we need to add, remove, replace, and read registry data. Some of the more common properties and methods are listed below in Tables 18.1 and 18.2, respectively.

Table 18.1   Properties of the RegistryKey Class

PROPERTY	DESCRIPTION
Name	Name of the key.
SubKeyCount	Count of subkeys at the base level, for the current key.
ValueCount	Count of values in the key.

Table 18.2   Methods of the RegistryKey Class

METHOD	DESCRIPTION
Close	Closes a key.
CreateSubKey	Creates anew subkey, or if one exists, it will open the existing one.
DeleteSubKey	Deletes a specified subkey.
DeleteSubKeyTree	Deletes a subkey and any children.
DeleteValue	Deletes a specified value from a key.
GetSubKeyNames	Returns an array of strings that contain all of the subkey names.
GetValue	Returns the specified value.
GetValueNames	Retrieves an array of strings that contain all of the value names associated with key.
OpenSubKey	Opens a subkey.
SetValue	Sets a specified value.

T U T O R I A L

CREATING THE PROJECT

Given the overview of the classes, properties, and methods that we'll be using, let's create the program:

1. Start VB.NET and create a new Windows application. Let's create a simple GUI for our application by adding three TextBox controls to the form. You can resize the form, rename its Text property, and position the TextBoxes so that they look something like Figure 18.4.

2. Add labels to the form that will allow you to see the information that the controls will contain. You can use Figure 18.5 as a guide to adding these labels.

3. Rename the TextBox controls so that their names correspond to the labels. Starting from the top and moving down, you can rename them as follows:

   • txtLoggedIn
   • txtSpeed
   • txtProdID

4. Add another label to the control, and a single ListBox and position— renaming the Text property of the label—so that they appear similar to Figure 18.6.

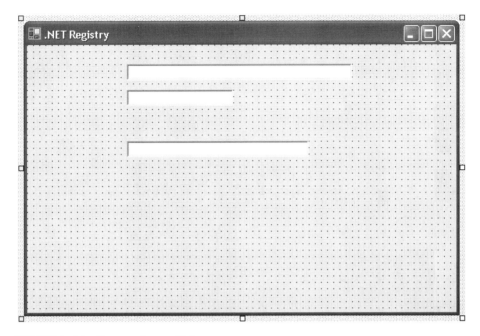

FIGURE 18.4   The first step for our GUI.

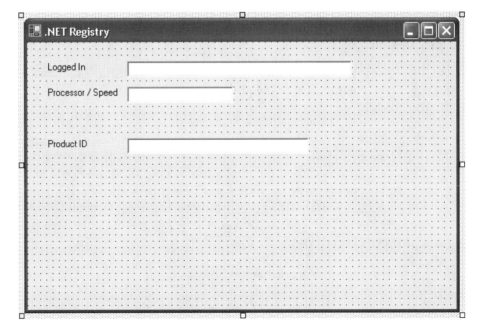

FIGURE 18.5   Labels are added to the form.

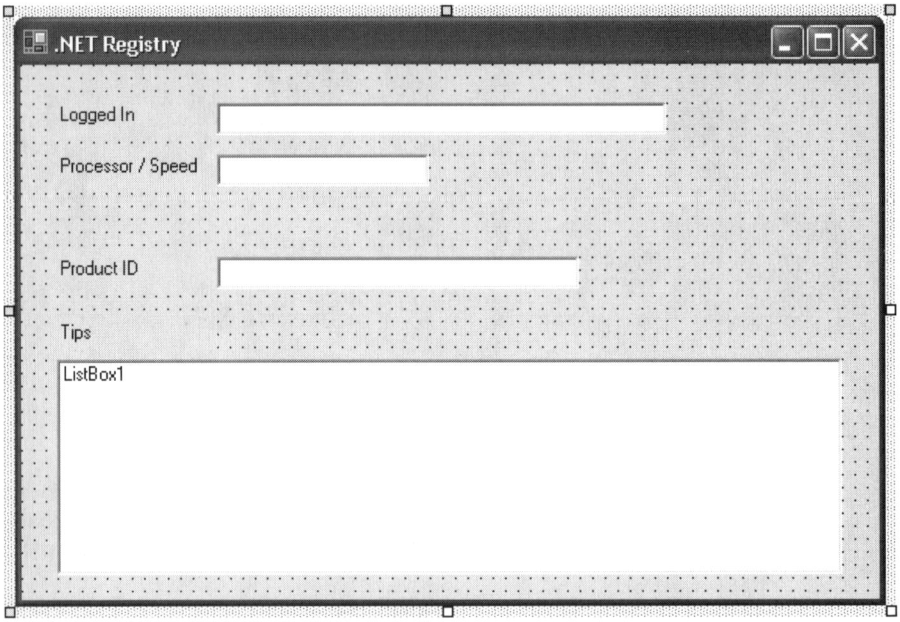

FIGURE 18.6 The final GUI.

ADDING SOME CODE

We'll begin writing code for this application by adding the following namespace to the project:

```
Imports Microsoft.Win32
```

You should add the Imports statement above all other code in the project. All of the remaining code for this project will be in the Form Load event, so select Base Class Events from the left drop-down list and then Load from the right drop-down to create the event.

We'll begin this procedure by creating a variable called reg as type RegistryKey:

```
Dim reg as RegistryKey
```

Next, we can create a variable called Temp and SubKeyName as Strings and a variable called X as an integer:

```
Dim temp, subKeyName As String
Dim x As Integer
```

Now, we can concentrate on the code for the application. First, let's set reg equal to `Registry.Users` to place us in the HKEY_USERS key:

```
reg = Registry.Users
```

Next, we can use a simple `If...Then` loop to check if the registry contains a value for the current user. If it does, we set `txtLoggedIn` equal to the value contained in `"Logon User Name"`. Otherwise, we'll set it to `"No User Found"`:

```
    If Not reg Is Nothing Then
            For Each subKeyName In reg.GetSubKeyNames
                reg = Registry.Users.OpenSubKey(subKeyName &
"\Software\Microsoft\Windows\CurrentVersion\Explorer", False)
                If Not reg Is Nothing Then
                    If reg.GetValue("Logon User Name") =
Nothing Then
                            'nothing
                    Else
                        txtLoggedIn.Text = reg.GetValue("Logon
User Name")
                    End If
                End If
            Next
        Else
            txtLoggedIn.Text = "No User Found"
        End If
```

Now, we can go through the same process for the other items in the application. We're going to check the processor speed, the type of processor used, and the Windows product key:

```
    reg =
Registry.LocalMachine.OpenSubKey("Hardware\Description\system\Centr
alProcessor\0", False)
            txtSpeed.Text = reg.GetValue("~Mhz")
```

```
        reg =
Registry.LocalMachine.OpenSubKey("HARDWARE\\DESCRIPTION\\System\\Ce
ntralProcessor\\0")
        txtSpeed.Text = txtSpeed.Text & " Mhz " &
reg.GetValue("VendorIdentifier")

        reg =
Registry.LocalMachine.OpenSubKey("Software\Microsoft\Windows\Curren
tVersion\", False)
        txtProdID.Text = reg.GetValue("ProductID")
```

The final aspect of our program is to go through all 40 tips that are stored in \Microsoft\Windows\CurrentVersion\Explorer\Tips\ and add each of them to the ListBox. We don't have a particular reason for wanting this information, but it's a good way to see how we can get several values at one time.

Here's the code:

```
For x = 1 To 40
        reg =
Registry.LocalMachine.OpenSubKey("Software\Microsoft\Windows\Curren
tVersion\Explorer\Tips\", False)
        temp = reg.GetValue(CStr(x))
        ListBox1.Items.Add("Tip # " & x & " : " & temp)
    Next
```

TESTING THE APPLICATION

We can now save the application and test it in the IDE. When you run it, you should see something like Figure 18.7. This will display all of the information for your machine.

 The information contained in ProductID is fictitious and is only there for an example.

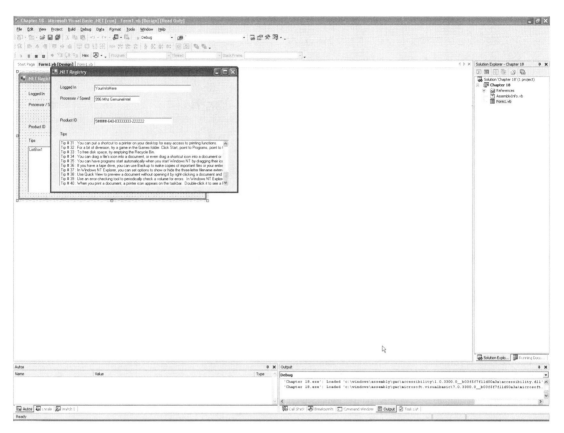

FIGURE 18.7   The final application being tested in the IDE.

FINAL CODE LISTING

This is the complete code listing for the application:

```
Imports Microsoft.Win32

Public Class Form1
    Inherits System.Windows.Forms.Form


    Private Sub Form1_Load(ByVal sender As System.Object,
ByVal e As System.EventArgs) Handles MyBase.Load
        Dim reg As RegistryKey 'the reg key
```

```
            Dim temp, subKeyName As String
            Dim x As Integer

            reg = Registry.Users
            If Not reg Is Nothing Then
                    For Each subKeyName In reg.GetSubKeyNames
                        reg =
Registry.Users.OpenSubKey(subKeyName &
"\Software\Microsoft\Windows\CurrentVersion\Explorer", False)
                        If Not reg Is Nothing Then
                            If reg.GetValue("Logon User Name") =
Nothing Then
                                'nothing
                                Else
                                    txtLoggedIn.Text
=reg.GetValue("Logon User Name")
                                End If
                            End If
                    Next
            Else
                txtLoggedIn.Text = "No User Information Found"
            End If


            reg =
Registry.LocalMachine.OpenSubKey("Hardware\Description\system\Centr
alProcessor\0", False)
            txtSpeed.Text = reg.GetValue("~Mhz")

            reg =
Registry.LocalMachine.OpenSubKey("HARDWARE\\DESCRIPTION\\System\\Ce
ntralProcessor\\0")
            txtSpeed.Text = txtSpeed.Text & " Mhz " &
reg.GetValue("VendorIdentifier")

            reg =
Registry.LocalMachine.OpenSubKey("Software\Microsoft\Windows\Curren
tVersion\", False)
            txtProdID.Text = reg.GetValue("ProductID")

            For x = 1 To 40
                    reg =
Registry.LocalMachine.OpenSubKey("Software\Microsoft\Windows\Curren
tVersion\Explorer\Tips\", False)
```

```
                           temp = reg.GetValue(CStr(x))
                           ListBox1.Items.Add("Tip # " & x & " : " &
temp)
                   Next

           End Sub


       End Class
```

CHAPTER REVIEW

In this chapter, we built an application that retrieves information from the registry. We can also save or alter existing information. However, because a wrong move with a registry setting can render your system useless without a reinstall of the OS, we've decided to stay away from this here. You can experiment on your own by looking up `CreateSubKey` and `SetValue` in the VB.NET help.

In the next chapter, we're going to build an application that can retrieve the source of a Web page from the Internet.

RETRIEVING WEB PAGE SOURCE FROM THE INTERNET

I n the previous chapter, we created an application that could retrieve settings from the system registry. In this chapter, we're going to get back to the networking abilities of the .NET Framework. Specifically, we're going to develop an application that can retrieve the source of a Web page (see Figure 19.1).

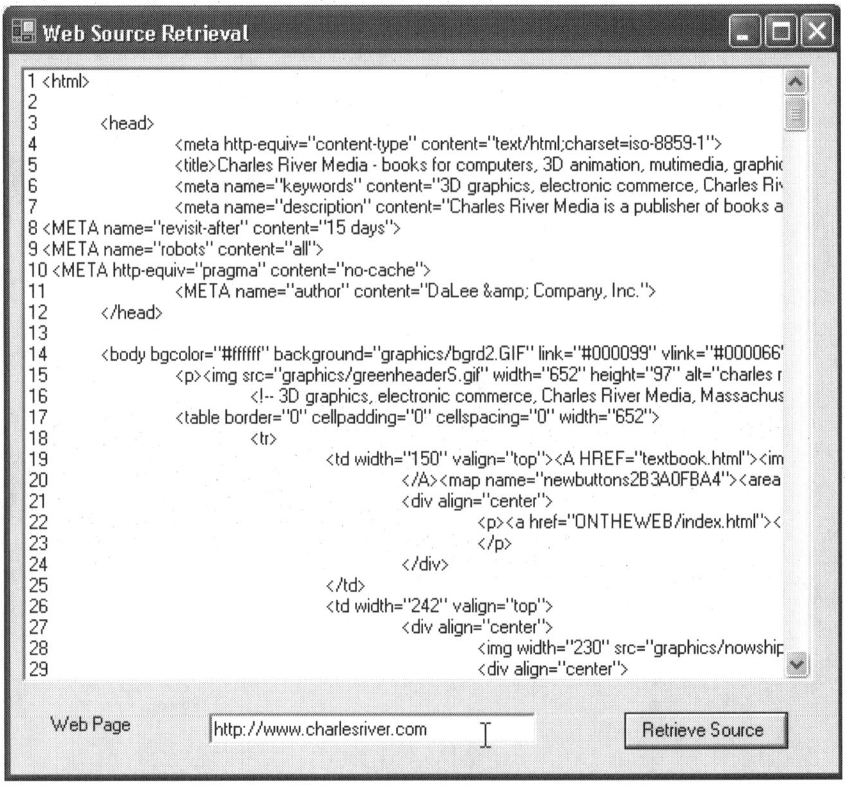

FIGURE 19.1 The final application having retrieved the source from a Web page.

PROJECT OVERVIEW

In previous versions of Visual Basic, we could have used the Internet Transfer Control or the WinInet API to do this type of application. Now, in .NET, the `System.NET` Namespace provides the `WebRequest` class. Using this class, we can obtain a stream that represents a response for a particular request. Once we have a stream, we can read the response as easily as we can from a file that's on the local machine.

TUTORIAL

GETTING STARTED

1. Create a new VB.NET Windows application.
2. Add a ListBox control to the form and a single button. The button can have its Text property set to "Retrieve Source". The form and controls can be positioned as in Figure 19.2.
3. Finally, add a TextBox to the form and a label that can be used to identify the control. The TextBox can be renamed to txtURL and its Text property can be set to an empty string. You can position them similarly to Figure 19.3.

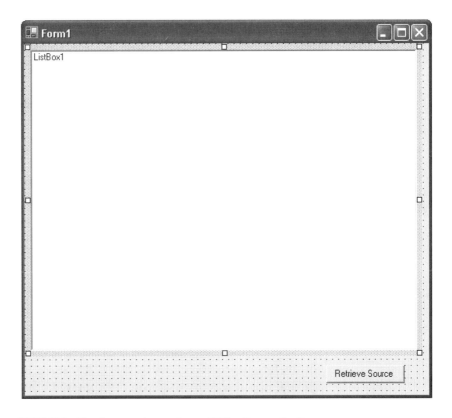

FIGURE 19.2   The first step in creating a GUI for the application.

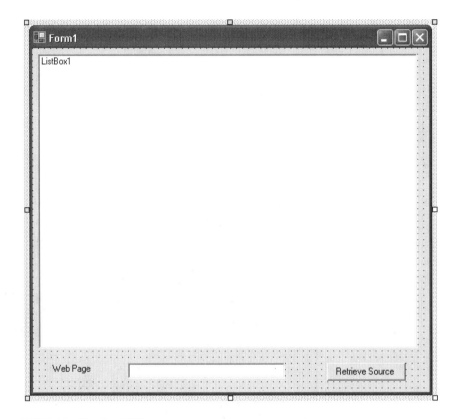

FIGURE 19.3 The final GUI.

PROGRAMMING

We can now write the code for the program, beginning with the `Imports` statement for `System.NET` and `System.IO`. These statements must be used prior to any other declarations:

```
Imports System.Net
Imports System.IO
```

We're going to use the `Form Load` event to change the `Text` property for the form to be `"Web Source Retrieval"`. Select Base Class Events from the left drop-down list and Load from the right drop-down list to create the event. Add the following code to the event:

```
Me.Text = "Web Source Retrieval"
```

The next step is to create the `Click` event for `Button1`. You can do this by selecting `Button1` from the left drop-down and then `Click` from the right. Inside this procedure, we'll retrieve the page source.

We can produce a new `WebRequest` by using the `Create` method of the `WebRequest` class:

```
Dim wrGETURL As WebRequest
wrGETURL = WebRequest.Create(sURL)
```

The next step might be optional for some users but it will be required for many of them. If you're behind a proxy server on a network, you'll need to create a `WebProxy` object and provide it to the `WebRequest` object. We're going to use the `Proxy` property of `wrGETURL` to assign the default proxy that uses the settings in Internet Explorer:

```
wrGETURL.Proxy = WebProxy.GetDefaultProxy()
```

Now that we have a request set up with the proxy information, we can use it to obtain a `Stream` object that corresponds to the response of our request:

```
Dim objStream As Stream
objStream = wrGETURL.GetResponse.GetResponseStream()
```

We can use the stream to read through the data that is retrieved line by line and add those lines to the `ListBox` control. We'll use a `Do...While` loop to loop through it and use the `Add` method of the `ListBox` to add the lines to it. We're also going to add a number to the `ListBox` so that the lines are separated with numbers at the beginning. The loop ends when the `ReadLine` method returns `Nothing`.

Here's the code:

```
Dim objReader As New StreamReader(objStream)
Dim sLine As String = ""
Dim i As Integer = 0

Do While Not sLine Is Nothing
        i += 1
        sLine = objReader.ReadLine
        If Not sLine Is Nothing Then

            ListBox1.Items.Add(i & " " & sLine)

        End If
```

The last step is to create a message box that can be displayed when a line is clicked on in the ListBox. This allows us to see a complete line at a single time as the ListBox isn't going to be wide enough to handle the entire lengths that are sent to it.

First, select ListBox1 from the left drop-down list and from the right drop-down, you can choose SelectedIndexChanged. This creates the appropriate event. Inside the procedure, we need to create the message box as follows:

```
MsgBox("The current line is : " & ListBox1.SelectedItem,
MsgBoxStyle.OKOnly, "Entire Line of Code")
```

TESTING THE APPLICATION

You can now save the application and then run it inside the IDE. When you run the program, a screen like Figure 19.4 is displayed.

FIGURE 19.4   The application as displayed on startup.

Next, enter *http://www.charlesriver.com* in the `TextBox` and then click the Retrieve Source button. If everything is working correctly, you'll see the source appear in the `ListBox` control (see Figure 19.5).

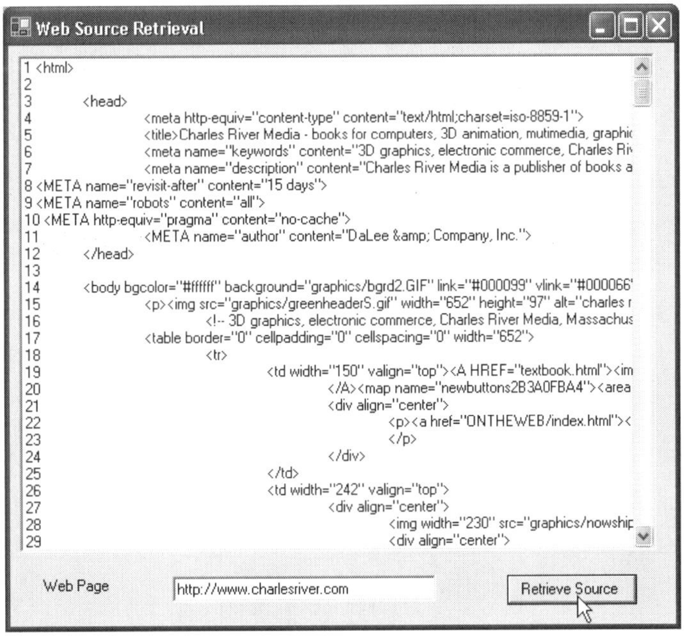

FIGURE 19.5   The source is retrieved from the Web.

If you click on any of the lines of code, you'll see a message box that displays the complete line of code (see Figure 19.6).

FIGURE 19.6   A message box displays information that was otherwise hidden.

FINAL CODE LISTING

This is the final listing for the application:

```
Imports System.Net
Imports System.IO

Public Class Form1
Inherits System.Windows.Forms.Form


Private Sub Form1_Load(ByVal sender As System.Object, ByVal
e As System.EventArgs) Handles MyBase.Load
      Me.Text = "Web Source Retrieval"
End Sub

Private Sub Button1_Click(ByVal sender As System.Object,
ByVal e As System.EventArgs) Handles Button1.Click

      Dim wrGETURL As WebRequest
      wrGETURL = WebRequest.Create(txtURL.Text)

      wrGETURL.Proxy = WebProxy.GetDefaultProxy()

      Dim objStream As Stream
      objStream = wrGETURL.GetResponse.GetResponseStream()

      Dim objReader As New StreamReader(objStream)
      Dim sLine As String = ""
      Dim i As Integer = 0

      Do While Not sLine Is Nothing
          i += 1
          sLine = objReader.ReadLine
          If Not sLine Is Nothing Then

              ListBox1.Items.Add(i & " " & sLine)

          End If
      Loop

End Sub
```

```
    Private Sub ListBox1_SelectedIndexChanged(ByVal sender As
System.Object, ByVal e As System.EventArgs) Handles
ListBox1.SelectedIndexChanged
        MsgBox("The current line is : " &
ListBox1.SelectedItem, MsgBoxStyle.OKOnly, "Entire Line of Code")
    End Sub
    End Class
```

CHAPTER REVIEW

In this chapter, we created an application that can retrieve the source code from a Web page. We used the WebRequest class to retrieve the pages and the StreamReader to read the information.

In the next chapter, we're going to create a simple slot machine game in VB.NET.

.NET SLOTS

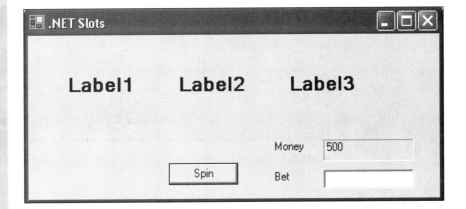

n the last chapter, we developed an application that retrieves the source from a Web page. It displays the source in a ListBox where we could look through it. In this chapter, we're going to create a slot machine game using standard controls and random numbers that are generated by the Rnd function (see Figure 20.1).

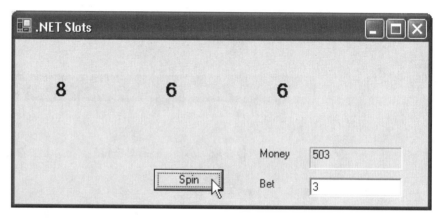

FIGURE 20.1   The final game.

TUTORIAL

GETTING STARTED

1. Create a Windows application in VB.NET.
2. Resize the form so that it's approximately 450x200. You can also change the Text property to ".NET Slots". Your graphical user interface (GUI) should look something like Figure 20.2 at this time.
3. Add three labels to the form. The labels will be used to display numbers that, if matched, will increase the amount of money that you have by double the amount you bet. If the numbers are unequal, you'll lose the amount of money you bet. The labels can be positioned like Figure 20.3.
4. You may have noticed that the labels are larger than normal in Figure 20.3. You can change the size of the labels by clicking on the Font property, choosing size 16, and also selecting Bold. This makes the labels much larger so that they stick out. You can change the names of the labels as follows:

   - lbl1
   - lbl2
   - lbl3

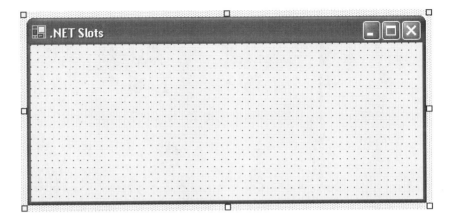

FIGURE 20.2   The form is the correct size.

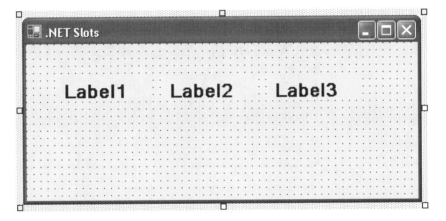

FIGURE 20.3   The labels are placed on the form.

5. Add another label to the form and then set the border style to fixed3D in the Properties window. Then change its name to *lblScore*. You can position the label as shown in Figure 20.4.
6. Add a TextBox to the form that will be used for entering a bet. You can set the Text property to an empty string and change its name to txtBet. You can position it near *lblScore* as shown in Figure 20.5.
7. Finally, finish the GUI by adding a button called btnSpin to the form. Change its Text property to read Spin and position it, along with a couple of label controls, to label the Money and Bet controls as shown in Figure 20.6.

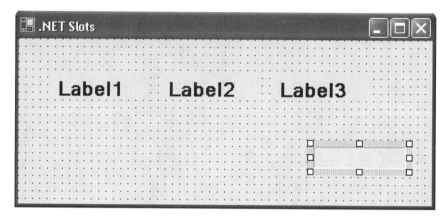

FIGURE 20.4   The label is in the correct position.

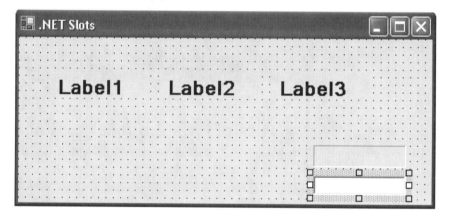

FIGURE 20.5   The GUI is nearly complete.

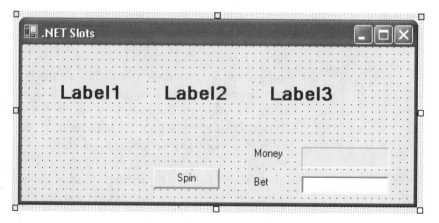

FIGURE 20.6   The final GUI.

WRITING THE CODE

We'll now move on to writing the code for the application. Let's begin with the `Form Load` event where we can initialize the value held in *lblScore*. You can select Base Class Events form the left drop-down list and Load from the right drop-down to create the code that handles the event. Inside the created `Sub` procedure, add the following line:

```
lblScore.Text = "500"
```

We'll now focus our attention on the `btnSpin` click event. Choose `btnSpin` from the left drop-down list and Click from the right. This will create the click event code for us. We're going to use the `Rnd` function to create a random number that will be used to assign values to the label controls.

The `Rnd` function creates a round number between 0 and 1. So, to create a number between 1 and 10, we need to multiply the number times 10 and add 1 to it. We then convert it to an integer value and we end up with a value between 1 and 10. An example of this follows:

```
CInt(Int((10 * Rnd()) + 1))
```

Before we go through the process of creating random numbers, we're going to test the value of `txtBet` to make sure it's greater than or equal to 1. This makes sure that a bet is placed before the spin can occur. Here's the code:

```
If txtBet.Text > 1 Then

End If
```

We can then go through the process of assigning each label to the random numbers that we're going to create. Add the following lines to the `If…Then` statement that we just created:

```
lbl1.Text = CInt(Int((10 * Rnd()) + 1))
lbl2.Text = CInt(Int((10 * Rnd()) + 1))
lbl3.Text = CInt(Int((10 * Rnd()) + 1))
```

After assigning values, we need to check them to see if we have won the game or lost. We use another `If…Then` statement to check to see if the values are equal:

```
If lbl1.Text = lbl2.Text Or lbl1.Text = lbl3.Text Or lbl2.Text
= lbl3.Text Then

End If
```

We can add or subtract the money as necessary. Here's the complete If...Then statement:

```
If lbl1.Text = lbl2.Text Or lbl1.Text = lbl3.Text Or lbl2.Text
= lbl3.Text Then
        lblScore.Text += CInt(txtBet.Text)
Else
        lblScore.Text -= CInt(txtBet.Text)
End If
```

We'll now return to the original check of the bet where we made sure that it was greater than or equal to 1. We haven't yet dealt with the possibility that the value is less than 1. If the value is less than 1, we need to display a message box to inform the user. Here's the Else statement for this:

```
Else
MsgBox("Please Enter a bet greater than $1",
MsgBoxStyle.Critical, "Invalid Bet")
```

At this time, the application would work perfectly. However, if the user were to enter a bet of *A* or some other invalid character, it would cause an error. We'll catch this exception error and if its number is 13 (this error refers to trying to change a string to type Double), we'll display a message box that informs the user that they entered an invalid bet. We'll also catch any other exceptions and display an error number and message for them.

Here's the complete Sub procedure as there are several loops. Due to the addition of Try/Catch exception handling, it's fairly complicated to see how this all goes together unless we look at it at one time:

```
Private Sub btnSpin_Click(ByVal sender As System.Object,
ByVal e As System.EventArgs) Handles btnSpin.Click
        Try
            If txtBet.Text > 1 Then
```

```
                    lbl1.Text = CInt(Int((10 * Rnd()) + 1))
                    lbl2.Text = CInt(Int((10 * Rnd()) + 1))
                    lbl3.Text = CInt(Int((10 * Rnd()) + 1))

                    If lbl1.Text = lbl2.Text Or lbl1.Text =
            lbl3.Text Or lbl2.Text = lbl3.Text Then
                            lblScore.Text += CInt(txtBet.Text)
                    Else
                            lblScore.Text -= CInt(txtBet.Text)
                    End If

                Else
                        MsgBox("Please Enter a bet greater than $1",
            MsgBoxStyle.Critical, "Invalid Bet")
                    End If

                Catch ex As Exception When Err.Number = 13 'Cast from
            string to type double is not valid
                    MsgBox("You need to input a number for a bet.",
            MsgBoxStyle.Critical, "Invalid Bet")
                    Exit Try

                Catch ex As Exception
                    MsgBox(ex.Message & " " & Err.Number,
            MsgBoxStyle.OKOnly, "Error in Application")

                End Try

            End Sub
```

TESTING THE APPLICATION

We're now at a point where we can save the program and then test it in the IDE. Running the application displays a screen like the one shown in Figure 20.7.

Enter a bid amount of 0 and click the Spin button. This will display a message box with an error (see Figure 20.8).

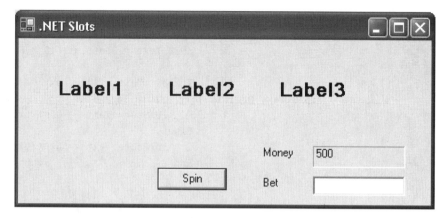

FIGURE 20.7   The final application is running.

FIGURE 20.8   An error message is given with a
bet of 0.

Click the OK button to close the message box and then enter a value
of *B* as a bet. This will display an entirely different message box, like the
one shown in Figure 20.9, informing the user that they've placed an invalid bet.

FIGURE 20.9   An invalid bet has been placed.

Now that you've tested the error handling, you can try a real value such as 5 for a bet. You can then click the Spin button and test if the application adds and subtracts values accordingly (see Figure 20.10).

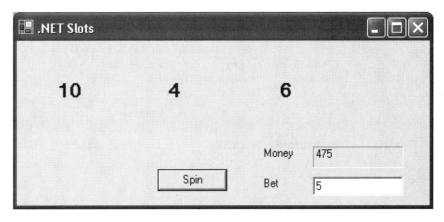

FIGURE 20.10 Several games have now been played and the money values have changed.

FINAL CODE LISTING

The final code listing for this application is as follows:

```
Public Class Form1
Inherits System.Windows.Forms.Form



    Private Sub btnSpin_Click(ByVal sender As System.Object,
ByVal e As System.EventArgs) Handles btnSpin.Click
        Try
            If txtBet.Text > 1 Then

                lbl1.Text = CInt(Int((10 * Rnd()) + 1))
                lbl2.Text = CInt(Int((10 * Rnd()) + 1))
                lbl3.Text = CInt(Int((10 * Rnd()) + 1))

                If lbl1.Text = lbl2.Text Or lbl1.Text
=lbl3.Text Or lbl2.Text = lbl3.Text Then
                    lblScore.Text += CInt(txtBet.Text)
                Else
                    lblScore.Text -= CInt(txtBet.Text)
                End If
```

```
                Else
                    MsgBox("Please Enter a bet greater than
$1",MsgBoxStyle.Critical, "Invalid Bet")
                End If

            Catch ex As Exception When Err.Number = 13 'Cast from
string to type double is not valid
                MsgBox("You need to input a number for a bet.",
MsgBoxStyle.Critical, "Invalid Bet")
                Exit Try

            Catch ex As Exception
                MsgBox(ex.Message & "  " & Err.Number,
MsgBoxStyle.OKOnly, "Error in Application")

            End Try

        End Sub

        Private Sub Form1_Load(ByVal sender As System.Object, ByVal
e As System.EventArgs) Handles MyBase.Load
            lblScore.Text = "500"
        End Sub

        End Class
```

CHAPTER REVIEW

In this chapter, we created an application that simulated a simple slot machine. We used various options for error handling and displayed errors that were encountered via message boxes. If the end user won a spin, the value of their money increased by double the amount that was placed as a bet. Likewise, if they lost a spin, the bet money was subtracted from their money. You could add a few additional checks such as a maximum bet, ending the game if a user got to 0 money, and so on.

In the next chapter we're going to create a word processor in VB.

WORD PROCESSOR

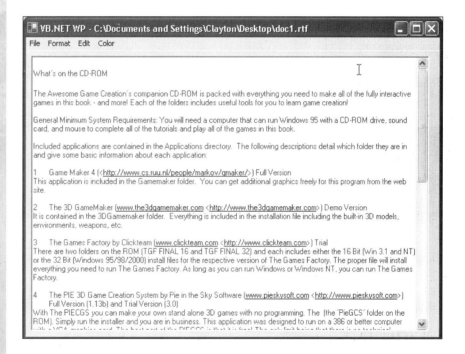

n the previous chapter, we created a slot machine game using the Rnd function and several of the built-in components. The next application that we're going to create is a word processor. We'll use a RichTextBox control, a MainMenu control, and several of the dialog controls to create a user interface that you'd expect for a word processor (see Figure 21.1).

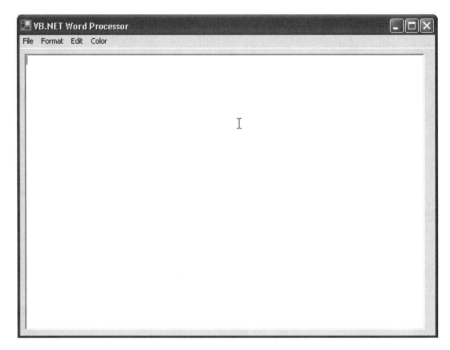

FIGURE 21.1   We're going to create a word processor like this one.

PROJECT OVERVIEW

The creation of a word processor will begin with the RichTextBox, which will be the control that's used to capture the user input of text information. We'll use several of its properties and methods to do standard formatting of text such as underlining, bold, and italics. We'll also use OpenFileDialog, SaveFileDialog, FontDialog, ColorDialog, and MainMenu controls.

TUTORIAL

GUI

We have a good idea of how we're going to put this application together and we know the controls that we're going to use. We'll start by creating a new Windows application in VB.NET:

1. Resize the form to 640x480 and then add a RichTextBox control to the form. The RichTextBox control can be resized as shown in Figure 21.2.

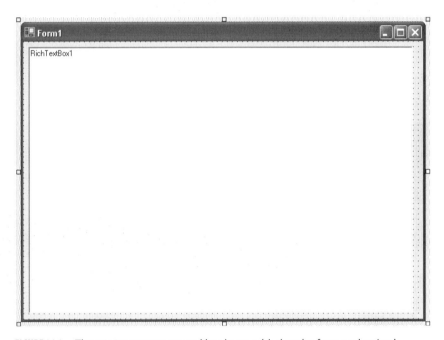

FIGURE 21.2   The RichTextBox control has been added to the form and resized.

2. Add a MainMenu control to the project. The control will be visible at the bottom of the screen and will also add an area at the top of the form that says Type Here. Click on this text and change it to read &File. The form should now look like Figure 21.3.

The ampersand (&) character instructs the menu to create a shortcut to a menu item that you create. For this example (&File), the letter F will now be underlined and you will be able to access it during runtime by using Alt-F key combination.

3. After you create this menu item, you'll notice that there are two additional areas that contain Type Here text. Click on the area immediately beneath the File item and type &Open.

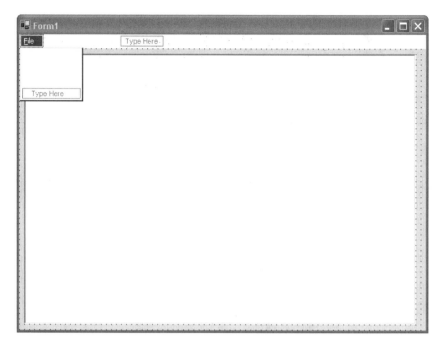

FIGURE 21.3 A menu is beginning to take shape.

4. At the lower-right corner of your screen in the Properties window, change the name of this item to reflect the item, if you would prefer to do so.

ON THE CD *In the example that's on the CD-ROM, and in the code in this chapter, the menu items are left at their default settings.*

5. Continue adding items beneath the File menu as follows:

&Save
E&xit

Your complete menu structure at this time will consist of a File menu with Open, Save, and Exit options.

6. Include the additional menus in our application. Click on the Type Here area immediately to the right of File and type Format.

7. Add the following items beneath Format:

Font
Caps
Center Justify
Left Justify
Right Justify

8. Include two additional menu items: Edit and Color. The Edit menu consists of the following items:

Copy
Paste
Cut

The Color menu will have the following items beneath it:

Font
Background

At this time, you should have all of the appropriate menus and your screen should look something like Figure 21.4.

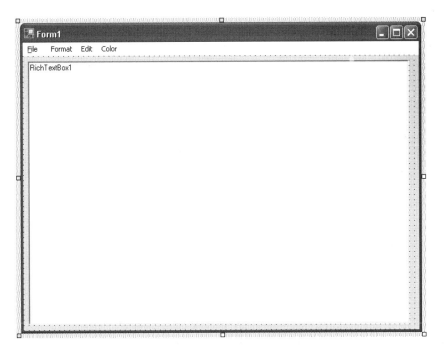

FIGURE 21.4   The menus have been created.

9. The final step in the creation of a GUI is to add several dialog controls: `OpenFile`, `SaveFile`, `Font`, and `Color`. As you probably expected, the dialog controls don't really change the GUI except as place holders that can be seen beneath the visible part of the GUI (see Figure 21.5).

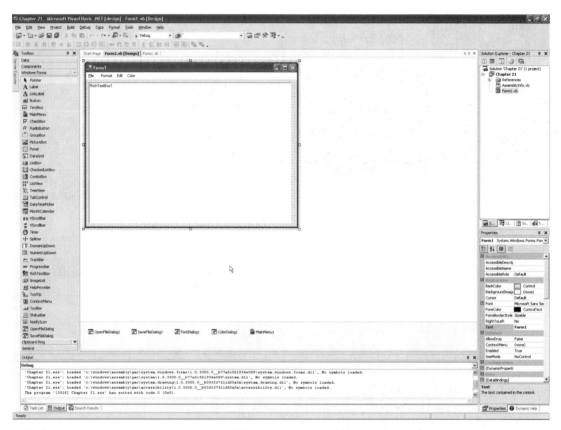

FIGURE 21.5   The final GUI.

THE CODE

Now that the GUI is out of the way, we'll move on to the code. You can open the code editor and then choose Base Class Events from the left drop-down list and Load from the right one. This will create the Form Load event for us. We're going to set the content of the RichTextBox equal to an empty string and the Text property of the Form to "VB.NET Word Processor":

```
Private Sub Form1_Load(ByVal sender As System.Object, ByVal e
As System.EventArgs) Handles MyBase.Load
    RichTextBox1.Text = ""
    Me.Text = "VB.NET Word Processor"
End Sub
```

We can now look at what will happen as the various menu items are clicked. We'll go through them one by one beginning with the File menu. The File item (MenuItem1) won't actually need to be dealt with as we are only clicking on it so that it'll expose the items beneath it.

MenuItem2 is the Open menu. We'll use the FileOpenDialog and the Load method of the RichTextBox control to open the contents of a Rich-Text file (RTF) and place it in the RichTextBox for editing. We'll also set the Text property of the form to be equal to "VB.NET WP -" followed by the filename so that the filename is visible in the caption of the form. To create the event, you can choose MenuItem2 from the left drop-down list and then choose Click from the right drop-down list. This approach will be the same for all of the events for the menu items.

Here's the code for the procedure:

```
Private Sub MenuItem2_Click(ByVal sender As System.Object,
ByVal e As System.EventArgs) Handles MenuItem2.Click
    'File Open
    OpenFileDialog1.ShowDialog()
    RichTextBox1.LoadFile(OpenFileDialog1.FileName)
    Me.Text = "VB.NET WP - " & OpenFileDialog1.FileName
End Sub
```

Saving the file is the next section to deal with. This section is Menu-Item3, and as such, you can create its click event by selecting MenuItem3 from the drop-down list and Click from the right one. We can use the SaveFileDialog and SaveFile methods of the RichTextBox control to handle the saving of a file. We can also set the Text property of the form to be equal to the SaveFileDialog.

Here's the code:

```
Private Sub MenuItem3_Click(ByVal sender As System.Object,
ByVal e As System.EventArgs) Handles MenuItem3.Click
    'File Save
    SaveFileDialog1.ShowDialog()
    RichTextBox1.SaveFile(SaveFileDialog1.FileName)
End Sub
```

The next menu item, MenuItem4, is for exiting the application:

```
Private Sub MenuItem4_Click(ByVal sender As System.Object,
ByVal e As System.EventArgs) Handles MenuItem4.Click
    'Exit
    Me.Close()
End Sub
```

`MenuItem6` will be the next menu item that we'll deal with as `Menu-Item5` is the Format item. This is a menu item that will change the font for the `RichTextBox` control. We can use the `FontDialog`'s `ShowDialog` method to display a dialog box on the screen, and then when a user clicks OK to make changes, we can set the `Font` property of the dialog equal to the `Font` property of the `FontDialog`.

Here's the code:

```
Private Sub MenuItem6_Click(ByVal sender As System.Object,
ByVal e As System.EventArgs) Handles MenuItem6.Click
    'Font
    FontDialog1.ShowDialog()
    RichTextBox1.SelectionFont = FontDialog1.Font
End Sub
```

`MenuItem7` the Caps menu item. This is a menu item that will change the selected text of the `RichTextBox` control to all capital letters. We can use the `SelectedText` property of the `RichText` as follows:

```
Private Sub MenuItem7_Click(ByVal sender As System.Object,
ByVal e As System.EventArgs) Handles MenuItem7.Click
    'Convert to all caps
    RichTextBox1.SelectedText = RichTextBox1.SelectedText.ToUpper
End Sub
```

We're going to handle the Left Justify, Right Justify, and Center Justify menu items (`MenuItems` 8, 9, and 10). These procedures will all use the `SelectionAlignment` property to set the appropriate justification:

```
Private Sub MenuItem8_Click(ByVal sender As System.Object,
ByVal e As System.EventArgs) Handles MenuItem8.Click
    'Center Justify
    RichTextBox1.SelectionAlignment = HorizontalAlignment.Center
End Sub
```

```
Private Sub MenuItem9_Click(ByVal sender As System.Object,
ByVal e As System.EventArgs) Handles MenuItem9.Click
    'Left Justify
    RichTextBox1.SelectionAlignment = HorizontalAlignment.Left
End Sub
```

```
Private Sub MenuItem10_Click(ByVal sender As Object, ByVal e As
System.EventArgs) Handles MenuItem10.Click
    'Right Justify
```

```
RichTextBox1.SelectionAlignment = HorizontalAlignment.Right
End Sub
```

The next three menu items (12, 13, and 14) will deal with Copy, Paste, and Cut. We can use the built-in `Copy`, `Paste`, and `Cut` methods that are provided in the `RichTextBox` control to provide the functions to our application:

```
Private Sub MenuItem12_Click(ByVal sender As System.Object,
ByVal e As System.EventArgs) Handles MenuItem12.Click
    'Copy
    RichTextBox1.Copy()
End Sub

Private Sub MenuItem13_Click(ByVal sender As System.Object,
ByVal e As System.EventArgs) Handles MenuItem13.Click
    'Paste
    RichTextBox1.Paste()
End Sub

Private Sub MenuItem14_Click(ByVal sender As System.Object,
ByVal e As System.EventArgs) Handles MenuItem14.Click
    'Cut
    RichTextBox1.Cut()
End Sub
```

The final two items will deal with the font color and background color of the `RichTextBox`. We can use the `ColorDialog`, `ForeColor`, and `BackColor` properties of the `RichTextBox` to handle this:

```
Private Sub MenuItem16_Click(ByVal sender As System.Object,
ByVal e As System.EventArgs) Handles MenuItem16.Click
    'Font Color
    ColorDialog1.ShowDialog()
    RichTextBox1.ForeColor = ColorDialog1.Color
End Sub

Private Sub MenuItem17_Click(ByVal sender As System.Object,
ByVal e As System.EventArgs) Handles MenuItem17.Click
    'Background Color
    ColorDialog1.ShowDialog()
    RichTextBox1.BackColor = ColorDialog1.Color
End Sub
```

TUTORIAL

TESTING THE WORD PROCESSOR

Now that the application is complete, you can test it by saving it and then running it in the IDE. It'll display a window similar to the one shown in Figure 21.6 when it's first opened.

These steps can be completed to test the application:

1. Choose File | Open to display an Open dialog box like the one shown in Figure 21.7.

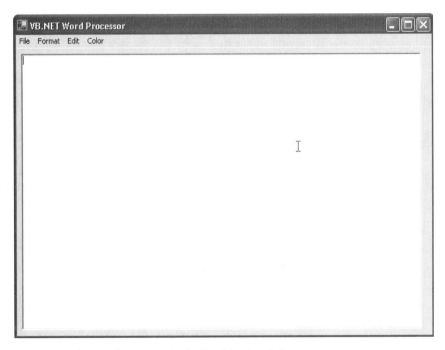

FIGURE 21.6 The word processor looks like this when it first opens.

2. Choose an RTF file from your hard drive to display its contents. You'll see the file loaded into our application and the caption of the form will change to read the name of the new file (see Figure 21.8).
3. Test the application further by changing the font (see Figure 21.9), applying justification (Figures 21.10, 21.11, and 21.12), and adding colors (Figures 21.13 and 21.14).

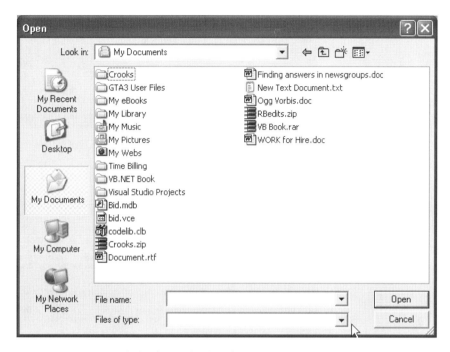

FIGURE 21.7   An Open dialog box is displayed.

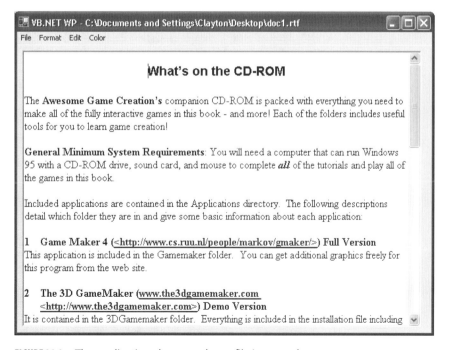

FIGURE 21.8   The application changes when a file is opened.

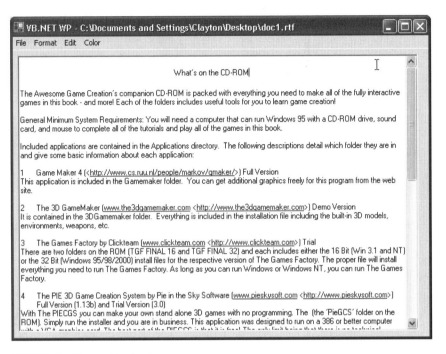

FIGURE 21.9   Change the font.

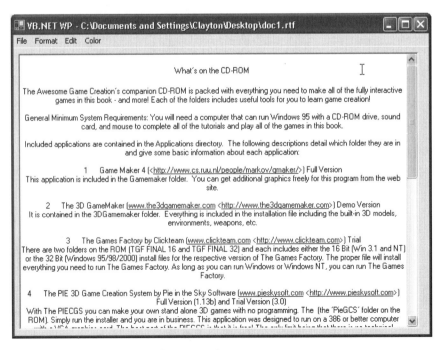

FIGURE 21.10   Apply center justification to the text.

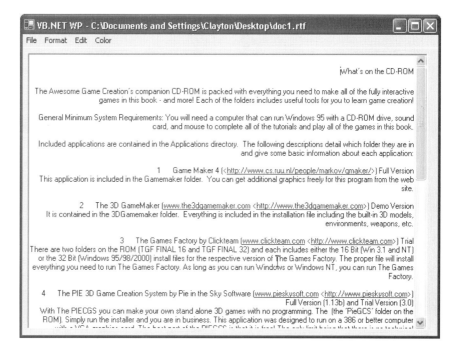

FIGURE 21.11   Apply right justification to the text.

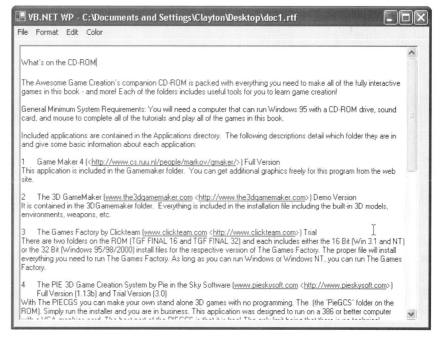

FIGURE 21.12   Change our text back to left justification.

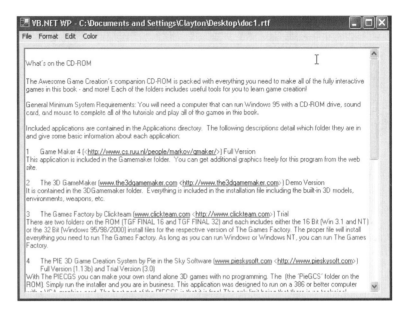

FIGURE 21.13 The text color has been changed from black to red. (See the full-color version on the book's companion CD-ROM.)

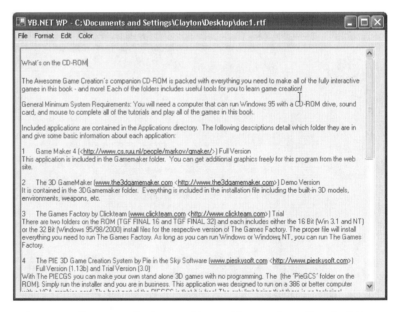

FIGURE 21.14 Change our background from white to yellow. (See the full-color version on the book's companion CD-ROM.)

FINAL CODE LISTING

The following is the complete code listing for this application:

```
Public Class Form1
Inherits System.Windows.Forms.Form

Private Sub MenuItem2_Click(ByVal sender As System.Object,
ByVal e As System.EventArgs) Handles MenuItem2.Click
      'File Open
      OpenFileDialog1.ShowDialog()
      RichTextBox1.LoadFile(OpenFileDialog1.FileName)
      Me.Text = "VB.NET WP - " & OpenFileDialog1.FileName
End Sub

Private Sub MenuItem3_Click(ByVal sender As System.Object,
ByVal e As System.EventArgs) Handles MenuItem3.Click
      'File Save
      SaveFileDialog1.ShowDialog()
      RichTextBox1.SaveFile(SaveFileDialog1.FileName)
      Me.Text = "VB.NET WP - " & SaveFileDialog1.FileName
End Sub

Private Sub MenuItem4_Click(ByVal sender As System.Object,
ByVal e As System.EventArgs) Handles MenuItem4.Click
      'Exit
      Me.Close()
End Sub

Private Sub MenuItem6_Click(ByVal sender As System.Object,
ByVal e As System.EventArgs) Handles MenuItem6.Click
      'Font
      FontDialog1.ShowDialog()
      RichTextBox1.SelectionFont = FontDialog1.Font
End Sub

Private Sub MenuItem7_Click(ByVal sender As System.Object,
ByVal e As System.EventArgs) Handles MenuItem7.Click
      'Convert to all caps
      RichTextBox1.SelectedText =
RichTextBox1.SelectedText.ToUpper
End Sub

Private Sub MenuItem8_Click(ByVal sender As System.Object,
ByVal e As System.EventArgs) Handles MenuItem8.Click
```

```
            'Center Justify
            RichTextBox1.SelectionAlignment =
HorizontalAlignment.Center
        End Sub

        Private Sub MenuItem9_Click(ByVal sender As System.Object,
ByVal e As System.EventArgs) Handles MenuItem9.Click
            'Left Justify
            RichTextBox1.SelectionAlignment =
HorizontalAlignment.Left
        End Sub

        Private Sub MenuItem10_Click(ByVal sender As Object, ByVal
e As System.EventArgs) Handles MenuItem10.Click
            'Right Justify
            RichTextBox1.SelectionAlignment =
HorizontalAlignment.Right
        End Sub

        Private Sub MenuItem12_Click(ByVal sender As System.Object,
ByVal e As System.EventArgs) Handles MenuItem12.Click
            'Copy
            RichTextBox1.Copy()
        End Sub

        Private Sub MenuItem13_Click(ByVal sender As System.Object,
ByVal e As System.EventArgs) Handles MenuItem13.Click
            'Paste
            RichTextBox1.Paste()
        End Sub

        Private Sub MenuItem14_Click(ByVal sender As System.Object,
ByVal e As System.EventArgs) Handles MenuItem14.Click
            'Cut
            RichTextBox1.Cut()
        End Sub

        Private Sub MenuItem16_Click(ByVal sender As System.Object,
ByVal e As System.EventArgs) Handles MenuItem16.Click
            'Font Color
            ColorDialog1.ShowDialog()
            RichTextBox1.ForeColor = ColorDialog1.Color
        End Sub
```

```
      Private Sub MenuItem17_Click(ByVal sender As System.Object,
ByVal e As System.EventArgs) Handles MenuItem17.Click
          'Background Color
          ColorDialog1.ShowDialog()
          RichTextBox1.BackColor = ColorDialog1.Color
      End Sub

      Private Sub Form1_Load(ByVal sender As System.Object, ByVal
e As System.EventArgs) Handles MyBase.Load
          RichTextBox1.Text = ""
          Me.Text = "VB.NET Word Processor"
      End Sub
```

CHAPTER REVIEW

In this chapter, we created a word processor by relying on the properties and methods of the RichTextBox control. We used several of the dialog controls to change various aspects of the text in the application.

In the next chapter, we're going to add the ability to encrypt or decrypt the text that's in the application.

ENCRYPTION AND DECRYPTION

I n the last chapter, we created an application that could load and save rich text format (RTF) files. We're going to expand that application to include some basic encryption and decryption capabilities (see Figure 22.1). We'll allow the user to encrypt a message and then decrypt it at a later time. The file can be encrypted and decrypted with or without saving it.

FIGURE 22.1   The text in the word processor has been encrypted.

TUTORIAL

PROJECT OVERVIEW

Instead of creating an entire application from scratch, we're going to add encryption and decryption capabilities to the example from the previous chapter. Because most of this application is already available to us, this chapter is going to be a very quick read. We can simply add two additional menu items to finish the graphical user interface (GUI). These items will allow us to add encryption and decryption capabilities to the word processor:

1. Click on the Type Here area at the far right of the menu. Add Encryption in this space.

2. Click on the newly created Type Here text that's now visible beneath the Encryption text.
3. Change the text to Encrypt and then create another menu item, Decrypt. These are menu items 19 and 20.

WRITING SOME CODE

We really didn't have much to do with the GUI so we're able to move on quickly to the programming aspect of this project. We only have two Sub procedures that we need to create. The first one will be the routine that will be used to encrypt the text.

The following steps will begin the code writing process:

1. Open the code editor and then select MenuItem19 from the left drop-down list.
2. Select Click from the right drop-down list to create the click event for the Encrypt button in the menu.

To perform the encryption, we're going to use the Asc and Chr functions. We use the Asc function to get the character code for an individual character, and then use this to value in a calculation. The calculated result will then convert back into a character for displaying on the screen. If we've done everything correctly, the characters will look totally different. This is the general process for encrypting a string. To decrypt it, we can simply reverse the process to get the original string back.

Encrypting

We'll begin this Sub procedure with the creation of a variable that will be used to obtain data from the clipboard. You might wonder why we're going to deal with the clipboard. While there are several ways that we could attack this problem, we're going to use the RichTextBox Cut method to send the current text to the clipboard. We'll then retrieve this information and store it in a string variable where we can then begin to manipulate it.

Here's the first line of code for creating the clipboard variable:

```
Dim data As IDataObject = Clipboard.GetDataObject()
```

The next step is to create the global variables for the string (str) and the encrypted string (estr). You can place the following line at the top of the code directly beneath the Inherits line:

```
Dim str, estr As String
```

The last variable we need to create is an integer variable that will be used to count through every character of the string.
Here's the variable declaration:

```
Dim i As Integer
```

We'll now use the SelectAll and Cut methods offered by the Rich-TextBox control to select all of the text in the control and then cut it from the control. Cutting will remove the text from the RichTextBox control and also make it available on the clipboard.
Here's the code:

```
RichTextBox1.SelectAll()
RichTextBox1.Cut()
```

We can now retrieve the string from the clipboard and set the variable str equal to the contents that is converted to a string:

```
str = data.GetData(DataFormats.Text).ToString()
```

At this time, the variable str contains the unconverted text. We'll now count through from 1 to the length of the str variable. During this loop, we'll set our other variable estr equal to the current encrypted character.

We're going to calculate the encrypted character by taking the Asc value of the character and adding 30 to it. The 30 is an arbitrary number that was picked, so feel free to change it as you feel necessary. You'll probably want to use something larger than 20 for a value as there can be some problems with characters less than this size. We then convert this value back to a string and store it in estr.
Here's the code:

```
For i = 1 To Len(Str)
    estr = estr & Chr(Asc(Mid(str, i, 1)) + 30)
Next i
```

We're now in the position to add the new `estr` string to the `RichText` box and then set the `str` string back to an empty string. This will display our final encrypted string.

Here's the code:

```
RichTextBox1.Text = estr
str = ""
```

Here's the complete `Sub` procedure:

```
Private Sub MenuItem19_Click(ByVal sender As System.Object,
ByVal e As System.EventArgs) Handles MenuItem19.Click
        'Encryption

        Dim data As IDataObject = Clipboard.GetDataObject()
        Dim i As Integer

        RichTextBox1.SelectAll()
        RichTextBox1.Cut()
        str = data.GetData(DataFormats.Text).ToString()

        For i = 1 To Len(Str)
            estr = estr & Chr(Asc(Mid(str, i, 1)) + 30)
        Next i

        RichTextBox1.Text = estr

        str = ""

    End Sub
```

Decrypting

We've created a completely functional encryption routine, but as of yet, we cannot decrypt this information so that it's back in its original form. This procedure is going to take the `estr` value that we already have. We'll then convert it back to the proper character by taking the individual character codes and subtracting 30 from them before converting the codes into characters. At this point, you should create a new click event for `MenuItem20`.

We'll again use a variable to count through the characters so this is our first entry in the newly created procedure:

```
Dim i As Integer
```

The next step is simply to convert the value back into the string. We'll follow the same format as for encryption by counting through each of the characters using a For...Next loop. We'll take each character, convert it to a character code, and then subtract a value of 30 from it. Then, we'll convert it to a character and set the variable str equal to itself and the new character. This keeps the existing characters so that we can continue to store them until we finally set the RichTextBox Text property equal to the entire string at one time.

Here's the code:

```
For i = 1 To Len(estr)
    str &= Chr(Asc(Mid(estr, i, 1)) - 30)
Next i
RichTextBox1.Text = str
estr = ""
<t>The entire Sub procedure follows:
    Private Sub MenuItem20_Click(ByVal sender As System.Object,
ByVal e As System.EventArgs) Handles MenuItem20.Click
        Dim i As Integer
        'Encryption

        For i = 1 To Len(estr)
            str &= Chr(Asc(Mid(estr, i, 1)) - 30)
        Next i
        RichTextBox1.Text = str

        estr = ""

    End Sub
```

TUTORIAL TESTING THE APPLICATION

It's now time to test the program to see if it can now encrypt and decrypt the information as we would expect:

1. Save the application and then run it. A window like Figure 22.2 will be displayed.
2. Create a basic text string in the application. Try typing your name or some other simple string into the RichTextBox. For example, Figure 22.3 displays *Hello World* as an example string.

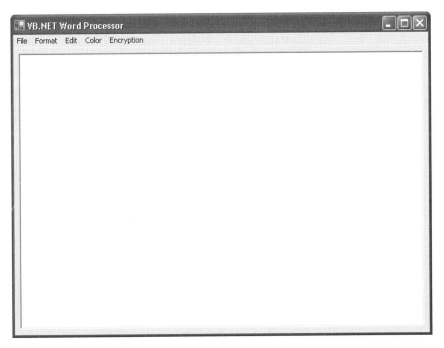

FIGURE 22.2   The application appears like this at startup.

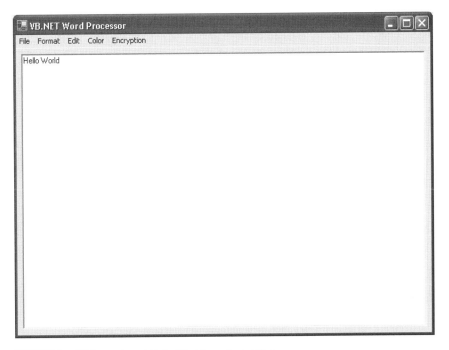

FIGURE 22.3   We've entered *Hello World* as a test string.

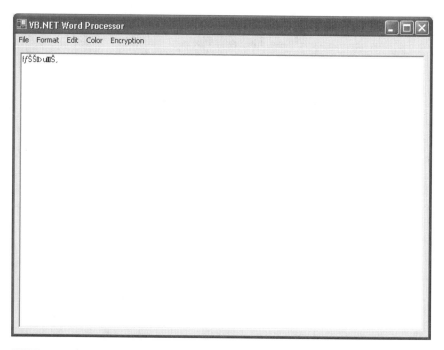

FIGURE 22.4   The string is unrecognized.

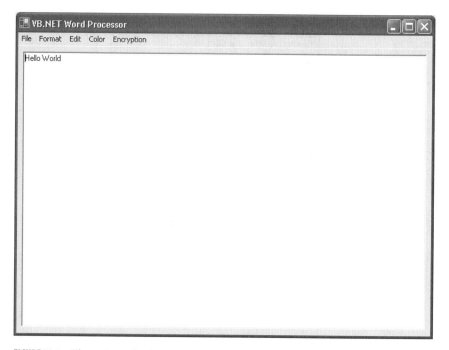

FIGURE 22.5   The string is back in its original format.

3. Choose Encryption | Encrypt. The text should now be unrecognizable as real words (see Figure 22.4).

If you now choose Encryption | Decrypt, your string will reappear as shown in Figure 22.5.

FINAL CODE LISTING

This is the final code listing for the application, including all of the code from the previous chapter, so that you can see how the new code has been added:

```
Public Class Form1
Inherits System.Windows.Forms.Form
Dim str, estr As String

Private Sub MenuItem2_Click(ByVal sender As System.Object,
ByVal e As System.EventArgs) Handles MenuItem2.Click
        'File Open
        Dim fn As String
        OpenFileDialog1.ShowDialog()
        fn = OpenFileDialog1.FileName
        RichTextBox1.LoadFile(fn)
        Me.Text = "VB.NET WP - " & fn
    End Sub

Private Sub MenuItem3_Click(ByVal sender As System.Object,
ByVal e As System.EventArgs) Handles MenuItem3.Click
        'File Save
        'Don't need a variable
        SaveFileDialog1.ShowDialog()
        RichTextBox1.SaveFile(SaveFileDialog1.FileName)
    End Sub

Private Sub MenuItem4_Click(ByVal sender As System.Object,
ByVal e As System.EventArgs) Handles MenuItem4.Click
        'Exit
        Me.Close()
    End Sub

Private Sub MenuItem6_Click(ByVal sender As System.Object,
ByVal e As System.EventArgs) Handles MenuItem6.Click
```

```vbnet
            FontDialog1.ShowDialog()
            RichTextBox1.SelectionFont = FontDialog1.Font

    End Sub


    Private Sub MenuItem7_Click(ByVal sender As System.Object,
ByVal e As System.EventArgs) Handles MenuItem7.Click
        'Convert to all caps
        RichTextBox1.SelectedText =
RichTextBox1.SelectedText.ToUpper
    End Sub


    Private Sub MenuItem8_Click(ByVal sender As System.Object,
ByVal e As System.EventArgs) Handles MenuItem8.Click
        'Center Justify
        RichTextBox1.SelectionAlignment =
HorizontalAlignment.Center
    End Sub


    Private Sub MenuItem9_Click(ByVal sender As System.Object,
ByVal e As System.EventArgs) Handles MenuItem9.Click
        'Left Justify
        RichTextBox1.SelectionAlignment =
HorizontalAlignment.Left
    End Sub


    Private Sub MenuItem10_Click(ByVal sender As Object, ByVal
e As System.EventArgs) Handles MenuItem10.Click
        'Right Justify
        RichTextBox1.SelectionAlignment =
HorizontalAlignment.Right
    End Sub


    Private Sub MenuItem12_Click(ByVal sender As System.Object,
ByVal e As System.EventArgs) Handles MenuItem12.Click
        'Copy
        RichTextBox1.Copy()
    End Sub


    Private Sub MenuItem13_Click(ByVal sender As System.Object,
ByVal e As System.EventArgs) Handles MenuItem13.Click
        'Paste
        RichTextBox1.Paste()
    End Sub
```

```
        Private Sub MenuItem14_Click(ByVal sender As System.Object,
ByVal e As System.EventArgs) Handles MenuItem14.Click
            'Cut
            RichTextBox1.Cut()
        End Sub

        Private Sub MenuItem16_Click(ByVal sender As System.Object,
ByVal e As System.EventArgs) Handles MenuItem16.Click
            'Font Color
            ColorDialog1.ShowDialog()
            RichTextBox1.ForeColor = ColorDialog1.Color
        End Sub

        Private Sub MenuItem17_Click(ByVal sender As System.Object,
ByVal e As System.EventArgs) Handles MenuItem17.Click
            'Background Color
            ColorDialog1.ShowDialog()
            RichTextBox1.BackColor = ColorDialog1.Color
        End Sub

        Private Sub Form1_Load(ByVal sender As System.Object, ByVal
e As System.EventArgs) Handles MyBase.Load
            'Set Form Load Properties
            RichTextBox1.Text = ""
            Me.Text = "VB.NET Word Processor"
        End Sub

        Private Sub MenuItem19_Click(ByVal sender As System.Object,
ByVal e As System.EventArgs) Handles MenuItem19.Click
            'Encryption

            Dim data As IDataObject = Clipboard.GetDataObject()
            Dim i As Integer

            RichTextBox1.SelectAll()
            RichTextBox1.Cut()
            str = data.GetData(DataFormats.Text).ToString()

            For i = 1 To Len(Str)
                estr = estr & Chr(Asc(Mid(str, i, 1)) + 30)
            Next i

            RichTextBox1.Text = estr
```

```
            str = ""

        End Sub

        Private Sub MenuItem20_Click(ByVal sender As System.Object,
    ByVal e As System.EventArgs) Handles MenuItem20.Click
            Dim i As Integer
            'Encryption

            For i = 1 To Len(estr)
                str &= Chr(Asc(Mid(estr, i, 1)) - 30)
            Next i
            RichTextBox1.Text = str

            estr = ""

        End Sub
    End Class
```

CHAPTER REVIEW

In this chapter, we added basic encryption and decryption information to our word processor application that had been created in the previous chapter. At this time, the application can only decrypt the information that has been previously encrypted. You could easily modify this application so that it could decrypt files that were previously encrypted and saved.

In the next chapter, we're going to create an application that creates screen captures.

23

SCREEN CAPTURE

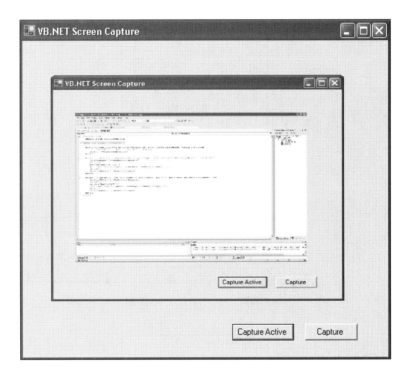

In the last chapter, we added encryption and decryption capabilities to the word processor that we originally developed in Chapter 21. In this chapter, we're going to create an application that can do screen captures (see Figure 23.1). To accomplish our goals, we're going to simulate key presses on a keyboard using the `System.Windows.Forms.SendKeys` class.

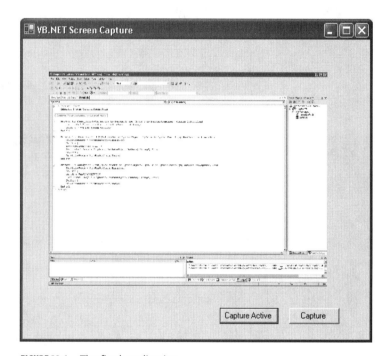

FIGURE 23.1 The final application.

PROJECT OVERVIEW

We're going to create a project that's capable of capturing the entire screen or the currently active window. Windows has built in a very simple screen capture with the PrntScrn (Print Screen) button on your keyboard. This button, when accompanied by the `Alt` key will only capture the window currently in focus. By itself, it'll capture the entire screen. We'll use this to our advantage when we simulate the key presses.

TUTORIAL   GUI

Follow these steps to start this project:

1. Create a new Windows application in VB.NET.
2. Add a PictureBox and two buttons to the form. You can resize the form and see how the controls have been positioned by referring to Figure 23.2.

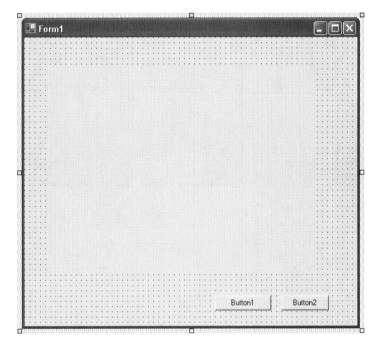

FIGURE 23.2   Create a GUI.

3. Set the properties for the controls. The buttons will be given the names of btnActive and btnCapture. The PictureBox can remain PictureBox1. You can set the Text properties of the button controls to Capture Active and Capture, respectively. Your GUI should now be complete (see Figure 23.3).

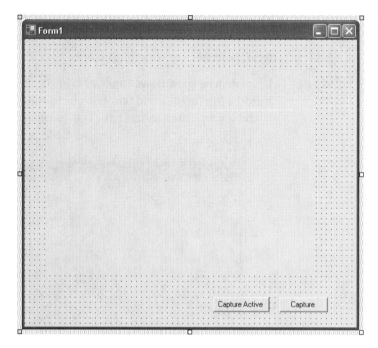

FIGURE 23.3   A simple GUI is now complete.

WRITING SOME CODE

Let's begin this application by creating the Form Load event. Open the code editor and then select Base Class Events form the left drop-down list and then Load from the right drop-down. This will create the event.

We're not going to do very much in this event. The SizeMode property of the PictureBox control needs to be set to PictureBoxSizeMode.StretchImage and the Text property of the form needs to be set to "VB.NET Screen Capture."

Here's the code:

```
Private Sub Form1_Load(ByVal sender As System.Object, ByVal e
As System.EventArgs) Handles MyBase.Load
    PictureBox1.SizeMode = PictureBoxSizeMode.StretchImage
    Me.Text = "VB.NET Screen Capture"
End Sub
```

We're now going to look at the basics of the `SendKey` class before we use it in the capture `Sub` procedures. Recall that Windows provides a very simple way to capture screen shots using the PrntScrn key. We'll use `SendKey` to simulate a user pressing the same PrntScrn button.

SendKeys

`SendKeys` is something that can be used easily, as the only information required to use it are the text characters (or character) that correspond to the key you wish to stimulate. To send normal letters or numbers, you can simply use the character or characters enclosed in quotation marks (""). For example, suppose you want to simulate the letter *S* being pressed. You can use:

```
SendKeys("S")
```

There are a few keys that have some special characters assigned to represent them. The following list details some of them:

SPECIAL CHARACTER	KEY
+	Shift
^	Ctrl
%	Alt
~ or {Enter}	Enter

To use these special characters, you must surround the character with braces ({}). For example, to specify the Alt key, you can use the following:

```
SendKeys("%")
```

Preceding a string with one of the special characters that we just looked at allows you to send a keystroke combination beginning with Shift, Ctrl, or Alt. For example, to simulate Alt followed by *A*, use %A. If you'd like to have the Shift, Ctrl, or Alt key be held down when another key is pressed, you can enclose the key or keys in parentheses (()) and precede it with the special character. For example, suppose you would like the Alt key to be held down and the letter *A* pressed while holding it down, you can use %(A).

You can specify certain action keys by using Table 23.1:

Table 23.1   Action Key Codes

KEY	CODE
Backspace	{BACKSPACE}, {BS}, or {BKSP}
Break	{BREAK}
Caps Lock	{CAPSLOCK}
Del or Delete	{DELETE} or {DEL}
Down Arrow	{DOWN}
End	{END}
Enter	{ENTER}or ~
Esc	{ESC}
Help	{HELP}
Home	{HOME}
Ins or Insert	{INSERT} or {INS}
Left Arrow	{LEFT}
Num Lock	{NUMLOCK}
Page Down	{PGDN}
Page Up	{PGUP}
Right Arrow	{RIGHT}
Scroll Lock	{SCROLLLOCK}
Tab	{TAB}
Up Arrow	{UP}
F1	{F1}
F2	{F2}
F3	{F3}
F4	{F4}
F5	{F5}
F6	{F6}
F7	{F7}
F8	{F8}
F9	{F9}
F10	{F10}
F11	{F11}
F12	{F12}
F13	{F13}
F14	{F14}
F15	{F15}
F16	{F16}

You also have a few additional options for using `SendKeys`. You can specify a key being pressed a certain number of times. For example, you can use (A 5) to simulate the A key being pressed five times.

Capturing the Screen

Now that you have a basic understanding of the `SendKeys` class, we'll use it to capture the screens. First, we need to select `btnActive` from the left drop-down list and then Click from the right drop-down. This will create the click event for `btnActive`.

We'll begin this procedure by minimizing the current window and also hiding it so that it won't be visible in the capture.

Here's the code:

```
Me.WindowState = FormWindowState.Minimized
Me.Hide()
```

The next step is to use the `Send` method of `SendKeys` to send Alt + PrntScrn to capture the active window. This will copy the image to the clipboard. We can then retrieve the image from the bitmap and load it into the `PictureBox` control. Lastly, we can show the form and set its state to Normal.

Here's the code:

```
SendKeys.Send("%({PRTSC})")
PictureBox1.Image = Clipboard.GetDataObject.GetData("Bitmap",
True)
Me.Show()
Me.WindowState = FormWindowState.Normal
```

That is all of the code we need for this procedure. The complete listing for this procedure follows:

```
Private Sub btnActive_Click(ByVal sender As System.Object,
ByVal e As System.EventArgs) Handles btnActive.Click
    Me.WindowState = FormWindowState.Minimized
    Me.Hide()
    SendKeys.Send("%({PRTSC})")
    PictureBox1.Image =
Clipboard.GetDataObject.GetData("Bitmap", True)
    Me.Show()
    Me.WindowState = FormWindowState.Normal
End Sub
```

The entire window capture is nearly identical to the active capture. You can minimize the window and hide it to start the procedure. Next, you can send the PrntScrn key to copy the entire window to the clipboard. This is the area of the procedure that differs as the previous one sent Alt + PrntScrn while this one sends only PrntScrn. Once the image is on the clipboard, we can retrieve it and display it as before. The last step again is to set the form to Normal.

Here's the entire procedure:

```
Private Sub btnCapture_Click(ByVal sender As System.Object,
ByVal e As System.EventArgs) Handles btnCapture.Click
        Me.WindowState = FormWindowState.Minimized
        Me.Hide()
        SendKeys.Send("({PRTSC})")
        PictureBox1.Image =
Clipboard.GetDataObject.GetData("Bitmap", True)
        Me.Show()
        Me.WindowState = FormWindowState.Normal
    End Sub
```

TESTING THE SCREEN CAPTURES

We can now test the application. First, you should save it and then run it. It'll display a window something like the one shown in Figure 23.4.

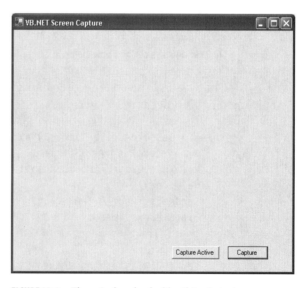

FIGURE 23.4   The window looks like this at startup.

The next step is to try the Capture Active and Capture buttons to make sure they work correctly (see Figures 23.5 and 23.6).

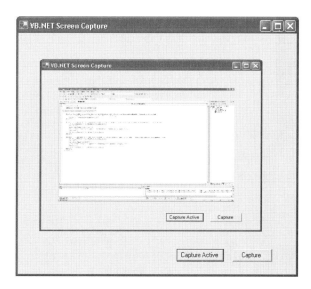

FIGURE 23.5   An active screen capture.

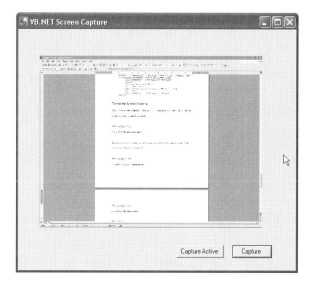

FIGURE 23.6   A screen capture.

FINAL CODE LISTING

This is the complete code listing for the application:

```
Public Class Form1
Inherits System.Windows.Forms.Form

Private Sub Form1_Load(ByVal sender As System.Object, ByVal
e As System.EventArgs) Handles MyBase.Load
    PictureBox1.SizeMode = PictureBoxSizeMode.StretchImage
    Me.Text = "VB.NET Screen Capture"
End Sub

Private Sub btnActive_Click(ByVal sender As System.Object,
ByVal e As System.EventArgs) Handles btnActive.Click
    Me.WindowState = FormWindowState.Minimized
    Me.Hide()
    SendKeys.Send("%({PRTSC})")
    PictureBox1.Image =
Clipboard.GetDataObject.GetData("Bitmap", True)
    Me.Show()
    Me.WindowState = FormWindowState.Normal
End Sub

Private Sub btnCapture_Click(ByVal sender As System.Object,
ByVal e As System.EventArgs) Handles btnCapture.Click
    Me.WindowState = FormWindowState.Minimized
    Me.Hide()
    SendKeys.Send("({PRTSC})")
    PictureBox1.Image =
Clipboard.GetDataObject.GetData("Bitmap", True)
    Me.Show()
    Me.WindowState = FormWindowState.Normal
End Sub
End Class
```

CHAPTER REVIEW

In this chapter, we used the SendKeys class to simulate the pressing of the PrntScrn button, which copies an image to the clipboard. Once we had the image on the clipboard, we could the display the image in a Picture-Box control.

In the next chapter, we're going to create a very simple drawing application.

24

DRAWING WITH VB.NET

The last project we created was an application that captured screen shots by simulating key presses (specifically the PrntScrn key). In this chapter, we're going to create an application that allows you to draw on a PictureBox control (see Figure 24.1). It'll allow you to open several different file types or just draw on an empty screen using several different tools.

FIGURE 24.1   The final application.

PROJECT OVERVIEW

This application will use several controls to create a working user interface. First, a PictureBox will be used to capture the mouse clicks and movement that in turn will be used to draw various shapes. A menu control will allow us to choose the various types of drawing tools and several dialog boxes will allow us to set various properties and open files.

CREATING A GUI

Creating a GUI for this application will be very simple as it'll consist of a single PictureBox control, a menu control, and several dialog controls. We'll begin by creating a new Windows application and then adding the PictureBox control to it. You can size the form and the PictureBox so that they're similar to Figure 24.2.

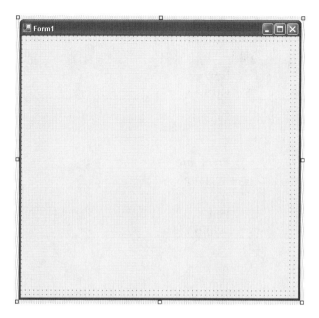

FIGURE 24.2   The beginning step of a GUI.

Next, you can add a MainMenu control to the form and create the following menu items:

MENUITEM NAME	TEXT PROPERTY
MenuItem1	File
mnuNew	New
mnuOpen	Open
mnuExit	Exit
MenuItem2	Drawing
mnuFreehand	Freehand
mnuRectangle	Rectangle
mnuArc	Arc
MenuItem3	Pen
mnuPenWidth	Width
MenuItem4	Color
mnuPenColor	Pen
mnuBGColor	Background

The structure appears as follows:

File
    New
    Open
    Exit

Drawing
    Freehand
    Rectangle
    Arc
    Pen
    Width

Color
    Pen

The final step in the creation of the GUI is to add an `OpenFileDialog` and `ColorDialog` to the form. Your final GUI should look something like Figure 24.3.

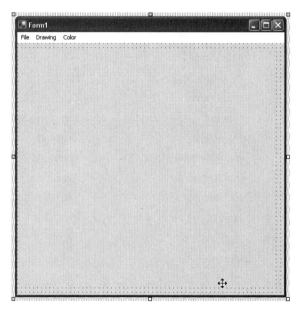

FIGURE 24.3 The final GUI looks like this.

WRITING SOME CODE

We're going to begin writing the code for this application by creating several variables that we'll use throughout the application. The following list will create variables that store the location of the mouse, the previous location of the mouse, the type of drawing we're making (freehand, rectangle, and so on), width of the drawing pen, and the color of the drawing pen.

Here are the declarations:

```
Dim XPrev, YPrev, X, Y As Single
Dim DrawType As String
Dim PenWidth As Integer
Dim PenColor As Color
```

The Menu Items

The next step is to handle the selection of the types of drawing. In other words, we need to create the click events for the following menu items:

- mnuFreehand
- mnuRectangle
- mnuArc
- mnuPenWidth
- mnuPenColor
- mnuBGColor
- mnuNew
- mnuOpen
- mnuExit

You can create the click events for each of them as we've done many times throughout the text.

The next step is to write the code for each of these click events. If you remember, we created a `DrawType` variable of type string. We're going to use this variable to instruct the program on the type of drawing we're going to be performing. For example, if we're doing freehand drawing, we'll set the `DrawType` variable equal to `"Freehand"`. We'll than capture the mouse movements in the `PictureBox` in a later step.

Here's the code for `mnuFreehand` and `mnuRectangle`:

```
Private Sub mnuFreehand_Click(ByVal sender As System.Object,
ByVal e As System.EventArgs) Handles mnuFreehand.Click
     DrawType = "Freehand"
```

```
    End Sub

    Private Sub mnuRectangle_Click(ByVal sender As System.Object,
ByVal e As System.EventArgs) Handles mnuRectangle.Click
        DrawType = "Rectangle"
    End Sub
```

Clicking on `mnuArc` will require a bit more work. We're going to use `InputBoxes` and ask the user to input various pieces of information that will then be used to draw an arc. They'll need to enter an `X` and `Y` coordinate, `Width`, `Height`, `Start Angle`, and a `Sweep Angle` before the arc is drawn. Unlike the freehand and rectangle options, we're not going to capture mouse positions to draw an arc. Instead, we're going to use the values that were input by the user and the `DrawMethod` of a `Graphics` object.

First, we'll create the `Graphics` object:

```
Dim g As Graphics = PictureBox1.CreateGraphics
```

Our next step is to create a new `Pen` with the current `Color` and `Width`. We haven't completed the settings for these at this time, but you can assume that the `PenColor` and `PenWidth` variables hold this information:

```
Dim p As New Pen(PenColor, PenWidth)
```

We'll then use a series of `InputBoxes` to capture input from the user, and once we have this information, we'll finally draw the arc:

```
XA = InputBox("Please Enter X : ", "Arc Drawing")
YA = InputBox("Please Enter Y : ", "Arc Drawing")
WA = InputBox("Please Enter Width : ", "Arc Drawing")
HA = InputBox("Please Enter Height : ", "Arc Drawing")
SA = InputBox("Please Enter Start Angle : ", "Arc Drawing")
SWA = InputBox("Please Enter Sweep Angle : ", "Arc Drawing")
g.DrawArc(p, XA, YA, WA, HA, SA, SWA)
```

Here's the complete `Sub` procedure:

```
    Private Sub mnuArc_Click(ByVal sender As System.Object, ByVal e
As System.EventArgs) Handles mnuArc.Click
        Dim g As Graphics = PictureBox1.CreateGraphics
        Dim p As New Pen(PenColor, PenWidth)
        Dim XA, YA, WA, HA, SA, SWA As Integer
        XA = InputBox("Please Enter X : ", "Arc Drawing")
```

```
    YA = InputBox("Please Enter Y : ", "Arc Drawing")
    WA = InputBox("Please Enter Width : ", "Arc Drawing")
    HA = InputBox("Please Enter Height : ", "Arc Drawing")
    SA = InputBox("Please Enter Start Angle : ", "Arc Drawing")
    SWA = InputBox("Please Enter Sweep Angle : ", "Arc Drawing")
    g.DrawArc(p, XA, YA, WA, HA, SA, SWA)
End Sub
```

It's a good time to handle the width of the pen and the color of the pen. The `mnuPenWidth` and `mnuPenColor` menu items are used to set the respective attributes. We can use an `InputBox` to set the `PenWidth` and the `ColorDialog` to set the color.

Here's the code for these procedures:

```
Private Sub mnuPenWidth_Click(ByVal sender As System.Object,
ByVal e As System.EventArgs) Handles mnuPenWidth.Click
    PenWidth = InputBox("Please Enter Width of Pen : ", "Pen
Settings", "1")
End Sub


Private Sub mnuPenColor_Click(ByVal sender As System.Object,
ByVal e As System.EventArgs) Handles mnuPenColor.Click
    ColorDialog1.ShowDialog()
    PenColor = ColorDialog1.Color
End Sub
```

Setting the background color (`mnuBGColor`) is very similar to the pen color:

```
Private Sub mnuBGColor_Click(ByVal sender As System.Object,
ByVal e As System.EventArgs) Handles mnuBGColor.Click
    ColorDialog1.ShowDialog()
    PictureBox1.BackColor = ColorDialog1.Color
End Sub
```

The New, Open, and Exit menu items (`mnuNew`, `mnuOpen`, and `mnuExit`) are all similar to activities we've done in past projects so a quick glance of the following code will get you up to speed:

```
Private Sub mnuNew_Click(ByVal sender As System.Object, ByVal e
As System.EventArgs) Handles mnuNew.Click
    PictureBox1.Image = Nothing
End Sub
```

```
    Private Sub mnuOpen_Click(ByVal sender As System.Object, ByVal
e As System.EventArgs) Handles mnuOpen.Click
        OpenFileDialog1.ShowDialog()
        PictureBox1.Image = Image.FromFile(OpenFileDialog1.FileName)
    End Sub

    Private Sub mnuExit_Click(ByVal sender As System.Object, ByVal
e As System.EventArgs) Handles mnuExit.Click
        Me.Close()
    End Sub
```

Form Load

In this application, we need to initialize the PenWidth and PenColor variables so that if the user draws something without first setting one of
them, it'll not cause a problem. Using the Form Load event, we'll set the
width equal to 1 and the color equal to black:

```
    Private Sub Form1_Load(ByVal sender As System.Object, ByVal e
As System.EventArgs) Handles MyBase.Load
        PenWidth = 1
        PenColor = Color.Black
    End Sub
```

Capturing the Mouse

The remaining part of this application revolves around capturing the position and movement of the mouse. We can use the MouseDown, MouseUp,
and MouseMove events for PictureBox1. You can create these events by
choosing PictureBox1 from the left drop-down list and then the respective events from the right drop-down.
We'll begin with the MouseDown event, and like the arc drawing Sub procedure, we start with the creation of a Graphics object and Pen:

```
    Dim g As Graphics = PictureBox1.CreateGraphics
    Dim p As New Pen(PenColor, PenWidth)
```

Next, we'll set the Xprev (previous position of the mouse X position)
and the YPrev (previous position for Y) equal to the current position of
the PictureBox down event:

```
    XPrev = e.X
    YPrev = e.Y
```

We need to check the type of button that was pressed and also the value of the `DrawType` variable to see what we're supposed to be drawing. Using an `If...Then` loop, we can check to see if we pressed the left mouse button (the only button we're interested in for drawing) and then the value of `DrawType`. If the value is `"Rectangle"`, we draw a small line to show the beginning position of the rectangle so that as the user moves the mouse, they can refer back to the beginning position.

Here's the code:

```
If e.Button = MouseButtons.Left And DrawType = "Rectangle" Then
    g.DrawLine(p, e.X, e.Y, e.X + 1, e.Y)
End If
```

If the button pressed is the left button and the `DrawType` is `"Freehand"`, then we can draw a small ellipse at the current position of the mouse. The series of small ellipses will appear to be a line as you move around. When we draw the ellipse, we need to subtract one-half of the width from the `X` and `Y` positions so that the ellipse is centered on the actual mouse point instead of being drawn to the right of the mouse. This further enhances the simulation of freehand drawing.

Here's the code:

```
If e.Button = MouseButtons.Left And DrawType = "Freehand" Then
    g.DrawEllipse(p, e.X - CInt(0.5 * PenWidth), e.Y - CInt(0.5
* PenWidth), PenWidth, PenWidth)
End If
```

Here's the code for the entire `Sub` procedure:

```
Private Sub PictureBox1_MouseDown(ByVal sender As Object, ByVal
e As System.Windows.Forms.MouseEventArgs) Handles
PictureBox1.MouseDown

    Dim g As Graphics = PictureBox1.CreateGraphics
    Dim p As New Pen(PenColor, PenWidth)
    XPrev = e.X
    YPrev = e.Y
    If e.Button = MouseButtons.Left And DrawType = "Rectangle"
Then
    g.DrawLine(p, e.X, e.Y, e.X + 1, e.Y)
    End If

    If e.Button = MouseButtons.Left And DrawType = "Freehand" Then
```

```
        g.DrawEllipse(p, e.X - CInt(0.5 * PenWidth), e.Y - CInt(0.5
* PenWidth), PenWidth, PenWidth)
        End If

    End Sub
```

We're now going to handle the mouse movements. The procedure begins, not surprisingly, with the creation of a Graphics object and a Pen:

```
Dim g As Graphics = PictureBox1.CreateGraphics
Dim p As New Pen(PenColor, PenWidth)
```

 We create the Graphics objects at the beginning of the procedure for uniformity, but it's a better option to create Graphics objects only when they're needed. An example of this is in the last Sub procedure within the If...Then loops so that the Graphics objects are created only if the other conditions are True.

We're now going to test the mouse button to see if the left one is pressed and if the drawing type is "Freehand". We then check the pen width to see if it's less than 1. If it's less than 1, we draw a line from the previous x position (XPrev) and previous y position (YPrev) to the current positions. This allows us to create pens that are very thin. On the other hand, if it's larger than 1, we can use the same DrawEllipse method as for MouseDown.

The last step is to set the XPrev and YPrev variables equal to the current positions so that the next time the mouse is moved, these will actually become the previous values:

```
If e.Button = MouseButtons.Left And DrawType = "Freehand" Then
    If PenWidth <= 1 Then g.DrawLine(p, XPrev, YPrev, e.X, e.Y)
    If PenWidth > 1 Then g.DrawEllipse(p, e.X - CInt(0.5 *
PenWidth), e.Y - CInt(0.5 * PenWidth), PenWidth, PenWidth)
    XPrev = e.X
    YPrev = e.Y
```

Here's the entire procedure:

```
Private Sub PictureBox1_MouseMove(ByVal sender As Object, ByVal
e As System.Windows.Forms.MouseEventArgs) Handles
PictureBox1.MouseMove
    Dim g As Graphics = PictureBox1.CreateGraphics
    Dim p As New Pen(PenColor, PenWidth)
    If e.Button = MouseButtons.Left And DrawType = "Freehand" Then
```

```
      If PenWidth <= 1 Then g.DrawLine(p, XPrev, YPrev, e.X, e.Y)
      If PenWidth > 1 Then g.DrawEllipse(p, e.X - CInt(0.5 *
PenWidth), e.Y - CInt(0.5 * PenWidth), PenWidth, PenWidth)
      XPrev = e.X
      YPrev = e.Y
    End If
  End Sub
```

The last event that we need to deal with is the MouseUp event. This procedure will only deal with drawing the rectangle, but if you decide to add other options such as circles, lines, and so on, you can utilize this same event.

We'll begin by checking the DrawType variable to see if it's a rectangle that we're drawing, and if so, we'll create a Pen and Graphics object:

```
If DrawType = "Rectangle" Then
Dim g As Graphics = PictureBox1.CreateGraphics
Dim p As New Pen(PenColor, PenWidth)
End If
```

We'll then use a series of If…Then…Else statements to determine where the last point on the rectangle is located. A rectangle can be drawn only with the first X,Y coordinates in the upper-left area and the last X,Y coordinates in the lower right. Keeping this in mind, we'll need to do some calculations to draw the various types of rectangles seen in Figure 24.4.

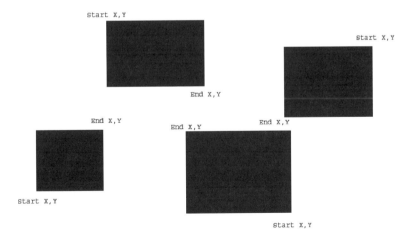

FIGURE 24.4   We can draw various types of rectangles.

To perform the calculations, we need to begin with determining which type of rectangle we're drawing using `If...Then...Else` statements. We can do this by checking the values of XPrev and YPrev against the current X and Y positions. Based on these checks, we can do the appropriate calculations.

We're going to draw the rectangles from the upper-left to the lower-right regardless of the intended drawing. We're going to calculate the upper-left and lower-right values based on the values of the XPrev, YPrev, `Current X`, and `Current Y` values. The calculations will be based on the type of rectangle that we're attempting to draw. For example, if we're trying to draw a rectangle where the XPrev value is greater than the `Current X` value and the YPrev value is greater than the `Current Y` value, then we need to draw the rectangle as follows:

UPPER LEFT X	UPPER LEFT Y	LOWER LEFT X	LOWER LEFT Y
Current X	Current Y	XPrev—Current X	YPrev—Current Y

Here's the code for the checks and calculations:

```
If XPrev <= e.X And YPrev <= e.Y Then
    g.DrawRectangle(p, XPrev, YPrev, e.X - XPrev, e.Y - YPrev)
ElseIf XPrev <= e.X And YPrev >= e.Y Then
    g.DrawRectangle(p, XPrev, e.Y, e.X - XPrev, YPrev - e.Y)
ElseIf XPrev >= e.X And YPrev >= e.Y Then
    g.DrawRectangle(p, e.X, e.Y, XPrev - e.X, YPrev - e.Y)
ElseIf XPrev >= e.X And YPrev <= e.Y Then
    g.DrawRectangle(p, e.X, YPrev, XPrev - e.X, e.Y - YPrev)
```

Here's the entire completed procedure:

```
Private Sub PictureBox1_MouseUp(ByVal sender As Object,
ByVal e As System.Windows.Forms.MouseEventArgs) Handles
PictureBox1.MouseUp
        If DrawType = "Rectangle" Then
            Dim g As Graphics = PictureBox1.CreateGraphics
            Dim p As New Pen(PenColor, PenWidth)

            If XPrev <= e.X And YPrev <= e.Y Then
                g.DrawRectangle(p, XPrev, YPrev, e.X - XPrev,
e.Y - YPrev)
            ElseIf XPrev <= e.X And YPrev >= e.Y Then
                g.DrawRectangle(p, XPrev, e.Y, e.X - XPrev,
YPrev - e.Y)
```

```
                    ElseIf XPrev >= e.X And YPrev >= e.Y Then
                        g.DrawRectangle(p, e.X, e.Y, XPrev - e.X, YPrev
 - e.Y)
                    ElseIf XPrev >= e.X And YPrev <= e.Y Then
                        g.DrawRectangle(p, e.X, YPrev, XPrev - e.X, e.Y
 - YPrev)
                    End If

                End If
            End Sub
```

TESTING THE PROGRAM

We can quickly test this program by running it in the IDE, but you should save it before doing so. Make sure that if there's an error and it crashes the program, you can recover your program, as is.

When you run the program, a window like the one in Figure 24.5 is displayed.

FIGURE 24.5   The application on startup.

The next step is to try the various drawing tools. You can experiment with each of the tools; examples of each of them can be seen in Figures 24.6 through 24.9.

FIGURE 24.6   A freehand drawing.

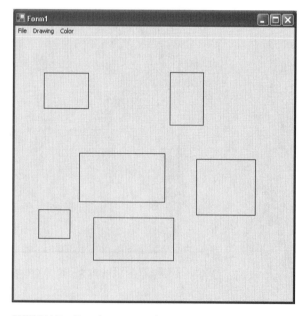

FIGURE 24.7   Drawing rectangles.

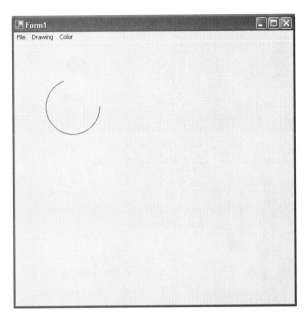

FIGURE 24.8   An arc drawn with X = 50, Y = 50, Width = 100, Height = 100, start angle = 0, and sweep angle = 245.

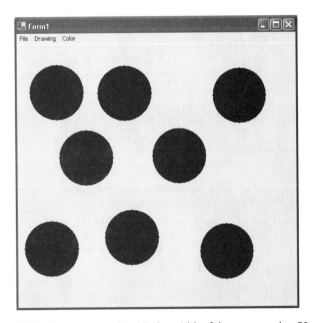

FIGURE 24.9   An example with the width of the pen equal to 50.

FINAL CODE LISTING

Here's the final code listing:

```
Public Class Form1
Inherits System.Windows.Forms.Form
Dim XPrev, YPrev, X, Y As Single
Dim DrawType As String
Dim PenWidth As Integer
Dim PenColor As Color

Private Sub PictureBox1_MouseDown(ByVal sender As Object,
ByVal e As System.Windows.Forms.MouseEventArgs) Handles
PictureBox1.MouseDown

        Dim g As Graphics = PictureBox1.CreateGraphics
        Dim p As New Pen(PenColor, PenWidth)
        XPrev = e.X
        YPrev = e.Y
        If e.Button = MouseButtons.Left And DrawType =
"Rectangle" Then
                g.DrawLine(p, e.X, e.Y, e.X + 1, e.Y)
        End If

        If e.Button = MouseButtons.Left And DrawType =
"Freehand" Then
                g.DrawEllipse(p, e.X - CInt(0.5 * PenWidth), e.Y -
CInt(0.5 * PenWidth), PenWidth, PenWidth)
        End If

    End Sub


    Private Sub PictureBox1_MouseMove(ByVal sender As Object,
ByVal e As System.Windows.Forms.MouseEventArgs) Handles
PictureBox1.MouseMove
        Dim g As Graphics = PictureBox1.CreateGraphics
        Dim p As New Pen(PenColor, PenWidth)
        If e.Button = MouseButtons.Left And DrawType =
"Freehand" Then
            If PenWidth <= 1 Then g.DrawLine(p, XPrev, YPrev,
e.X, e.Y)
            If PenWidth > 1 Then g.DrawEllipse(p, e.X -
CInt(0.5 * PenWidth), e.Y - CInt(0.5 * PenWidth), PenWidth,
PenWidth)
```

```
                XPrev = e.X
                YPrev = e.Y
            End If
        End Sub


        Private Sub PictureBox1_MouseUp(ByVal sender As Object,
ByVal e As System.Windows.Forms.MouseEventArgs) Handles
PictureBox1.MouseUp
            If DrawType = "Rectangle" Then
                Dim g As Graphics = PictureBox1.CreateGraphics
                Dim p As New Pen(PenColor, PenWidth)

                If XPrev <= e.X And YPrev <= e.Y Then
                    g.DrawRectangle(p, XPrev, YPrev, e.X - XPrev,
e.Y - YPrev)
                ElseIf XPrev <= e.X And YPrev >= e.Y Then
                    g.DrawRectangle(p, XPrev, e.Y, e.X - XPrev,
YPrev - e.Y)

                ElseIf XPrev >= e.X And YPrev >= e.Y Then
                    g.DrawRectangle(p, e.X, e.Y, XPrev - e.X, YPrev
- e.Y)

                ElseIf XPrev >= e.X And YPrev <= e.Y Then
                    g.DrawRectangle(p, e.X, YPrev, XPrev - e.X, e.Y
- YPrev)
                End If


            End If
        End Sub


        Private Sub mnuFreehand_Click(ByVal sender As
System.Object, ByVal e As System.EventArgs) Handles
mnuFreehand.Click
            DrawType = "Freehand"
        End Sub


        Private Sub mnuRectangle_Click(ByVal sender As
System.Object, ByVal e As System.EventArgs) Handles
mnuRectangle.Click
            DrawType = "Rectangle"
        End Sub


        Private Sub mnuArc_Click(ByVal sender As System.Object,
ByVal e As System.EventArgs) Handles mnuArc.Click
            Dim g As Graphics = PictureBox1.CreateGraphics
```

```
              Dim p As New Pen(PenColor, PenWidth)
              Dim XA, YA, WA, HA, SA, SWA As Integer
              XA = InputBox("Please Enter X : ", "Arc Drawing")
              YA = InputBox("Please Enter Y : ", "Arc Drawing")
              WA = InputBox("Please Enter Width : ", "Arc Drawing")
              HA = InputBox("Please Enter Height : ", "Arc Drawing")
              SA = InputBox("Please Enter Start Angle : ", "Arc
        Drawing")
              SWA = InputBox("Please Enter Sweep Angle : ", "Arc
        Drawing")
              g.DrawArc(p, XA, YA, WA, HA, SA, SWA)
        End Sub


        Private Sub mnuPenWidth_Click(ByVal sender As
System.Object, ByVal e As System.EventArgs) Handles
mnuPenWidth.Click
              PenWidth = InputBox("Please Enter Width of Pen : ",
        "Pen Settings", "1")
        End Sub


        Private Sub mnuPenColor_Click(ByVal sender As
System.Object, ByVal e As System.EventArgs) Handles
mnuPenColor.Click
              ColorDialog1.ShowDialog()
              PenColor = ColorDialog1.Color
        End Sub


        Private Sub Form1_Load(ByVal sender As System.Object, ByVal
e As System.EventArgs) Handles MyBase.Load
              PenWidth = 1
              PenColor = Color.Black
        End Sub


        Private Sub mnuBGColor_Click(ByVal sender As System.Object,
ByVal e As System.EventArgs) Handles mnuBGColor.Click
              ColorDialog1.ShowDialog()
              PictureBox1.BackColor = ColorDialog1.Color
        End Sub


        Private Sub mnuNew_Click(ByVal sender As System.Object,
ByVal e As System.EventArgs) Handles mnuNew.Click
              PictureBox1.Image = Nothing
        End Sub
```

```
        Private Sub mnuOpen_Click(ByVal sender As System.Object,
ByVal e As System.EventArgs) Handles mnuOpen.Click
            OpenFileDialog1.ShowDialog()
            PictureBox1.Image =
Image.FromFile(OpenFileDialog1.FileName)
        End Sub

        Private Sub mnuExit_Click(ByVal sender As System.Object,
ByVal e As System.EventArgs) Handles mnuExit.Click
            Me.Close()
        End Sub
    End Class
```

CHAPTER REVIEW

In this chapter, we created an application that can draw various types of shapes using a PictureBox control, Graphics object, and several other different methods.

In the next chapter, we're going to spend a little more time on graphics when we develop a drag-and-drop aware application that can convert images to various formats.

25

DRAG-AND-DROP
IMAGE CONVERSIONS

In the previous chapter, we created an application that allowed the user to draw in a PictureBox. We're going to work on a similar type of application in this chapter—a program that allows a user to drag-and-drop any type of picture onto it and then allows them to save it in another format (see Figure 25.1).

FIGURE 25.1 The final application.

CREATING THE GUI

The project we're going to create in this chapter will consist of a single PictureBox along with a button that will be used to display a Save File dialog box. You can create the user interface with this information. For approximate sizes, you can refer to Figure 25.2.

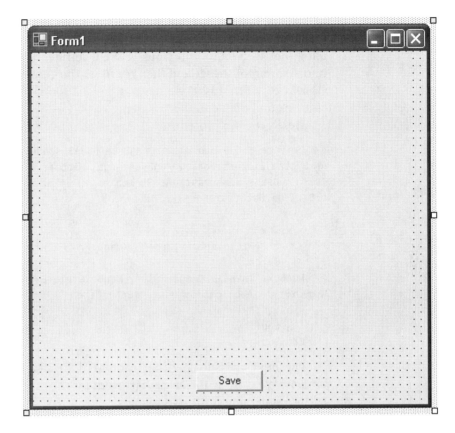

FIGURE 25.2   A simple GUI for our application.

WRITING THE CODE

We can begin writing this application by opening the code editor and creating a Form Load event. This event will allow us to set several important properties for the PictureBox. First, we can set AllowDrop equal to True, which allows the control to respond to dropped objects; let's set the color to Aqua so that it stands out. Next, we can set the Text property of the form equal to "Drag & Drop Image Conversion".

Here's the entire Sub procedure:

```
Private Sub Form1_Load(ByVal sender As System.Object, ByVal e
As System.EventArgs) Handles MyBase.Load
    PictureBox1.AllowDrop = True
    PictureBox1.BackColor = Color.Aqua
    Me.Text = "Drag & Drop Image Conversion"
End Sub
```

The next step is to handle the dropped objects using the `PictureBox` `DragDrop` event. We'll begin this procedure with the `Try`/`Catch` error handling that we've used previously. We'll retrieve the content of the file into an array of strings and then try to set the `Image` property of the `PictureBox` equal to this. If we have an invalid format, we'll display a message box and then end the `Try` loop.

Here's the `Sub` procedure:

```
Private Sub PictureBox1_DragDrop(ByVal sender As Object, ByVal e
As System.Windows.Forms.DragEventArgs) Handles PictureBox1.DragDrop
    Dim sFileArray() As String =
e.Data.GetData(DataFormats.FileDrop)

    Try
        PictureBox1.Image = Image.FromFile(sFileArray(0))
    Catch
    MsgBox("Invalid Image File", MsgBoxStyle.Exclamation Or
MsgBoxStyle.ApplicationModal, "Error")
        Return
    End Try
End Sub
```

Our next step is to check the content of the data coming into the `PictureBox`. We can use the `DragEnter` event for the `PictureBox`. We'll use an If…Then statement for this as follows:

```
Private Sub PictureBox1_DragEnter(ByVal sender As Object, ByVal e
As System.Windows.Forms.DragEventArgs) Handles PictureBox1.DragEnter
    If (e.Data.GetDataPresent(DataFormats.FileDrop)) Then
        e.Effect = DragDropEffects.Copy
    Else
        e.Effect = DragDropEffects.None
    End If
End Sub
```

The final event we need to handle is the `btnSave` click event. We can begin this event by checking the content of the `PictureBox` to be certain that there's actually some content to save. If there is content, then we'll continue. Otherwise, we display a message box to inform the user that there's nothing to save.

Here's the code:

```
If PictureBox1.Image Is Nothing Then
    MsgBox("There is nothing to save — please drop a file onto
the Picture Box!", MsgBoxStyle.Exclamation Or
MsgBoxStyle.ApplicationModal, "No Image")
```

```
        Return
    End If
```

If it passes this, we can then move forward and display the `SaveFile-Dialog`. We can then check the `SaveFileDialog` to make certain that a file-name is given:

```
SaveFileDialog1.ShowDialog()
If SaveFileDialog1.FileName = "" Then Return
```

The last thing we need to do is decide what format the file should be saved in. We can use a series of `If...Then` statements, along with the `EndsWith` method, to see what type of file extension was used, which instructs us on how to save a file. For example, if *abc.jpg* is the given name, we know that it ends in *jpg* so we can save the file as a Joint Photographic Experts Group (JPEG) file.

Here's the code:

```
    Dim imgFormat As Imaging.ImageFormat
    If (SaveFileDialog1.FileName.EndsWith("png")) Then
imgFormat = Imaging.ImageFormat.Png
    If (SaveFileDialog1.FileName.EndsWith("jpg")) Then
imgFormat = Imaging.ImageFormat.Jpeg
    If (SaveFileDialog1.FileName.EndsWith("bmp")) Then
imgFormat = Imaging.ImageFormat.Bmp
    If (SaveFileDialog1.FileName.EndsWith("gif")) Then
imgFormat = Imaging.ImageFormat.Gif
    If (SaveFileDialog1.FileName.EndsWith("tga")) Then
imgFormat = Imaging.ImageFormat.Tiff
```

The last thing we do is save the file using the image format that we just created. Using some error handling, we then save the file and catch any exceptions that occur:

```
Try
    PictureBox1.Image.Save(SaveFileDialog1.FileName, imgFormat)
    Catch ex As Exception
        MsgBox(ex.Message, MsgBoxStyle.Critical Or
MsgBoxStyle.ApplicationModal, "Error")
    End Try
End Sub
```

The entire procedure follows:

```
Private Sub btnSave_Click(ByVal sender As System.Object, ByVal
e As System.EventArgs) Handles btnSave.Click
    If PictureBox1.Image Is Nothing Then
```

```
        MsgBox("There is nothing to save - please drop a file
onto the Picture Box!", MsgBoxStyle.Exclamation Or
MsgBoxStyle.ApplicationModal, "No Image")
            Return
        End If

        SaveFileDialog1.ShowDialog()

        If SaveFileDialog1.FileName = "" Then Return

        Dim imgFormat As Imaging.ImageFormat
        If (SaveFileDialog1.FileName.EndsWith("png")) Then
imgFormat = Imaging.ImageFormat.Png
        If (SaveFileDialog1.FileName.EndsWith("jpg")) Then
imgFormat = Imaging.ImageFormat.Jpeg
        If (SaveFileDialog1.FileName.EndsWith("bmp")) Then
imgFormat = Imaging.ImageFormat.Bmp
        If (SaveFileDialog1.FileName.EndsWith("gif")) Then
imgFormat = Imaging.ImageFormat.Gif
        If (SaveFileDialog1.FileName.EndsWith("tga")) Then
imgFormat = Imaging.ImageFormat.Tiff

    Try
        PictureBox1.Image.Save(SaveFileDialog1.FileName, imgFormat)
        Catch ex As Exception ' If failed we get the exception (the
replacement of the error object in VB6)
            MsgBox(ex.Message, MsgBoxStyle.Critical Or
MsgBoxStyle.ApplicationModal, "Error")
        End Try
    End Sub
```

TESTING THE APPLICATION

You can now save the application and start it in VB.NET. Try dragging files of varying types onto the window. Figures 25.3 through 25.5 display several different files that were dragged onto the project.

FIGURE 25.3   A bitmap has been dropped onto the PictureBox.

FIGURE 25.4   A JPEG image appears in the PictureBox.

FIGURE 25.5   An error message
displays after a text file is dropped.

FINAL CODE LISTING

This is the final code listing for the project:

```
Public Class Form1
Inherits System.Windows.Forms.Form

Private Sub Form1_Load(ByVal sender As System.Object, ByVal
e As System.EventArgs) Handles MyBase.Load
      PictureBox1.AllowDrop = True
      PictureBox1.BackColor = Color.Aqua
      Me.Text = "Drag & Drop Image Conversion"
End Sub


Private Sub PictureBox1_DragDrop(ByVal sender As Object,
ByVal e As System.Windows.Forms.DragEventArgs) Handles
PictureBox1.DragDrop
      Dim sFileArray() As String =
e.Data.GetData(DataFormats.FileDrop)
      Try
          PictureBox1.Image = Image.FromFile(sFileArray(0))
      Catch
          MsgBox("Invalid Image File",
MsgBoxStyle.Exclamation Or MsgBoxStyle.ApplicationModal, "Error")
          Return
      End Try
End Sub
```

```vbnet
        Private Sub PictureBox1_DragEnter(ByVal sender As Object,
ByVal e As System.Windows.Forms.DragEventArgs) Handles
PictureBox1.DragEnter
        If (e.Data.GetDataPresent(DataFormats.FileDrop))
Then
            e.Effect = DragDropEffects.Copy
        Else
            e.Effect = DragDropEffects.None
        End If
    End Sub



        Private Sub btnSave_Click(ByVal sender As System.Object,
ByVal e As System.EventArgs) Handles btnSave.Click
        If PictureBox1.Image Is Nothing Then
            MsgBox("There is nothing to save -- please drop a
file onto the Picture Box!", MsgBoxStyle.Exclamation Or
MsgBoxStyle.ApplicationModal, "No Image")
            Return
        End If

        SaveFileDialog1.ShowDialog()

        If SaveFileDialog1.FileName = "" Then Return

        Dim imgFormat As Imaging.ImageFormat
        If (SaveFileDialog1.FileName.EndsWith("png")) Then
imgFormat = Imaging.ImageFormat.Png
        If (SaveFileDialog1.FileName.EndsWith("jpg")) Then
imgFormat = Imaging.ImageFormat.Jpeg
        If (SaveFileDialog1.FileName.EndsWith("bmp")) Then
imgFormat = Imaging.ImageFormat.Bmp
        If (SaveFileDialog1.FileName.EndsWith("gif")) Then
imgFormat = Imaging.ImageFormat.Gif
        If (SaveFileDialog1.FileName.EndsWith("tga")) Then
imgFormat = Imaging.ImageFormat.Tiff

        Try
            PictureBox1.Image.Save(SaveFileDialog1.FileName,
imgFormat)
        Catch ex As Exception
```

```
                MsgBox(ex.Message, MsgBoxStyle.Critical Or
        MsgBoxStyle.ApplicationModal, "Error")
                End Try
            End Sub
            End Class
```

CHAPTER REVIEW

In this chapter, we created an application that can be used for a variety of purposes. You learned about adding drag-and-drop capabilities to a form, which can be useful in a wide assortment of applications.

In the next chapter, we're going to look at one of the many ways we can create an MP3 player.

CREATING AN MP3 PLAYER

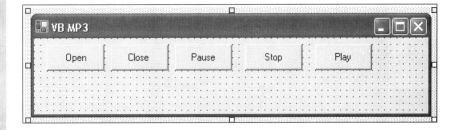

The popularity of MP3 music is unquestionable. There have been several lawsuits directed by the recording industry at companies that aid users in sharing files, which are often protected under copyright laws. The media attention to the format is incredible. So, with all the publicity, the user base of programs such as Kazaa continue to grow nearly exponentially. This isn't an endorsement of exchanging copyrighted materials, but rather an acknowledgement that regardless of the outcome of future lawsuits, the format itself is so popular that it'll undoubtedly remain in one capacity or another. Keeping this in mind, developing an MP3 player is a very good project for learning Visual Basic programming concepts.

PROJECT OVERVIEW

In this chapter, you'll develop an MP3 player. This project could be based around a number of commercial ActiveX controls, but the goal of this book is to allow you to complete most of the projects without spending any additional money.

Instead of an ActiveX control, you could also remotely control another application from a Visual Basic program. For instance, it would be relatively easy to write a program that would remotely control an existing MP3 player. Again, this option would require you to purchase additional software, which you shouldn't have to do.

Another problem with this approach would occur if you decided to distribute your application to other users. Controlling another application would require the user of your MP3 player to purchase another MP3 player. Instead of an ActiveX control or another application, the solution we'll use is the *winmm.dll* file and Multimedia Control Interface (MCI) commands.

TUTORIAL

THE PROJECT

To begin our project, we'll construct the basic graphical user interface (GUI) for the MP3 player:

1. Start the Visual Basic IDE. From the New Projects window, make sure that Visual Basic is selected. Choose the Windows Application option. You can change the name of the project to something you'd like; it's named *Chapter 26* on the CD-ROM and throughout the chapter.

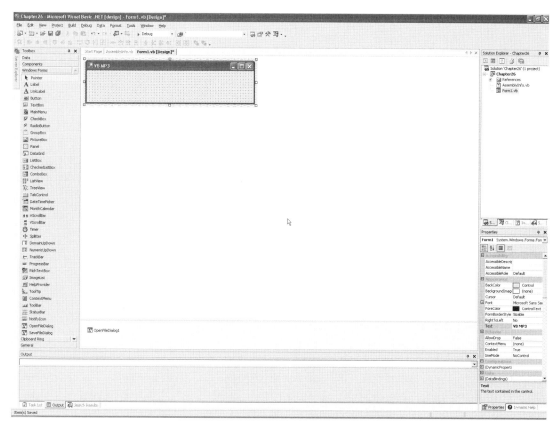

FIGURE 26.1   The File Open dialog box is visible beneath the form and with the Text property changed.

2. You'll need to place several controls on the form, one of which is the Open File dialog box. You can place this control anywhere you'd like as it's not visible at runtime. When you drag it onto the form, it'll be displayed beneath the form (see Figure 26.1).

3. Alter the Text property of the form to read VB MP3. You'll find this property in the Properties window.

4. Place a series of command buttons for the functions associated with an MP3 players like opening, stopping, and so on. The buttons can be arranged along the top side of the form, going from left to right, and can be named as follows:

- cmdOpen
- cmdPlay
- cmdStop

- cmdPause
- cmdClose

Their captions should also be altered to reflect their intended usage; for example, the `cmdOpen` button should have its caption property renamed to Open. When it's finished, the form should look something like Figure 26.2.

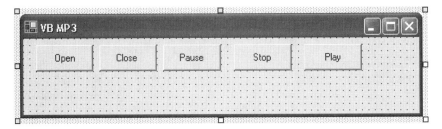

FIGURE 26.2   The interface is beginning to take shape with command buttons in place.

5. Add one `Label` control that will be used to display the filename of the song and another to identify the use of the control to the end user. You can name the control `lblCaption` and change the `Text` property to an empty string. (Erase anything inside the box in the Properties window). The last label control can be positioned to its left and given a `Text` property of `"Filename"`.

If a specific name isn't given, you can use the standard VB-assigned names.

Your final interface should appear something like Figure 26.3.

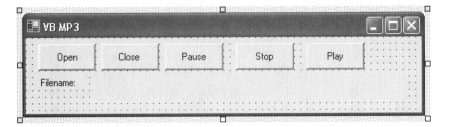

FIGURE 26.3   The final GUI.

SETTING UP

This application will use several variables to store information. If you double-click on the form, it'll display the code window and your cursor will be visible in the Form1_Load event. You can move above the cursor directly above this event and place the following variable declarations directly beneath "Inherits System. Inherits.System.Windows.Forms.Form":

```
    Private Declare Function mciSendString Lib "winmm.dll" _
Alias "mciSendStringA" (ByVal lpstrCommand As String, _
ByVal lpstrReturnString As String, ByVal uReturnLength _
As Long, ByVal hwndback As Long) As Long

    Dim strFileName As String
    Dim blnPlaying As Boolean
    Dim Temp As Integer
    Dim command As String
    Dim s As String
    Dim strFileNameTemp As String
```

 You may have noticed the underline character (_) located in the Private Declare *statement. This simply allows you to use multiple lines to display a line that should actually be located in a single line.*

Although there are several variables, the first line, which begins with Private Declare..., is the most interesting one. It's a Windows Application Programming Interface (API) call. For now, you don't need to concern yourself too much with API calls as they'll be discussed in detail in the next chapter, but you do need to understand that the mciSendString function is now available to the entire form.

The mciSendString function sends a command to a Multimedia Control Interface (MCI) device. The command strings used with this function can perform almost any task necessary for using a multimedia device installed on the computer. This approach provides a relatively easy way to perform multimedia output operations.

The Form1_Load event is called when the form is first displayed. We'll use this event to set up the lblCaption to read "–No Media". Enter the following code for the Form_Load event, which will set lblCaption to a value to inform the user that nothing is opened currently:

```
    Private Sub Form1_Load(ByVal sender As System.Object, _
        ByVal e As System.EventArgs) Handles MyBase.Load
```

```
      lblCaption.Text = " — No Media"

End Sub
```

PLAYING THE MP3 FILES

You've created a command button called cmdOpen that will be used by the program to open the MP3 file. We simply use the cmdOpen_Click event, which occurs when the button is clicked. Before we play the file, we need to check to see if a file is already playing. If one's playing, you should exit the procedure without opening a file. However, you should let the user know that they're trying to open the player when a file is open already. If a file isn't playing, you should continue opening a file that begins with initializing the File Open dialog control so that it displays only MP3 files. Lastly, you should use the mciSendString function to open the file.

The following code does all of this:

```
Private Sub cmdOpen_Click(ByVal sender As System.Object, _
ByVal e As System.EventArgs) Handles cmdOpen.Click


    On Error GoTo ErrorHandler
    If blnPlaying Then
        MsgBox("Player is Busy!", vbExclamation)
        Exit Sub
    End If
    OpenFileDialog1.Filter = "MP3 Files|*.MP3"
    OpenFileDialog1.ShowDialog()

    If OpenFileDialog1.FileName = "" Or _
OpenFileDialog1.FileName = strFileName Then

    Else

        strFileName = OpenFileDialog1.FileName
        strFileNameTemp = OpenFileDialog1.FileName
        FileCopy(strFileName, "C:\mciplay")
        strFileName = "C:\mciplay"

        mciSendString("open " & strFileName & " type
MPEGVideo", _
        0, 0, 0)
```

```
            lblCaption.Text = strFileNameTemp
        End If
    ErrorHandler:
    End Sub
```

There's an interesting problem with using the `mciSendString` method for playing MP3 audio files. The filename cannot be more than eight characters followed by 26 characters as an extension. It's obviously not practical to limit your application to use only files named in this format. So, we'll solve this by copying the file to the root directory of your hard drive and give it a name of *MCIPlay*. We'll then use this filename to play the file. The `mciSendString` command is very strict about its syntax; it uses quotation marks (?) and includes `MPEGVideo` as its type. Although it says video, it's the correct type for MP3 audio files as well.

THE REST OF THE FUNCTIONS

Once you've opened the file, you can use the command buttons you created for playing, stopping, pausing, and so on. The programming that's used in all of the procedure is nearly identical.

First, you need to see if a file is already playing by checking the `blnPlaying` variable, which is of type `Boolean`. A `Boolean` variable can display only two values—`True` or `False`. (You can also think of this as 0 or 1—Off or On). If a file is playing, you can send an MCI code to do the task. Lastly, you can change the `lblCaption` to reflect the command.

The following code lists all of the procedures:

```
Private Sub cmdClose_Click(ByVal sender As System.Object, _
 ByVal e As System.EventArgs) Handles cmdClose.Click
    If blnPlaying Then
        mciSendString("close " & strFileName, 0, 0, 0)
    End If
    blnPlaying = False
    lblCaption.Text = " --No Media"
End Sub

Private Sub cmdPause_Click(ByVal sender As System.Object, _
 ByVal e As System.EventArgs) Handles cmdPause.Click
    If blnPlaying Then
        mciSendString("pause " & strFileName, 0, 0, 0)
        blnPlaying = False
```

```
                    lblCaption.Text = OpenFileDialog1.Filename & " --
Paused"
            End If
        End Sub

        Private Sub cmdPlay_Click(ByVal sender As System.Object, _
        ByVal e As System.EventArgs) Handles cmdPlay.Click
            If strFileName <> "" Then
                mciSendString("play " & strFileName, 0, 0, 0)
                blnPlaying = True
                lblCaption.Text = OpenFileDialog1.Filename & " --
Playing"
            End If
        End Sub

        Private Sub cmdStop_Click(ByVal sender As System.Object, _
        ByVal e As System.EventArgs) Handles cmdStop.Click
            If blnPlaying Then
                mciSendString("stop " & strFileName, 0, 0, 0)
                blnPlaying = False
                lblCaption.Text = OpenFileDialog1.Filename & " --
Stopped"
            End If
        End Sub
```

The only procedure that differs slightly is `cmdPlay_Click`, which doesn't check the status of a playing file. Rather, it only needs to determine if the `strFileName` variable contains information. If it does, it knows that it must have a file open. If not, it exits the procedure.

Figure 26.4 represents what the finished MP3 player should look like when playing a file. If you were interested, you could add common functions, such as play lists or captions that display time-related information. This project will be used in the next chapter to add some interesting changes to the vanilla-looking GUI.

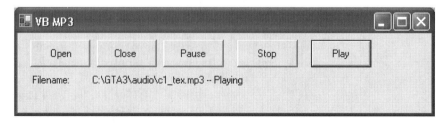

FIGURE 26.4 Play an MP3 file.

FINAL CODE LISTING

The following code is the complete listing for this chapter:

```
Private Declare Function mciSendString Lib "winmm.dll"
Alias "mciSendStringA" (ByVal lpstrCommand As String, ByVal
lpstrReturnString As String, ByVal uReturnLength As Long,
ByVal hwndback As Long) As Long

Dim strFileName As String
Dim strFileNameTemp As String
Dim blnPlaying As Boolean
Dim Temp As Integer
Dim command As String

Private Sub Form1_Load(ByVal sender As System.Object, ByVal
e As System.EventArgs) Handles MyBase.Load
    lblCaption.Text = " -- No Media"
End Sub

Private Sub cmdOpen_Click(ByVal sender As System.Object,
ByVal e As System.EventArgs) Handles cmdOpen.Click


    On Error GoTo ErrorHandler
    If blnPlaying Then
        MsgBox("Player is Busy!", vbExclamation)
        Exit Sub
    End If
    OpenFileDialog1.Filter = "MP3 Files|*.MP3"
    OpenFileDialog1.ShowDialog()

    If OpenFileDialog1.FileName = "" Or
OpenFileDialog1.FileName = strFileName Then

        Else

            strFileName = OpenFileDialog1.FileName
            strFileNameTemp = OpenFileDialog1.FileName
            FileCopy(strFileName, "C:\mciplay") 'Copy to c:\
            strFileName = "C:\mciplay" ' Create file with no
spaces

            mciSendString("open " & strFileName & " type
MPEGVideo", 0, 0, 0)
```

```
                    lblCaption.Text = strFileNameTemp
                End If
            ErrorHandler:
            End Sub

            Private Sub cmdClose_Click(ByVal sender As
            System.Object, ByVal e As System.EventArgs) Handles
cmdClose.Click
                If blnPlaying Then
                    mciSendString("close " & strFileName, 0, 0, 0)
                End If
                blnPlaying = False
                lblCaption.Text = " --No Media"
            End Sub

            Private Sub cmdPause_Click(ByVal sender As
            System.Object, ByVal e As System.EventArgs) Handles
            cmdPause.Click
                If blnPlaying Then
                    mciSendString("pause " & strFileName, 0, 0, 0)
                    blnPlaying = False
                    lblCaption.Text = OpenFileDialog1.FileName & " --
Paused"
                End If
            End Sub

            Private Sub cmdPlay_Click(ByVal sender As System.Object,
ByVal e As System.EventArgs) Handles cmdPlay.Click
                If strFileName <> "" Then
                    mciSendString("play " & strFileName, 0, 0, 0)
                    blnPlaying = True
                    lblCaption.Text = OpenFileDialog1.FileName & " --
Playing"
                End If
            End Sub



            Private Sub cmdStop_Click(ByVal sender As System.Object,
ByVal e As System.EventArgs) Handles cmdStop.Click
                If blnPlaying Then
                    mciSendString("stop " & strFileName, 0, 0, 0)
                    blnPlaying = False
                    lblCaption.Text = strFileName & " -- Stopped"
```

```
            End If
        End Sub
```

CHAPTER REVIEW

This chapter introduced you to a variety of new concepts, including basic API information and the `Variant` and `Boolean` data types. You also learned how to create and use arrays. You sent commands to the *winmm.dll* file by using `mciSendStrings`, which played the MP3 files. You also read tag information from an MP3 by opening it for binary reading and then checking the various fields to determine if information was present.

In the next chapter, we're going to add some effects to this application to enhance the way that it looks to an end user.

FORM EFFECTS

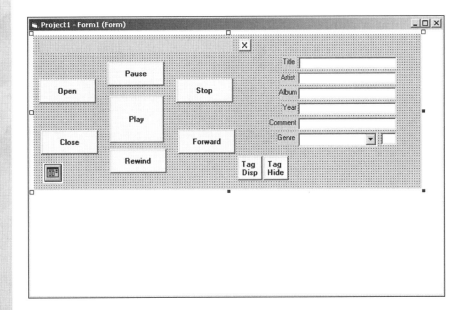

B y itself, Visual Basic provides the necessary basic ingredients for graphical user interface (GUI) design. Unfortunately, although you can change the colors and shapes of items such as forms and controls, you're severely limited to the variations that you can design. In this chapter, you'll create an application that doesn't really have a great deal of functionality, but instead focuses on designing a unique interface using the new GDI+ features of VB.NET that we first looked at in Chapter 6.

THE VB 6 WAY

We're going to take a slightly different approach in this chapter. We'll begin by looking at what we had to do in earlier versions of VB. This will help you understand how some of the new features in VB.NET make your job much easier. If you'd like to pass over this information, you can proceed to the section, "The VB.NET Way," later in this chapter.

ON THE CD

The VB 6 project is included on the CD-ROM but is different from the VB.NET project that's also included. The techniques are what we're interested in rather than the exact functions of the individual programs.

If you're not familiar with the *application programming interface (API)*, it's a collection of hundreds of ready-made functions and procedures that are available to you inside Visual Basic. The API routines are required in VB 6 to do this project and work very similar to Visual Basic's own internal functions. In fact, you're making calls to the API when you use Visual Basic keywords, properties, and methods. However, Visual Basic does a great job of shielding you from the intricacies of the calls.

All of the Windows API routines are stored in special files called dynamic linking libraries (DLLs), which are simply compiled programs that can be accessed only by other programs and usually have *.dll* as their file extension. Thousands of API routines are available and they can save you time in the programming development cycle.

The three following files hold most of the API routines, or functions, that you'll call from your Visual Basic applications:

- USER32.DLL: Contains functions related to the control of the program interface such as cursors, menus, and windows.
- GDI32.DLL: Provides functions that control output to the screen and other devices.
- KERNEL32.DLL: Gives you access to the internal Windows hardware and software interface along with memory, file, and directory functions.

If you take a quick glance through the folders for *Windows*, *Windows\System*, *WINNT*, and *WINNT\SYSTEM32* (for Windows NT, XP, or 2000), you'll see these and many more *.dll* files. The majority of them are copied to these directories when Windows is installed on your system. You can quickly see that linking to these files is fundamental to the operations of the Windows OS.

In order to access the Windows API, you must first let your program know that you'd like to use a particular DLL. Before you call a DLL procedure, it must be declared in your Visual Basic program using the `Declare` statement. `Declare` statements go in the general declaration area of form and code modules. The `Declare` statement informs your program about the name of the procedure, and the number and type of arguments that it takes.

The basic *call* to a DLL function is `Declare Function DLLFunction Lib nameofDLL [(argument list)] As type`. In the example, `nameofDLL` is a string specifying the name of the DLL file that contains the procedure, while `type` is the returned value type. A DLL *procedure* is slightly different: `Declare Sub DLLProcecure Lib nameofDLL [(argument list)]`.

If you place the calls in code modules, you need to preface the `Declare` statements with the keywords `Public` or `Private`, which indicate the procedure scope. This is not a concern in form modules as the only possible use is `Private`. As a result, you need to preface the `Declare` statement with `Private` in form modules.

The idea is to create a new user interface, with odd-shaped forms and buttons, giving a variety of effects to our project. This can be accomplished by using *regions*, which are areas on a form that are in the shape of rectangles, ellipses, or polygons, and are combined with other regions to form elaborate shapes.

 Remember that this information is for VB 6. We'll look at how easy it easy to accomplish this same task in VB.NET.

The reason you needed a brief explanation of the Windows API is VB 6 doesn't have the ability to access regions directly. On the other hand, the API allows you to create the regions and returns a handle to the region. A handle is simply an "address" that points to something such as a control or a form, or for our specific needs, the regions that you're going to create.

Recall that you'll be using the API to make regions. The following API calls can be used.

Creating Rectangles

This API function creates a rectangular region and provides a handle to it. Passing its upper-left and lower-right corners to the function specifies the rectangle defining the region.

Here's the function:

```
Public Declare Function CreateRectRgn Lib "gdi32" _
ByVal X1 As Long, ByVal Y1 As Long, ByVal X2 As _
Long, ByVal Y2 As Long) As Long
```

Creating Ellipses

This API function creates an elliptically shaped region. The ellipse that forms the region is specified by the bounding rectangle defined by the co-ordinates passed to the function. The function isn't used in our example, but you could substitute it if you would like.

Here's the function:

```
Public Declare Function CreateEllipticRgn Lib "gdi32" _
(ByVal X1 As Long, ByVal Y1 As Long, ByVal X2 As Long, _
ByVal Y2 As Long) As Long
```

Creating Rounded Rectangles

This API function creates a rectangle like the earlier CreateRectRgn, but allows you to specify X3 and Y3 coordinates for creating a rounded rectangle. This function is used for all the buttons and the form in the example that's created in this chapter.

Here's the function:

```
Public Declare Function CreateRoundRectRgn Lib "gdi32" _
(ByVal X1 As Long, ByVal Y1 As Long, ByVal X2 As Long, _
ByVal Y2 As Long, ByVal X3 As Long, ByVal Y3 As Long) As Long
```

Creating a Polygon or Custom Shape

This API call allows you to create any shape based on a series of points. Used to make an arrow effect in the example. Once you've created the regions, you can combine them with others and set the window's region to this newly created shape. Here are the API functions for creating a polygon region:

```
Public Declare Function CreatePolygonRgn Lib "gdi32" _
(lpPoint As POINTAPI, ByVal nCount As Long, ByVal _
nPolyFillMode As Long) As Long
```

Combining Regions

This API function combines two or more regions to form a third one. The two regions can be combined using a variety of logical operators, but the region that receives the combined regions must already be a region. You can complete a blank region to use for this purpose, or you could simply use any of the original regions.

Here's the function:

```
Public Declare Function CombineRgn Lib "gdi32" _
(ByVal hDestRgn As Long, ByVal hSrcRgn1 As Long, _
ByVal hSrcRgn2 As Long, ByVal nCombineMode As Long) As Long
```

The logical operators are as follows:

- RGN_AND: The combined region is the overlapping area of the two source regions.
- RGN_OR: The combined region is all the area contained in either of the two source regions, including any overlap.
- RGN_XOR: The combined region is all of the area contained in either of the two source regions, excluding any overlap.
- RGN_DIFF: The combined region is all the area of the first source region except for the portion also included in the second source region.
- RGN_COPY: The combined region is identical to the first source region. The second source region is ignored.

Initializing the Window

This is the function that changes the shape of the window. Any part of the form that's outside of the region isn't drawn, and so is invisible to the end user. Here's the function:

```
Public Declare Function SetWindowRgn Lib "user32" _
(ByVal hWnd As Long, ByVal hRgn As Long, ByVal bRedraw As
Boolean) As Long
```

SETTING UP THE FORM

If you refer to Figure 27.1, you'll notice that our new GUI will have several new command buttons for the extra operations that are needed for closing the program. You can create these command buttons and place them on the form at exact locations. Because the form will be rounded, the buttons could be placed in an area that isn't displayed and would obviously not provide their needed functionality.

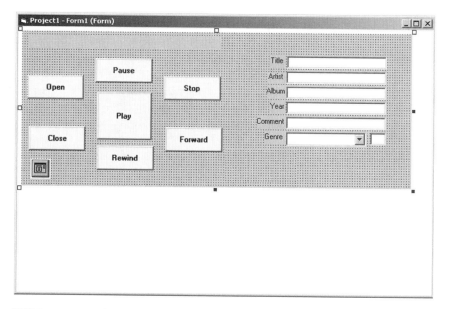

FIGURE 27.1 A GUI for the MP3 Player.

The following information will allow you to set the properties for the command buttons:

- cmdCloseForm: Top 110, Left 4734, Width 284 , Height 284, Caption X
- cmdDisplayTag: Top 2891, Left 4691, Width 575, Height 576, Caption Show Tag
- cmdHideTag: Top 2891, Left 5288, Width 575, Height 575, Caption Hide Tag

These buttons should look similar to the ones displayed in Figure 27.2.

The command buttons that were previously on the form can also be arranged to appear similar to the figure and their properties should be adjusted as well. Their background property should be changed to yellow (&H00C0FFFF&) and the following properties need to be set:

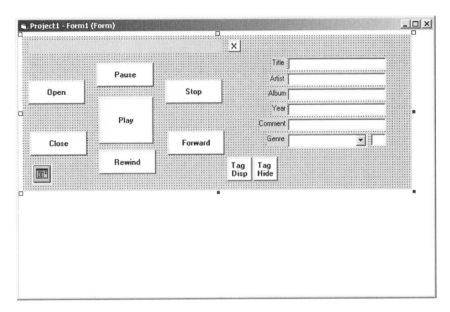

FIGURE 27.2   The new command buttons will provide extra features for the MP3 player.

- cmdPause, cmdOpen, cmdStop, cmdForward, cmdRewind, cmd-
Close: Width 1307, Height 572
- cmdPlay: Width 1250, Height 1115

Next, you need to set the form's border style to 0-None in the Properties window. The size of the form should also be altered to a Width of
9480 and Height of 3660.

Some Declarations

Because the form uses API calls, there are a few extra items that need to
be declared. In addition to the API calls, you'll also need a couple of new
variables as well. These variables will be mentioned once you use them.

You can enter the following information in the declarations of
Form1:

```
Private Declare Function CreatePolygonRgn Lib "gdi32"_ (lpPoint
As POINTAPI, ByVal nCount As Long, ByVal _ nPolyFillMode As Long)
As Long


Private Declare Function SetWindowRgn Lib "user32" _
(ByVal hwnd As Long, ByVal hRgn As Long, ByVal bRedraw_
```

```
As Boolean) As Long

Private Declare Function CreateRoundRectRgn Lib _
"gdi32" (ByVal X1 As Long, ByVal Y1 As Long, ByVal X2 _
As Long, ByVal Y2 As Long, ByVal X3 As Long, ByVal Y3 _
As Long)_ As Long

Private Declare Function CombineRgn Lib "gdi32"_
(ByVal hDestRgn As Long, ByVal hSrcRgn1 As Long,_
ByVal hSrcRgn2 As Long, ByVal nCombineMode As Long)_
As Long

Private Declare Sub ReleaseCapture Lib "user32" ()

Private Declare Function SendMessage Lib "user32" _
Alias "SendMessageA" (ByVal hwnd As Long, ByVal wMsg _
As Long, ByVal wParam As Integer, ByVal lParam As _
Long) As Long

Private Type POINTAPI
    X As Long
    Y As Long
End Type

Private ButtonRegion As Long
Private lngRegion As Long
Private lngRegion2 As Long

Private Const WM_NCLBUTTONDOWN = &HA1
Private Const HTCAPTION = 2
```

Changes to the Form_Load Event

The Form_Load event has several additions that need to be made to it. First, you need to set the lblCaption BorderStyle property to 1 so that you can see it more easily on the form. This becomes important once you set the BackStyle of the control to 0 to make it transparent. When you execute the MP3 player, you won't have the ability to move the form by clicking on the title bar. Instead, you can use an API call, which will only allow you to move the form if you're clicking directly on it. As a result, if you don't see the lblCaption, you might mistakenly forget it's there and attempt to move the form by clicking on it. You need to set all the label controls to a transparent BackStyle as well.

The following code can be entered below the previous last line of code but before the `End Sub` statement in the event:

```
lblCaption.BorderStyle = 1
lblCaption.BackStyle = 0
Label1.BackStyle = 0
Label2.BackStyle = 0
Label3.BackStyle = 0
Label27.BackStyle = 0
Label5.BackStyle = 0
Label6.BackStyle = 0
```

In Figure 27.2, you could see the `cmdTagHide` and `cmdTagShow` buttons that were made to look like arrows. To produce this effect, you need to initialize a variable called `PTS` that will be used to store the points that make up an arrow. The points can be thought of as a connect-the-dots type of game. As you can see in Figure 27.3, the arrows are very simple and easy to construct.

This will need to be done twice—once for each button and facing in opposite directions.

Next, you'll use the `SetWindowRgn` and `CreatePolygonRgn` API to draw the button in the shape. Now that the arrows are drawn, you can set the background of the form to an image of some type represented by the file, *background.jpg*. The following code will accomplish this:

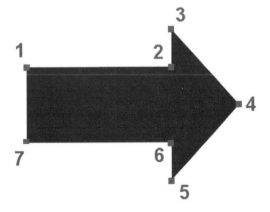

Image Points

FIGURE 27.3 Creating an array of points allows you to generate an arrow effect.

```
Dim pts(1 To 7) As POINTAPI
pts(1).X = 5
pts(1).Y = 15
pts(2).X = 15
pts(2).Y = 15
pts(3).X = 15
pts(3).Y = 5
pts(4).X = 25
pts(4).Y = 20
pts(5).X = 15
pts(5).Y = 35
pts(6).X = 15
pts(6).Y = 25
pts(7).X = 5
pts(7).Y = 25
cmdDisplayTag.Caption = ""
ButtonRegion = CreatePolygonRgn(pts(1),
UBound(pts), 1)
SetWindowRgn cmdDisplayTag.hwnd, ButtonRegion, True
pts(1).X = 5
pts(1).Y = 20
pts(2).X = 15
pts(2).Y = 35
pts(3).X = 15
pts(3).Y = 25
pts(4).X = 25
pts(4).Y = 25
pts(5).X = 25
pts(5).Y = 15
pts(6).X = 15
pts(6).Y = 15
pts(7).X = 15
pts(7).Y = 5
cmdHideTag.Caption = ""
ButtonRegion = CreatePolygonRgn(pts(1),
UBound(pts), 1)
SetWindowRgn cmdHideTag.hwnd, ButtonRegion, True
Set Me.Picture = LoadPicture(App.Path & _
"\background.jpg")
```

The command buttons that control the MP3 functions are made to appear in a rounded rectangular fashion. You can use the CreateRoundRectRgn API along with the SetWindowRgn API to handle the effect:

```
lngRegion = CreateRoundRectRgn(5, 5, 85, 34, 25, 25)
SetWindowRgn cmdOpen.hwnd, lngRegion, True
lngRegion = CreateRoundRectRgn(5, 5, 85, 34, 25, 25)
SetWindowRgn cmdPause.hwnd, lngRegion, True
lngRegion = CreateRoundRectRgn(5, 5, 85, 34, 25, 25)
SetWindowRgn cmdStop.hwnd, lngRegion, True
lngRegion = CreateRoundRectRgn(5, 5, 85, 34, 25, 25)
SetWindowRgn cmdClose.hwnd, lngRegion, True
lngRegion = CreateRoundRectRgn(5, 5, 85, 34, 25, 25)
SetWindowRgn cmdRewind.hwnd, lngRegion, True
lngRegion = CreateRoundRectRgn(5, 5, 85, 34, 25, 25)
SetWindowRgn cmdForward.hwnd, lngRegion, True
```

Lastly, you need to create a circular button for cmdPlay and the main part of the form should be adjusted to look like a rounded rectangle. Again, you can use the CreateRoundRectRgn and SetWindowRgn APIs to do this:

```
lngRegion = CreateRoundRectRgn(12, 6, 76, 65, 65, 65)
SetWindowRgn cmdPlay.hwnd, lngRegion, True
lngRegion = CreateRoundRectRgn(1, 1, 360, 230, 25, 25)
SetWindowRgn Me.hwnd, lngRegion, True
```

Moving the Form

When the title bar is removed from the form, you lose the ability to move the form by dragging it with the mouse. Instead, you're forced to use API calls to move the form whenever you click and drag it with the mouse. You can use the MouseDown event to capture any mouse activity and then call a procedure called MoveForm Mouse that contains the API calls.

The following procedures can be added to the project:

```
Private Sub Form_MouseDown(Button As Integer, Shift As Integer,
X As Single, Y As Single)
   If Button = 1 Then MoveFormMouse
   End Sub


Sub MoveFormMouse()
    Dim ReturnVal As Long
    ReleaseCapture
    ReturnVal = SendMessage(Form1.hwnd, WM_NCLBUTTONDOWN,_
    HTCAPTION, 0)
    If ReturnVal = 0 Then
```

```
        End If
    End Sub
```

FINISHING THE PROJECT

The final procedures that will finish the project use several of the same API calls that you've already used, mainly `CreateRoundRectRgn` and `SetWindowRgn` to simulate showing and hiding the tag information when the `cmdDisplayTag` and `cmdHideTag` buttons are clicked. The final step in the project is to exit it with the `cmdCloseForm` button.

These procedures can be added to the project:

```
Private Sub cmdDisplayTag_Click()
lngRegion = CreateRoundRectRgn(1, 1, 360, 230, 25, 25)
lngRegion2 = CreateRoundRectRgn(375, 1, 600, 230, 25, 25)
CombineRgn lngRegion2, lngRegion, lngRegion2, 3
SetWindowRgn Me.hwnd, lngRegion2, True
cmdDisplayTag.Visible = False
End Sub

Private Sub cmdHideTag_Click()
cmdDisplayTag.Visible = True
lngRegion = CreateRoundRectRgn(1, 1, 360, 230, 25, 25)
SetWindowRgn Me.hwnd, lngRegion, True
End Sub

Private Sub cmdCloseForm_Click()
    Unload Me
End Sub
```

THE VB.NET WAY

Before looking at the VB.NET approach, it's worth mentioning the VB 6 method. To begin, we had to use several relatively obscure API calls as VB 6 is fairly limited in built-in graphics features. On the other hand, .NET offers the GDI+ namespace that contains basically everything we need for this project.

We'll begin this project by opening it from the previous chapter. We'll use the same code for all of the playing and so on but we're going to change the way the form looks. we'll begin by adding the following line:

```
Imports System.Drawing.Drawing2D
```

We'll also add a new variable of type `Point` beneath the variables from the previous chapter (the others are listed for your convenience):

```
Dim strFileName As String
Dim strFileNameTemp As String
Dim blnPlaying As Boolean
Dim Temp As Integer
Dim command As String
Private mouse_offset As Point
```

In the `Form Load` event, we need to add a little new code. First, we'll change the opacity of the form to a value of `0.75` so that you can see through it. This is one of the more powerful new features offered to us. By changing the opacity property, we can produce in a single line what would be difficult in earlier versions of VB.

Here's the line of code:

```
Me.Opacity = 0.75
```

We'll now create regions and points for drawing the shape of the form. We'll set a series of points to draw the shape, change the `BackColor` property of `cmdOpen` and `cmdClose` to navy blue, and we'll also set `cmdOpen.Text` equal to an empty string.

Here's the entire `Form Load` procedure:

```
Private Sub Form1_Load(ByVal sender As System.Object, ByVal e
As System.EventArgs) Handles MyBase.Load
      lblCaption.Text = "—No Media"
      Me.Opacity = 0.75 ' New Code

      Dim windowRegion As Region
      Dim regionPoints(5) As Point
      Dim regionTypes(5) As Byte
      regionPoints(0) = New Point(0, 0)
      regionPoints(1) = New Point(Me.Width, 0)
      regionPoints(2) = New Point(Me.Width—50, Me.Height)
      regionPoints(3) = New Point(50, Me.Height)
      regionPoints(4) = New Point(0, 0)

      Dim Cnt As Long
      For Cnt = 0 To 5
```

```
        regionTypes(Cnt) = PathPointType.Line
    Next Cnt
    Dim regionPath As New GraphicsPath(regionPoints, regionTypes)
    Me.Region = New Region(regionPath)

    cmdOpen.Text = ""  ' Remove existing text
    cmdOpen.BackColor = Color.Navy
    cmdClose.BackColor = Color.Navy

End Sub
```

The next step is to create the Form1 Paint event. You already know
how to create the event using the drop-down lists. We're going to use the
Paint event to draw a gradient background from red to yellow in the
form.

Here's the code:

```
Private Sub Form1_Paint(ByVal sender As Object, ByVal e As
System.Windows.Forms.PaintEventArgs) Handles MyBase.Paint
        Dim r As Rectangle = New Rectangle(0, 0, Me.Width, Me.Height)
        Dim g As Graphics = e.Graphics
        Dim lb As LinearGradientBrush = New LinearGradientBrush(r,
Color.Red, Color.Yellow, LinearGradientMode.BackwardDiagonal)
        g.FillRectangle(lb, r)
    End Sub
```

We now need to remove the border from the form by changing the
FormBorderStyle property of the form to None in the form editor. This removes the border and the Close button that's at the upper-right of most
Windows applications and looks like an *x*. We'll add a new button to the
form, give it a Text property of "x," and then place it on the form. You'll
see an example of this in Figure 27.4.

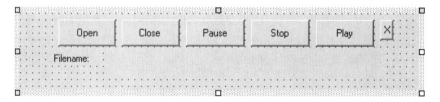

FIGURE 27.4   A new button is added to the form.

Now that we have the button, we need to add the click event for it and instruct the application to close when it's clicked:

```
Private Sub cmdExit_Click(ByVal sender As System.Object, ByVal
e As System.EventArgs) Handles cmdExit.Click
      Me.Close()
End Sub
```

Because we removed the border, we won't have a built-in way to move the form by clicking and dragging it. Instead, we'll use the `Mouse-Down` and `MouseMove` events of the form to do this for us:

```
Private Sub Form1_MouseDown(ByVal sender As Object, ByVal e As
System.Windows.Forms.MouseEventArgs) Handles MyBase.MouseDown
      mouse_offset = New Point(-e.X, -e.Y)
End Sub

Private Sub Form1_MouseMove(ByVal sender As Object, ByVal e As
System.Windows.Forms.MouseEventArgs) Handles MyBase.MouseMove
      If e.Button = MouseButtons.Left Then
          Dim mousePos As Point = Control.MousePosition
          mousePos.Offset(mouse_offset.X, mouse_offset.Y)
          Location = mousePos
      End If
End Sub
```

We'll now have a form that looks much different than a standard VB form but we're not finished. We're going to utilize the `cmdOpen Paint` event and the `cmdClose Paint` event to change the way those two buttons work. If we were interested in completing the application, we would follow the same procedure for the remaining buttons. But for this example, the two buttons will work.

Begin by creating both events. Next, instantiate a new instance of the `GraphicsPath` class in the `cmdOpen Paint` event:

```
Dim myGraphicsPath As New
System.Drawing.Drawing2D.GraphicsPath()
```

Next, we need to specify a string that we'll draw. In this case, we'll use `"Open"`, and specify the font family to be `"Arial"`, and the font style to be `"Bold"`:

```
Dim stringText As String = "Open"
```

```
Dim family As FontFamily = New FontFamily("Arial")
Dim fontStyle As FontStyle = fontStyle.Bold
```

Our next step is to specify the size of an imaginary square that will be used to house the string we're going to draw and a point at which the text will start. We'll use a size of 20:

```
Dim emSize As Integer = 20
Dim origin As PointF = New PointF(0, 0)
```

The last steps are to create a StringFormat object that will specify the text formatting information, such as line spacing and alignment. We'll also need to use the AddString method to create the string. Lastly, we'll need to set the control's Region property to the instance of the GraphicsPath class that we created earlier:

```
Dim format As StringFormat = StringFormat.GenericDefault

    myGraphicsPath.AddString(stringText, family, fontStyle,
emSize, origin, format)

    cmdOpen.Region = New Region(myGraphicsPath)Running the
Application
```

We don't need to test the application because the basics of file playback were tested in the previous chapter. We only need to run it to see if it's now drawn appropriately. We can also test the ability of the program to be moved with the mouse to make sure you can drag it around the screen. You can see an example of the form in Figure 27.5.

FINAL CODE LISTING

Here's the complete listing for both the cmdOpen Paint event and cmdClose Paint event:

```
    Private Sub cmdOpen_Paint(ByVal sender As Object, ByVal e
As System.Windows.Forms.PaintEventArgs) Handles cmdOpen.Paint
    Dim myGraphicsPath As New
System.Drawing.Drawing2D.GraphicsPath()

    Dim stringText As String = "Open"
    Dim family As FontFamily = New FontFamily("Arial")
```

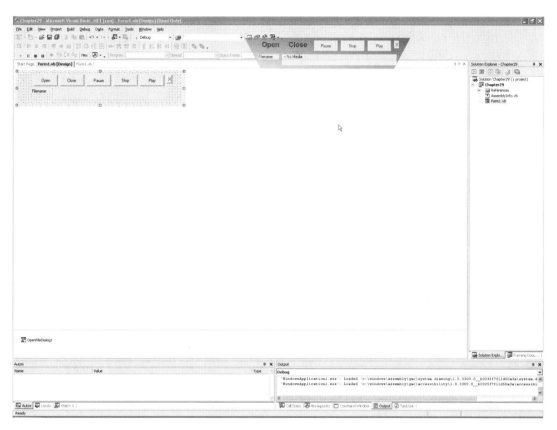

FIGURE 27.5   The final application.

```vb
        Dim fontStyle As FontStyle = fontStyle.Bold
        Dim emSize As Integer = 20

        Dim origin As PointF = New PointF(0, 0)

        Dim format As StringFormat = StringFormat.GenericDefault

        myGraphicsPath.AddString(stringText, family, fontStyle,
    emSize, origin, format)

        cmdOpen.Region = New Region(myGraphicsPath)

        End Sub
```

```
        Private Sub cmdClose_Paint(ByVal sender As Object, ByVal e
As System.Windows.Forms.PaintEventArgs) Handles cmdClose.Paint

        Dim myGraphicsPath As New
System.Drawing.Drawing2D.GraphicsPath()

        Dim stringText As String = "Close"

        Dim family As FontFamily = New FontFamily("Arial")

        Dim fontStyle As FontStyle = fontStyle.Bold

        Dim emSize As Integer = 20

        Dim origin As PointF = New PointF(0, 0)

        Dim format As StringFormat = StringFormat.GenericDefault

            myGraphicsPath.AddString(stringText, family, fontStyle,
emSize, origin, format)

        cmdClose.Region = New Region(myGraphicsPath)
        End Sub
        End Class
```

CHAPTER REVIEW

In this chapter, we added some very interesting effects that turn the very basic form into something more indicative of the functions provided by the application. We looked at how this type of task can be handled in VB.NET and also looked at how the same thing could have been done in VB 6. The simplistic VB.NET solution highlights the enhancements that have been made to an already powerful language.

In the next chapter, we are going to design an application that can calculate prime numbers.

28 FINDING PRIME NUMBERS

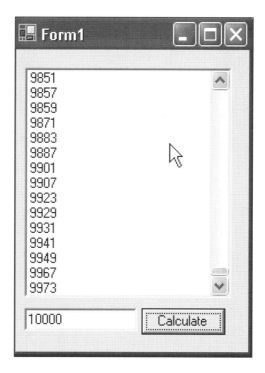

n this chapter, we're going to find prime numbers using an algorithm developed thousands of years ago. The approach, known as the "Sieve of Eratosthenes," is easy to follow, works very well on a PC, and has withstood the test of time. Simply put, the *sieve* is a mathematical device that was originated by Eratosthenes in about 230 B.C. for the purpose of segregating the composite from the prime numbers. Our application will look like Figure 28.1 when it's complete.

FIGURE 28.1   The final application.

DEFINITIONS

If you're unfamiliar when the concept, a *prime number* is a positive whole number (natural number) that's divisible by itself along with the number 1, and no other natural number. Other natural numbers that are greater than 1 are called *composite numbers*. The number 1 is interesting in that it's neither a prime nor composite number, which helps to avoid complicating many theories, including this one. For example, suppose that 1 is a prime. Then, by definition, all other primes would be composite as they would be divisible by 1. This would make 1 the only prime—something that wouldn't be all that exciting.

ALGORITHM

Eratosthenes was a Greek mathematician from Alexandria and derived this method of calculating primes. You may have heard his name in a mathematics course or even a history lesson as he was also the first person to measure the circumference of the earth accurately. The basis of his approach to calculating primes is much like a sieve that you would use in the kitchen. You toss the numbers into it and the sieve separates them out.

Before we build an application, we'll take a look at how we can find prime numbers by hand. As you remember from the definition, a prime number is divisible by itself along with the number 1 and no other natural number. So, for example, 2 is a prime number as it's divisible by itself and one. Going through a few numbers, we'll see that 3 is a prime number as is 5. Here are the calculations through 5:

    2: 2 / 1
    3: 3 / 1
    4: 2 / 2, 4 / 1
    5: 5 / 1

We can continue fairly easily for quite awhile, but it becomes increasingly difficult when we get to much larger numbers, such as 199,889. There's a fairly simple method for making a list of small primes. We'll start with a list of all of the numbers from 2 to 100:

    2 3 4 5 6 7 8 9 10
    11 12 13 14 15 16 17 18 19 20
    21 22 23 24 25 26 27 28 29 30
    31 32 33 34 35 36 37 38 39 40
    41 42 43 44 45 46 47 48 49 50
    51 52 53 54 55 56 57 58 59 60
    61 62 63 64 65 66 67 68 69 70
    71 72 73 74 75 76 77 78 79 80
    81 82 83 84 85 86 87 88 89 90
    91 92 93 94 95 96 97 98 99 100

We'll begin with a known prime (2), and then cross out every second number after 2:

    2 3 4 5 6 7 8 9 ~~10~~
    11 ~~12~~ 13 ~~14~~ 15 ~~16~~ 17 ~~18~~ 19 ~~20~~
    21 ~~22~~ 23 ~~24~~ 25 ~~26~~ 27 ~~28~~ 29 ~~30~~
    31 ~~32~~ 33 ~~34~~ 35 ~~36~~ 37 ~~38~~ 39 ~~40~~

41 ~~42~~ 43 ~~44~~ 45 ~~46~~ 47 ~~48~~ 49 ~~50~~
51 ~~52~~ 53 ~~54~~ 55 ~~56~~ 57 ~~58~~ 59 ~~60~~
61 ~~62~~ 63 ~~64~~ 65 ~~66~~ 67 ~~68~~ 69 ~~70~~
71 ~~72~~ 73 ~~74~~ 75 ~~76~~ 77 ~~78~~ 79 ~~80~~
81 ~~82~~ 83 ~~84~~ 85 ~~86~~ 87 ~~88~~ 89 ~~90~~
91 ~~92~~ 93 ~~94~~ 95 ~~96~~ 97 ~~98~~ 99 ~~100~~

You can see from the preceding list that 3 is the next prime, so we can cross out every third number after 3. If we happen upon a number that's already crossed out, you can continue on to the next:

2 3 4 5 ~~6~~ 7 ~~8~~ ~~9~~ ~~10~~
11 ~~12~~ 13 ~~14~~ ~~15~~ ~~16~~ 17 ~~18~~ 19 ~~20~~
~~21~~ ~~22~~ 23 ~~24~~ 25 ~~26~~ ~~27~~ ~~28~~ 29 ~~30~~
31 ~~32~~ ~~33~~ ~~34~~ 35 ~~36~~ 37 ~~38~~ ~~39~~ ~~40~~
41 ~~42~~ 43 ~~44~~ ~~45~~ ~~46~~ 47 ~~48~~ 49 ~~50~~
~~51~~ ~~52~~ 53 ~~54~~ 55 ~~56~~ ~~57~~ ~~58~~ 59 ~~60~~
61 ~~62~~ ~~63~~ ~~64~~ 65 ~~66~~ 67 ~~68~~ ~~69~~ ~~70~~
71 ~~72~~ 73 ~~74~~ ~~75~~ ~~76~~ 77 ~~78~~ 79 ~~80~~
~~81~~ ~~82~~ 83 ~~84~~ 85 ~~86~~ ~~87~~ ~~88~~ 89 ~~90~~
91 ~~92~~ ~~93~~ ~~94~~ 95 ~~96~~ 97 ~~98~~ ~~99~~ ~~100~~

Continuing, we can do the same thing with 5 and 7:

2 3 4 5 ~~6~~ 7 ~~8~~ ~~9~~ ~~10~~
11 ~~12~~ 13 ~~14~~ ~~15~~ ~~16~~ 17 ~~18~~ 19 ~~20~~
~~21~~ ~~22~~ 23 ~~24~~ ~~25~~ ~~26~~ ~~27~~ ~~28~~ 29 ~~30~~
31 ~~32~~ ~~33~~ ~~34~~ ~~35~~ ~~36~~ 37 ~~38~~ ~~39~~ ~~40~~
41 ~~42~~ 43 ~~44~~ ~~45~~ ~~46~~ 47 ~~48~~ ~~49~~ ~~50~~
~~51~~ ~~52~~ 53 ~~54~~ ~~55~~ ~~56~~ ~~57~~ ~~58~~ 59 ~~60~~
61 ~~62~~ ~~63~~ ~~64~~ ~~65~~ ~~66~~ 67 ~~68~~ ~~69~~ ~~70~~
71 ~~72~~ 73 ~~74~~ ~~75~~ ~~76~~ ~~77~~ ~~78~~ 79 ~~80~~
~~81~~ ~~82~~ 83 ~~84~~ ~~85~~ ~~86~~ ~~87~~ ~~88~~ 89 ~~90~~
~~91~~ ~~92~~ ~~93~~ ~~94~~ ~~95~~ ~~96~~ 97 ~~98~~ ~~99~~ ~~100~~

This gives us every prime from 1 to 100:

2 3 5 7 11 13 17 19 23 29 31 37 41 43 47 53 59 61 67 71 73 79 83 89 97

You can see that calculating primes isn't difficult but as you get to larger numbers, the process takes a much longer time. This is where the sieve comes into place. It suggests that a prime can be derived by testing all primes that are less than or equal to the square root of a number. At first glance, this may seem a bit strange. However, if you look at it further, it becomes logical as all integers are a product of primes and no prime number will be divisible by a number greater than its square root without a number lesser than its square root also being a divisor. This allows us to test all primes less than the square root of a number to determine if it's prime. Like the preceding tables, we'll seed our list with the number 2 and then calculate the primes between 2 and *n*—a number that we'll be able to enter in our program.

A Simple User Interface

You can begin this project by creating a new Windows form application so that we can build a simple user interface. There are only three controls that we need: ListBox for storing the primes; a TextBox that allows us to input the number we're willing to test to; and a button that we can click to start the calculation. Figure 28.2 displays the final GUI.

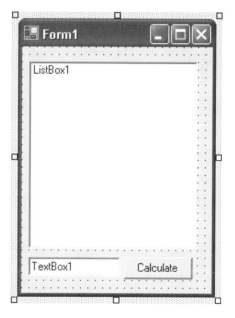

FIGURE 28.2   The final GUI for our application.

Adding Some Code

We can now write some code. Open the code editor and create the Form_Load event. We're going to add code to clear the ListBox and initialize the TextBox with a value of 100:

```
    Private Sub Form1_Load(ByVal eventSender As System.Object,
ByVal eventArgs As System.EventArgs) Handles MyBase.Load
        ListBox1.Items.Clear()
        TextBox1.Text = "100"
    End Sub
```

The next step is to handle the `Button1_Click` event. Clicking this button will begin the process of calculating the primes. We begin by initializing an array called `Primes` to a value of 2. We have yet to declare this variable, so you can add the following line to your application, placing it beneath `Inherits`:

```
    Public Primes() As Long
```

Now let's return to to the `Button1_Click` event. The next step is to clear the `ListBox` control so that any previous values are removed. We then call a `CalcPrimes` Sub, passing the `TextBox1.Text` value after converting it to an `Integer`. Lastly, we display the values in the `ListBox`:

```
    Private Sub Button1_Click(ByVal sender As System.Object, ByVal
e As System.EventArgs) Handles Button1.Click

        ReDim Primes(0)
        Primes(0) = 2
        ListBox1.Items.Clear()

        Dim Value As Long

        CalcPrimes(CInt(TextBox1.Text))

        For Each Value In Primes
            ListBox1.Items.Add((Value))
        Next Value

        Exit Sub

    End Sub
```

The `CalcPrimes` Sub will take the value passed from the `TextBox` and then loop from 2 to the maximum value that we created. It stores the prime values, and other than that, this is a simple procedure that calls `IsPrime`, which we'll create next:

```
Private Sub CalcPrimes(ByVal Max As Long)
    Dim I As Integer

    For I = 2 To Max
        If (IsPrime(I)) Then
            ReDim Preserve Primes(UBound(Primes) + 1)
            Primes(UBound(Primes)) = I
        End If
    Next

End Sub
```

This is the function that actually does the calculation. We'll return a `True` or `False` value so we'll begin by setting the function to `False`. We pass in a value `Number` that will be used for calculations. We'll use a loop to count from `Primes` lower bound to `Primes` upper bound. We'll also be certain to use `System.Windows.Forms.Application.DoEvents()` so that we can do other things in Windows and this window will not appear to be frozen. Of course, you could import this namespace along with `System.Math`, which is also used in this `Sub` procedure. However, because they were both used a single time, it didn't really make much of a difference.

We'll divide the number we think might be a prime by `Primes`. Of course, if it's divisible by a prime, then it's not a prime itself and we can exit. Otherwise, we do a second test to compare the square root of the value that we're checking against the square root of the number we passed into the function. If we've reached the square root of the number that was passed into the function without being able to divide the possible prime, then we have a new prime to add to the array.

Here's the code:

```
Private Function IsPrime(ByVal Number As Long) As Boolean
    IsPrime = False
    Dim I As Integer
    For I = LBound(Primes) To UBound(Primes)
        System.Windows.Forms.Application.DoEvents()
        If (Number Mod Primes(I) = 0) Then Exit Function
        If (Primes(I) >= System.Math.Sqrt(Number)) Then Exit
For
    Next
    IsPrime = True
End Function
```

TESTING THE APPLICATION

At this time, we're ready to save the application and then test it. When you run it, the window should look something like Figure 28.3.

The next step is to try a few values to see how they work (see Figures 28.4 through 28.6).

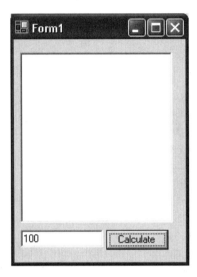

FIGURE 28.3 The window looks like this on startup.

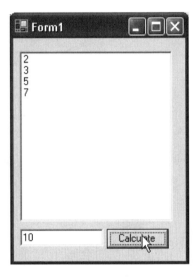

FIGURE 28.4 Testing with 10.

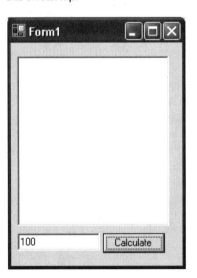

FIGURE 28.5 Testing with 100.

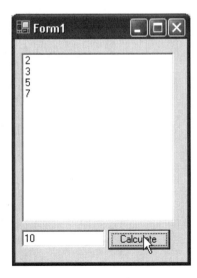

FIGURE 28.6 Testing with 10000.

FINAL CODE LISTING

This is the complete source code listing:

```
Public Class Form1
Inherits System.Windows.Forms.Form
Public Primes() As Long

Private Sub Form1_Load(ByVal eventSender As System.Object,
ByVal eventArgs As System.EventArgs) Handles MyBase.Load
    ListBox1.Items.Clear()
    TextBox1.Text = "100"
End Sub

Private Sub Button1_Click(ByVal sender As System.Object,
ByVal e As System.EventArgs) Handles Button1.Click

    ReDim Primes(0)
    Primes(0) = 2
    ListBox1.Items.Clear()

    Dim Value As Long

    CalcPrimes(CInt(TextBox1.Text))

    For Each Value In Primes
        ListBox1.Items.Add((Value))
    Next Value

    Exit Sub

End Sub

Private Sub CalcPrimes(ByVal Max As Long)
    Dim I As Integer

    For I = 2 To Max
        If (IsPrime(I)) Then
            ReDim Preserve Primes(UBound(Primes) + 1)
            Primes(UBound(Primes)) = I
        End If
    Next

End Sub
```

```
Private Function IsPrime(ByVal Number As Long) As Boolean
    Console.Write(Number)
    Console.Write(" ")

    IsPrime = False
    Dim I As Integer
    For I = LBound(Primes) To UBound(Primes)
        System.Windows.Forms.Application.DoEvents()
        If (Number Mod Primes(I) = 0) Then Exit Function
        If (Primes(I) >= System.Math.Sqrt(Number)) Then
Exit For
    Next
    IsPrime = True
End Function

End Class
```

CHAPTER REVIEW

The Sieve of Eratosthenes is one way to calculate all of the prime values between 2 and *n*. We created a program that basically implemented this sieve allowing a user to enter the value *n* and then proceeding to calculate the resulting prime numbers between 2 and the entered number.

In the next chapter, we're going to use the printing capabilities offered in VB.NET to add functions to the Word Processor application we created in Chapter 21.

PRINTING IN VB.NET

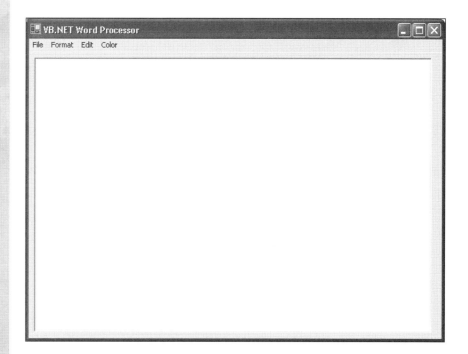

In previous versions of VB, developers would use the `Printer` object whenever they wanted to build an application that needed printing functionality. In VB.NET, the functionally of the printer object can now be found in the `System.Drawing.Printing` namespace. In this chapter, we'll use the basic word processor we built in Chapter 21 and add printing capabilities to it.

THE SYSTEM.DRAWING.PRINTING NAMESPACE

The `PrintDocument` member, which is located within the aforementioned `System.Drawing.Printing` namespace, contains the functionality that we're interested in. To print from an application, there are a few things that we need to do. First, we must create an instance of `PrintDocument`. Next, we use the classes `PrinterSettings` and `PageSettings` to set the properties for what we'd like to print. Once we set the properties, we call the `Print` method to print the document.

WRITING SOME CODE

We're going to use the example that we created in Chapter 21. If you remember, the word processor that we created in that chapter was based around the `RichTextBox` (see Figure 29.1). It included some basic functionality for opening and saving files and formatting text. We'll add the printing capability to this already existing framework

You can begin this application by opening the .NET IDE and adding Print to the menu that already exists. If you have trouble adding this to the File menu, you can refer back to Chapter 21. The menu can be placed anywhere you would like, but for simplicity, it's been added at the bottom of the screen as in Figure 29.2.

Open the code editor and then add the `Imports` line as the first line of code:

```
Imports System.Drawing.Printing
```

ADD THE PRINTING CODE

The next step is to create the Print menu click event so that it can contain the code for printing. Once you create this, you'll need to declare an instance of the `PrintDocument` class as shown here:

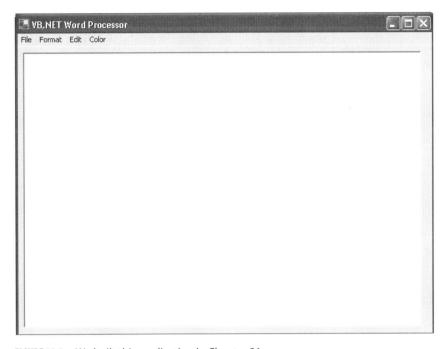

FIGURE 29.1   We built this application in Chapter 21.

FIGURE 29.2   Print has been added to the menu.

```
Dim myDoc As New Printing.PrintDocument()
```

This will be used to print the text contained in the RichTextBox. Next, we'll declare a PrintDialog Object so that we can use it to get information about the printer settings for our application:

```
Dim myPrinter As New PrintDialog()
myPrinter.Document = myDoc
```

We'll then check the result of the Printer dialog box. If it's OK, we'll then print the page using the `PrintPage` procedure that we've yet to create:

```
If myPrinter.ShowDialog() = DialogResult.OK Then
    AddHandler myDoc.PrintPage, AddressOf Me.PrintPage
myDoc.Print()
```

Before we move on, here's the entire procedure:

```
Private Sub MenuItem18_Click(ByVal sender As System.Object,
ByVal e As System.EventArgs) Handles MenuItem18.Click
    Dim myDoc As New Printing.PrintDocument()
    Dim myPrinter As New PrintDialog()
    myPrinter.Document = myDoc
    If myPrinter.ShowDialog() = DialogResult.OK Then
        AddHandler myDoc.PrintPage, AddressOf Me.PrintPage
        myDoc.Print()
    End If
End Sub
```

The next step is to create the `PrintPage` `Sub` procedure that will contain the code necessary for our application:

```
Private Sub PrintPage(ByVal sender As Object, ByVal ev As
PrintPageEventArgs)
    End Sub
```

We'll begin the process by determining the lines per page and the starting position:

```
LinesPerPage = ev.MarginBounds.Height / _
    RichTextBox1.Font.GetHeight(ev.Graphics)
Start = ev.MarginBounds.Top
```

We'll then use a loop to go through the lines in the `RichTextBox` and print them out using GDI+ `DrawString` method. The GDI+ library is used to draw the current line of the document to the printer. You can use this same approach to draw bitmaps or other graphics shapes to the printer:

```
For Each strPrint In RichTextBox1.Lines
    Start = ev.MarginBounds.Top + _
        RichTextBox1.Font.GetHeight(ev.Graphics) * LineNumber

    ev.Graphics.DrawString(strPrint, _
```

```
            RichTextBox1.Font, _
            Brushes.Black, _
            ev.MarginBounds.Left, Start)
        LineNumber = LineNumber + 1
    Next
```

Here's the entire procedure:

```
    Private Sub PrintPage(ByVal sender As Object, ByVal ev As
PrintPageEventArgs)
    Dim LinesPerPage As Single = 0
    Dim Start As Single = 0
    Dim strPrint As String
    Dim LineNumber As Short = 0

    LinesPerPage = ev.MarginBounds.Height / _
    RichTextBox1.Font.GetHeight(ev.Graphics)
    Start = ev.MarginBounds.Top

    For Each strPrint In RichTextBox1.Lines
        Start = ev.MarginBounds.Top + _
        RichTextBox1.Font.GetHeight(ev.Graphics) * LineNumber

      ev.Graphics.DrawString(strPrint, _
          RichTextBox1.Font, _
          Brushes.Black, _
          ev.MarginBounds.Left, Start)
      LineNumber = LineNumber + 1
    Next
    End Sub
```

FINAL CODE LISTING

The final code listing for this application follows:

```
        Imports System.Drawing.Printing

        Public Class Form1
        Inherits System.Windows.Forms.Form


        Private Sub MenuItem2_Click(ByVal sender As System.Object,
ByVal e As System.EventArgs) Handles MenuItem2.Click
```

```vb
        'File Open
        OpenFileDialog1.ShowDialog()
        RichTextBox1.LoadFile(OpenFileDialog1.FileName)
        Me.Text = "VB.NET WP - " & OpenFileDialog1.FileName
    End Sub

    Private Sub MenuItem3_Click(ByVal sender As System.Object, _
ByVal e As System.EventArgs) Handles MenuItem3.Click
        'File Save
        SaveFileDialog1.ShowDialog()
        RichTextBox1.SaveFile(SaveFileDialog1.FileName)
        Me.Text = "VB.NET WP - " & SaveFileDialog1.FileName
    End Sub

    Private Sub MenuItem4_Click(ByVal sender As System.Object, _
ByVal e As System.EventArgs) Handles MenuItem4.Click
        'Exit
        Me.Close()
    End Sub

    Private Sub MenuItem6_Click(ByVal sender As System.Object, _
ByVal e As System.EventArgs) Handles MenuItem6.Click
        'Font
        FontDialog1.ShowDialog()
        RichTextBox1.SelectionFont = FontDialog1.Font
    End Sub

    Private Sub MenuItem7_Click(ByVal sender As System.Object, _
ByVal e As System.EventArgs) Handles MenuItem7.Click
        'Convert to all caps
        RichTextBox1.SelectedText = _
RichTextBox1.SelectedText.ToUpper
    End Sub

    Private Sub MenuItem8_Click(ByVal sender As System.Object, _
ByVal e As System.EventArgs) Handles MenuItem8.Click
        'Center Justify
        RichTextBox1.SelectionAlignment = _
HorizontalAlignment.Center
    End Sub

    Private Sub MenuItem9_Click(ByVal sender As System.Object, _
ByVal e As System.EventArgs) Handles MenuItem9.Click
        'Left Justify
```

```vb
            RichTextBox1.SelectionAlignment =
HorizontalAlignment.Left
        End Sub


        Private Sub MenuItem10_Click(ByVal sender As Object, ByVal
e As System.EventArgs) Handles MenuItem10.Click
            'Right Justify
            RichTextBox1.SelectionAlignment =
HorizontalAlignment.Right
        End Sub


        Private Sub MenuItem12_Click(ByVal sender As System.Object,
ByVal e As System.EventArgs) Handles MenuItem12.Click
            'Copy
            RichTextBox1.Copy()
        End Sub


        Private Sub MenuItem13_Click(ByVal sender As System.Object,
ByVal e As System.EventArgs) Handles MenuItem13.Click
            'Paste
            RichTextBox1.Paste()
        End Sub


        Private Sub MenuItem14_Click(ByVal sender As System.Object,
ByVal e As System.EventArgs) Handles MenuItem14.Click
            'Cut
            RichTextBox1.Cut()
        End Sub


        Private Sub MenuItem16_Click(ByVal sender As System.Object,
ByVal e As System.EventArgs) Handles MenuItem16.Click
            'Font Color
            ColorDialog1.ShowDialog()
            RichTextBox1.ForeColor = ColorDialog1.Color
        End Sub


        Private Sub MenuItem17_Click(ByVal sender As System.Object,
ByVal e As System.EventArgs) Handles MenuItem17.Click
            'Background Color
            ColorDialog1.ShowDialog()
            RichTextBox1.BackColor = ColorDialog1.Color
        End Sub
```

```
        Private Sub Form1_Load(ByVal sender As System.Object, ByVal
e As System.EventArgs) Handles MyBase.Load
            RichTextBox1.Text = ""
            Me.Text = "VB.NET Word Processor"
        End Sub

        Private Sub MenuItem18_Click(ByVal sender As System.Object,
ByVal e As System.EventArgs) Handles MenuItem18.Click
            Dim myDoc As New Printing.PrintDocument()
            Dim myPrinter As New PrintDialog()
            myPrinter.Document = myDoc
            If myPrinter.ShowDialog() = DialogResult.OK Then
                AddHandler myDoc.PrintPage, AddressOf Me.PrintPage
                myDoc.Print()
            End If
        End Sub

        Private Sub PrintPage(ByVal sender As Object, ByVal ev As
PrintPageEventArgs)
            Dim LinesPerPage As Single = 0
            Dim Start As Single = 0
            Dim strPrint As String
            Dim LineNumber As Short = 0

            LinesPerPage = ev.MarginBounds.Height / _
                RichTextBox1.Font.GetHeight(ev.Graphics)

            Start = ev.MarginBounds.Top

            For Each strPrint In RichTextBox1.Lines
                Start = ev.MarginBounds.Top + _
                    RichTextBox1.Font.GetHeight(ev.Graphics) *
LineNumber

                ev.Graphics.DrawString(strPrint, _
                    RichTextBox1.Font, _
                    Brushes.Black, _
                    ev.MarginBounds.Left, Start)
                LineNumber = LineNumber + 1
            Next
        End Sub
    End Class
```

CHAPTER REVIEW

In this chapter, we added printing capabilities to the application that we created originally in Chapter 21. The `System.Drawing.Printing` namespace and GDI + were used to handle the process of drawing the text to the printer. Using a similar approach, you can include the ability to print shapes or additional bitmap graphics to a printer.

In the next chapter, we'll create a basic Text To Speech application using Microsoft Agent.

30

GETTING STARTED WITH MICROSOFT AGENT

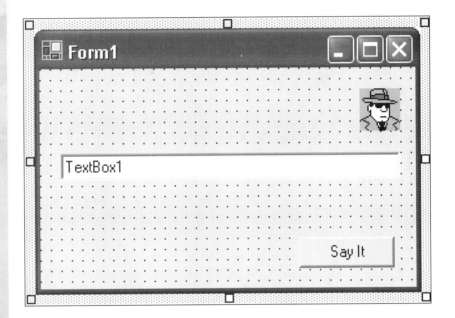

n this chapter, we're going to use the Microsoft Agent ActiveX control that's available freely from Microsoft and is included as a standard part of some of the various flavors of Windows. The standard character set includes four unique identities:

- Peedy the Parrot
- Genie
- Merlin the Wizard
- Robby the Robot

In addition to the standard varieties, there are many characters that have been created by third parties. These characters can be simple creations or very intricate. Some of them are freely available for download and others are available commercially. We'll use the Genie (see Figure 30.1) in this chapter although you'll soon find that it's very easy to switch characters .

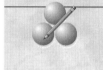

TUTORIAL   STARTING THE APPLICATION

Follow these steps to begin this application:

1. Open Visual Basic and select Windows Application.
2. Right-click on the toolbar that contains the standard controls and select Customize Toolbox from the pop-up menu (Figure 30.2).
3. The Customize Toolbox window is displayed and contains two tabs (Figure 30.3). Make sure that the first tab, COM Components, is selected and then scroll the list of available controls until you find Microsoft Agent Control 2.0.

If you cannot find the control, you can visit the Agent Web site at http://www. microsoft.com/products/msagent/downloads.htm to download the Agent control, characters, and Text To Speech engine. All of these are available for free from the Web site although you'll probably have them already if you're using a machine that's capable of running VB.NET.

4. Once you find the Agent control, select it from the window and click the OK button. You'll now find the Agent control available in the Toolbox among the other controls although you'll probably need to scroll to the bottom of the list (see Figure 30.4).
5. Add the Agent control to the window as you would any standard control. Although it's invisible to the end user, the control is seen at design time and is visible in Figure 30.5.

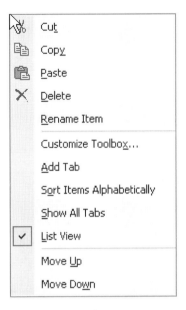

FIGURE 30.1   Merlin is one of many characters available for Microsoft Agent.

FIGURE 30.2   Use the pop-up menu.

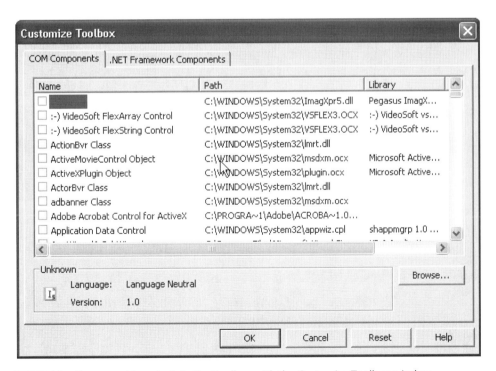

FIGURE 30.3   You can add controls to the Toolbox with the Customize Toolbox window.

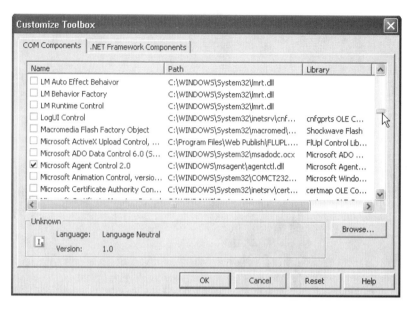

FIGURE 30.4   The control is available in the Toolbox.

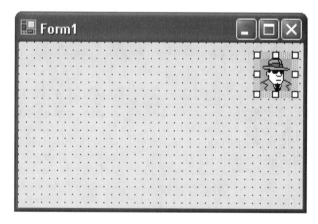

FIGURE 30.5   The control is placed on the window.

DECLARING THE CHARACTER FILE

The next step is to open the code editor in order to declare `Agent` as type `AgentObjects.IAgentCtlCharacterEx`:

```
Dim Agent As AgentObjects.IAgentCtlCharacterEx
```

We'll now set up a constant named `Datapath` that will store the location of the Agent character file named *Merlin.acs*:

```
Const DATAPATH As String = "C:\WINDOWS\MSAGENT\CHARS\merlin.acs"
```

 The previous line assumed that the merlin.acs file was available at a specific location. You can search your local hard drive to locate the file if it's at a different location and change the previous line to reflect the location.

INITIALIZING THE CHARACTER

We're now in a position where we need to initialize the character. We'll do this in the Form_Load event. Before following the first step in dealing with the Agent character, we can set the Text property of the form to "Say It Text To Speech". Next, we'll load the Merlin character using the Load method of Agent1 (the control that we added to the form). We'll then set an optional property of Agent called LanguageID, which sets the language used for Agent speech. In this case, we'll use English, which is an ID of &H409S.

Here is the code for these lines:

```
Me.Text = "Say It Text to Speech"
Agent1.Characters.Load("Merlin", DATAPATH)
Agent = Agent1.Characters("Merlin")
Agent.LanguageID = &H409S
```

We can now add a TextBox to the form (see Figure 30.6). The TextBox will be used to enter a string of characters.

The character will convert the text information to speech when the user instructs it to do so. In our application, we'll use a Button control for

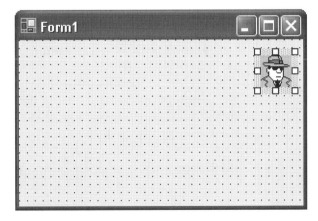

FIGURE 30.6   A TextBox is added to the form.

this. Add it to the form and change its `Text` property as seen in Figure 30.7.

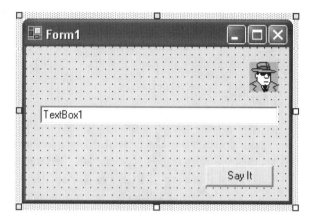

FIGURE 30.7   The `Button` control is added to the form.

There's a single line of code that we need to add to the `Form_Load` event. This code will set the `Text` property of `TextBox1` to `"Hello World!"`:

```
TextBox1.Text = "Hello World!"
```

The entire procedure is listed here:

```
Private Sub Form1_Load(ByVal eventSender As System.Object,
ByVal eventArgs As System.EventArgs) Handles MyBase.Load
        Me.Text = "Say It Text to Speech"
        Agent1.Characters.Load("Merlin", DATAPATH)
        Agent = Agent1.Characters("Merlin")
        Agent.LanguageID = &H409S
        TextBox1.Text = "Hello World!"
End Sub
```

We can now concentrate on the `Button1_Click` event, which will handle the Agent's speech, and hiding and showing the Agent. First, we'll use `Agent.Show` to display the Agent:

```
Agent.Show()
```

Next, we can use the `Speak` method of the `Agent` control to get the character to speak. You can use any arrangement of characters, and in our case, we'll use the Text property of TextBox1. The text will appear inside a bubble and will also be heard:

```
Agent.Speak(TextBox1.Text)
```

Once he has spoken, we'll hide the character again until the button is clicked:

```
Agent.Hide()
```

Here's the final procedure:

```
Private Sub Button1_Click(ByVal sender As System.Object, ByVal
e As System.EventArgs) Handles Button1.Click
    Agent.Show()
    Agent.Speak(TextBox1.Text)
    Agent.Hide()
End Sub
```

TESTING THE APPLICATION

At this time, the application is finished and you can save it. To test the application, you can run it in the IDE. On opening, the window should look like Figure 30.8.

You can click the Say It button, which should display the Agent as in Figure 30.9. Next, the Agent will speak the contents of the TextBox

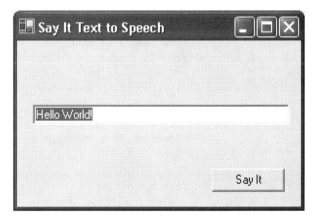

FIGURE 30.8 The opening screen.

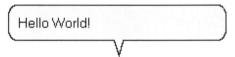

FIGURE 30.9   Displaying the Agent character, Merlin.

FIGURE 30.10   The Agent is speaking.

(Figure 30.10). Lastly, the Agent will be hidden and the original window will be displayed.

You can change the contents of the TextBox and then click the Say It button to test the application further.

FINAL CODE LISTING

This is the final code listing for the application:

```
Public Class Form1
Inherits System.Windows.Forms.Form

Dim Agent As AgentObjects.IAgentCtlCharacterEx
Const DATAPATH As String =
"C:\WINDOWS\MSAGENT\CHARS\merlin.acs"

Private Sub Form1_Load(ByVal eventSender As System.Object,
ByVal eventArgs As System.EventArgs) Handles MyBase.Load
    Me.Text = "Say It Text to Speech"
    Agent1.Characters.Load("Merlin", DATAPATH)
    Agent = Agent1.Characters("Merlin")
    Agent.LanguageID = &H409S
    TextBox1.Text = "Hello World!"
End Sub

Private Sub Button1_Click(ByVal sender As System.Object,
ByVal e As System.EventArgs) Handles Button1.Click
    Agent.Show()
```

```
        Agent.Speak(TextBox1.Text)
        Agent.Hide()
    End Sub
    End Class
```

CHAPTER REVIEW

In this chapter, we built our first Agent application. Using only a few lines of code, we were able to create an application that converted text information into speech.

In the next chapter, we're going to learn much more about Agent programming and we'll also build a simple guess-the-number game.

31

MORE MICROSOFT AGENT

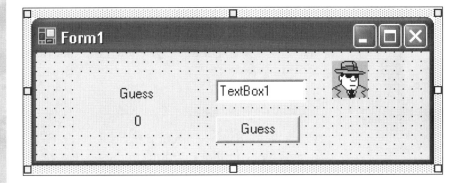

In the previous chapter, we built our first Microsoft Agent application that could convert plain text into speech output. We're going to spend the first part of this chapter looking at some additional options that are available to you with Agent. Then, once we've looked at some of the additional features, we'll put them to use when we build an application that plays a number guessing gamc.

SOME AGENT COMMANDS

We looked at some of the commands that we can give to Agents in the last chapter. We're going to look at some of the additional commands and brief explanations about what they allow us to do. A single line of code can make the Agent do very simple tasks that can be combined into very realistic sequences.

Making an Agent Think

The code to make an Agent think is very simple and will work with any Agent character that conforms to the correct specifications:

```
Agent.Think ("This is a Message.")
```

An example of this code in a real program would be as follows:

```
Agent.Think ("I am thinking of a number.")
```

This would make the words ("I am thinking of a number.") appear in a balloon above the Agent's head. The Agent doesn't speak these words aloud.

Moving an Agent

You can move an Agent around the screen by giving it the coordinates that you'd like it to move to.

```
Agent.MoveTo 1,1
```

An example of this follows:

```
Agent.MoveTo 50,100
```

This would move the Agent to X coordinate 50 and Y coordinate 100.

Stopping the Agent

If you need to stop an Agent at any time, you can use the Stop method as follows:

```
Agent.Stop
```

This will stop the Agent from anything it's doing including speaking, moving, playing an animation, and so on.

CHANGING ANIMATIONS

In addition to the functions, it's easy to change the animation that the character is displaying.

Processing Animations

An Agent has various animations that are built-in to the characters. You can change between these animations very quickly and easily as listed in Table 31.1.

Table 31.1   Agent Animation Commands

DESCRIPTION	COMMAND
Writes for a short time and then stops.	Agent.Play("Write")
Writes in a looping mode.	Agent.Play("Writing")
Reads for a short time then stops.	Agent.Play("Read")
Reads in a looping mode.	Agent.Play("Reading")
Plays then stops animation process.	Agent.Play("Process")
Plays process in looping mode.	Agent.Play("Processing")
Searches and then stops.	Agent.Play("Search")
Searches until you stop the Agent.	Agent.Play("Searching")

Facial Expressions

In addition to processing animations, Agents can also display various facial expressions as listed in Table 31.2.

Table 31.2   Agent Facial Expressions

DESCRIPTION	COMMAND
Acknowledge something.	Agent.Play("Acknowledge")
Agent looks alert.	Agent.Play("Alert")
Blink animation.	Agent.Play("Blink")
Character is confused.	Agent.Play("Confused")
The agent declines.	Agent.Play("Decline")
Doesn't recognize.	Agent.Play("DontRecognize")
Agent appears to listen (look left).	Agent.Play("Hearing_1")
Agent appears to listen (look right).	Agent.Play("Hearing_2")
Listening and looking both ways.	Agent.Play("Hearing_3")
Agent looks happy.	Agent.Play("Pleased")
Agent looks unhappy.	Agent.Play("Sad")
Will look startled.	Agent.Play("Surprised")
Agent doesn't understand.	Agent.Play("Uncertain")

Looking in Direction

The characters can look in many different directions as listed in Table 31.3.

Table 31.3   Directional Looking

DESCRIPTION	COMMAND
Agent looks down.	Agent.Play("LookDown")
Looks down and blinks.	Agent.Play("LookDownBlink")
Stops looking and rests.	Agent.Play("LookDownReturn")
Looks up when directed.	Agent.Play("LookUp")
Looks up and blinks.	Agent.Play("LookUpBlink")
Stops looking and rests.	Agent.Play("LookUpReturn")
Looks to the right.	Agent.Play("LookRight")

(continues)

Table 31.3   *(continued)*

DESCRIPTION	COMMAND
Looks right and blinks.	Agent.Play("LookRightBlink")
Stops looking and returns.	Agent.Play("LookRightReturn")
Looks left when directed.	Agent.Play("LookLeft")
Looks left and blinks.	Agent.Play("LookLeftBlink")
Stops looking and returns.	Agent.Play("LookLeftReturn")

Gesturing Animations

Agent characters can also appear to simulate various gestures. The gestures have standard names but could be different depending on the character. For example, one character could clap when `"Congratulate_1"` is played while another might simply smile. Table 31.4 lists the gesturing animations.

Table 31.4   Gesturing Animations

DESCRIPTION	COMMAND
Agent explaining something.	Agent.Play("Explain")
Get the user's attention.	Agent.Play("GetAttention")
Greeting a user.	Agent.Play("Greet")
Make an announcement.	Agent.Play("Announce")
Some type of congratulation.	Agent.Play("Congratulate_1")
Another congratulation.	Agent.Play("Congratulate_2")
Doing magic on screen.	Agent.Play("DoMagic1")
Variation of magic.	Agent.Play("DoMagic2")
Appears to be listening.	Agent.Play("StartListening")
Stops listening animation.	Agent.Play("StopListening")

Directional Gestures

You can also make the Agent gesture in certain directions or even specific x,y screen locations. Table 31.5 lists these gestures.

Table 31.5   Directional Gesturing

DESCRIPTION	COMMAND
Directional gesture up.	Agent.Play("GestureUp")
Gesture down.	Agent.Play("GestureDown")
Gesture right.	Agent.Play("GestureRight")
Gesture left.	Agent.Play("GestureLeft")
Agent gesture to specific location.	Agent.GestureAt X,Y

 `Agent.Gesture At X,Y` *is used to gesture at a specific location. You'll substitute actual screen locations such as 150,500 into the* X,Y *values. For example,* `Agent.GestureAt 150,500.`

AGENT EVENTS

There are several events that occur when you're using Agents. These events can be used to add advanced functionality to your application.

IdleStart

When the Agent is `Idle`, the `Agent_IdleStart` event is raised. We can use this to control exactly what the Agent does while in an `Idle` state. The following list details some of the various animations that you can play (some of these are unavailable on certain characters):

```
Agent.Play("Idle1_1")
Agent.Play("Idle1_2")
Agent.Play("Idle1_3")
Agent.Play("Idle1_4")
Agent.Play("Idle1_5")
Agent.Play("Idle1_6")
Agent.Play("Idle2_1")
Agent.Play("Idle2_2")
Agent.Play("Idle2_3")
Agent.Play("Idle3_1")
Agent.Play("Idle3_2")
Agent.Play("Idle3_3")
```

Complete Event

When the `Idle` event is finished, the `Agent_Complete` event is raised. We can use this to change what the character is doing after it's finished in the `Idle` state. We can use any method that's available to the character. For example, we can tell the character to go back to its default animation with the following line:

```
Agent.Play("Restpose")
```

Click Event

The Agent, like most things in VB, can respond when clicked with the mouse. This raises the `Agent_Click` event, and like the complete event, you can do a variety of things with the Agent by using any of its available methods. For example, you could use the `Speak` method to say something when the user clicks:

```
Agent.Speak("Hello")
```

Move Event

When you move an Agent around the screen (either programmatically or by clicking and dragging it), an `Agent_Move` event is raised. This allows you to set what happens to the Agent when it's moved. For example, you could instruct the Agent to play a certain animation when moved:

```
Agent.Play("Surprised")
```

DragStart Event

When the user begins to drag an Agent, the `DragStart` event is raised. You can use this event to do something such as playing a certain animation:

```
Agent.Play("Surprised")
```

DragStop Event

The opposite event occurs when you stop dragging the Agent and it's equally useful. For example, suppose you'd like to move the Agent back to its original position and tell the user that they wouldn't like to be dragged again:

```
Agent.MoveTo 100,100
Agent.Play("Surprised")
Agent.Speak("Please don't move me again!")
```

BalloonHide and BalloonShow Events

These two events can be used when the Agent's speech balloon is hidden or displayed. These events are available to change what's happening to the Agent when the events occur. For example, suppose you hide the balloon in your application. You could then have the Agent inform the user as to how they can get the balloon back:

```
Agent.Speak("My speech balloon was hidden.")
Agent.Speak("You can get this back by clicking")
Agent.Speak("on the balloon button.")
```

AGENT PROPERTIES

Along with the methods and properties that we've already looked at, there are an equally impressive number of properties that we have access to when dealing with an Agent.

SoundEffectsOn and SoundEffectsOff Properties

You can use the SoundEffectsOn property to set the Agent sounds effects on or off. The sound effects are played when different things happen to an Agent. If you would like the Agent to enable its effects, you can turn this on. However, if your application requires silence except for Text To Speech output, you can turn off the Agent's sound effects.

This code turns on the sound effects:

```
Agent.SoundEffectsOn = True
```

This turns it off:

```
Agent.SoundEffectsOn = False
```

IdleMode On or Off Properties

You can turn Idle on or off, which will effect whether the Agent can use its Idle mode and corresponding Idle events. To turn it off:

```
Agent.IdleOn = False
```

To turn it back on:

```
Agent.IdleOn = True
```

AutoPopupMenu Property

You can turn the pop-up menu that appears when the Agent is right-clicked. By default, the menu is on with the only option being hide. To turn it off:

```
Agent.AutoPopupMenu = False
```

To turn it back on:

```
Agent.AutoPopupMenu = True
```

CREATING A GAME

We're now going to take advantage of some of the properties and methods exposed by Microsoft Agent and create a game that allows us to guess a random number between 1 and 10.

User Interface

The user interface for this application will be very simple and is similar to the one created in the last example. We'll use a `TextBox` control, the `Agent` control, two `Label` controls and a `Button`. You can set their properties as follows:

TYPE	NAME	TEXT
Label	Label1	Guess
Label	lblGuesses	0
TextBox1	TextBox1	TextBox1
Button	Button1	Guess
Agent	Agent1	

The form should be rectangular with the dimensions of 360 × 128 and the controls should be arranged similarly to Figure 31.1.

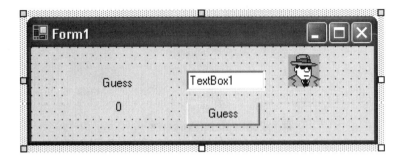

FIGURE 31.1   The user interface is complete.

WRITING SOME CODE

We'll begin writing some code by creating several variables for our application. You're already familiar with the first two that are needed:

```
Dim Agent As AgentObjects.IAgentCtlCharacterEx

Const DATAPATH As String = _
"C:\WINDOWS\MSAGENT\CHARS\merlin.acs"
```

The next two will be used to store information about the random number and if the application is being run for the first time:

```
Dim Number As Integer
Dim FirstTime As Boolean
```

We're now going to go through the individual Sub procedures for our application, beginning with Form1_Load.

Form1_Load

The Form1_Load Sub procedure is going to be used to set up a few values for our game. We'll also call another Sub procedure that we've not yet created called InitializeAgent:

```
Private Sub Form1_Load(ByVal eventSender As System.Object,
ByVal eventArgs As System.EventArgs) Handles MyBase.Load
    Me.Text = "Number Guess"
    FirstTime = True
    InitializeAgent()
End Sub
```

The `InitializeAgent` Sub procedure will contain a great deal of code that will hinge upon whether this is the first time that the game is being executed in a given session. If it is, the Agent will take a moment to introduce the user to the various elements of the user interface and how the game will be played. This is a simple game, so this step is probably unnecessary, but it allows us to use some of the methods that we looked at earlier in the chapter.

At the end of the `Sub`, we call `GenerateNum`, the next `Sub` procedure we'll look at. Here's the code for `InitializeAgent`:

```
Private Sub InitializeAgent()
    If FirstTime Then
        Agent1.Characters.Load("Merlin", DATAPATH)
        Agent = Agent1.Characters("Merlin")
        Agent.LanguageID = &H409S
        Agent.MoveTo(Me.Left + Me.Width - Agent.Width,
Me.Top, 10)
        FirstTime = False
        With Agent
            .Show()
            .Play("Wave")
            .Speak("Hello, I am " & Agent.Name & ".")
            .Speak("Welcome to our guessing game.")
            .Speak("I will pick a random number")
            .Speak("between 1 and 10.  Your job will be")
            .Speak("to guess the number with as few
guesses")
            .Speak("as possible.")
            .MoveTo(Me.Left + Agent.Width, Me.Top, 5)
            .Play("GestureRight")
            .Speak("This area will display the number of
guesses.")
            .MoveTo(Me.Left, Me.Top, 5)
            .Play("GestureLeft")
            .Speak("You can type your guess into ")
            .Speak("this box and then click the Guess
Button.")
            .MoveTo(Me.Left + Me.Width - Agent.Width,
Me.Top, 10)
            .Speak("Good luck!")
        End With
    End If

    TextBox1.Text = ""
```

```
    GenerateNum()
End Sub
```

The `GenerateNum` `Sub` procedure does exactly what its name implies. It generates the random number that we're going to try to guess. Again, using methods that we looked at earlier in the chapter, we can generate the number and have the Agent let the user know what's going on at this time.

Here's the code:

```
Private Sub GenerateNum()
    Randomize()
    lblGuesses.Text = "0"
    Agent.Think("I am generating the number now.")
    Number = CInt(Int((10 * Rnd()) + 1))
    Agent.Play("Process")
    Agent.Speak("I have a number, please guess.")
End Sub
```

The next `Sub` procedure that we need to create is `Button1_Click`. This event will be triggered once the user has entered a guess and the number. We convert the string located in `TextBox1` to an integer and call `CheckGuess`, the last function that we need to create for the game.

Here's the code for `Button1_Click`:

```
Private Sub Button1_Click(ByVal sender As System.Object, ByVal
e As System.EventArgs) Handles Button1.Click
    Dim Temp As Integer
    Temp = CInt(lblGuesses.Text)
    Temp = Temp + 1
    lblGuesses.Text = CStr(Temp)
    Agent.StopAll()
    CheckGuess(CInt(TextBox1.Text))
End Sub
```

The final function for our game will check the value stored in the variable `Number` and the value that was passed to it (X). If the numbers are equal, the Agent will let the user know that they've won the game. If they are incorrect, the Agent will instruct the user if they are too high or too low with their current guess.

If the user wins the game, an `InputBox` will be used to capture a "Y" or "N" value to see if the user wants to play again. If so, `InitializeAgent` is called again. Because the value stored in `FirstTime` is set to `False`, the game will skip over the Agent handing out instructions. If the player wishes to exit, the application then ends.

Here's the code for this function:

```
Function CheckGuess(ByVal X As Integer)
    Dim Temp As String
    If X = Number Then
        Agent.Speak("You are correct!")
        Agent.Play("Pleased")
        Agent.Speak("The number was " & CStr(X))
        Temp = InputBox("Would you like to play again (Y/N)?")
        If Temp = "Y" Then InitializeAgent()
        If Temp = "N" Then End
    ElseIf X < Number Then
        Agent.Speak("Sorry, you are too low.")
    ElseIf X > Number Then
        Agent.Speak("Sorry, you have guessed too high.")
    End If
End Function
```

FINAL CODE LISTING

This is the complete code listing for the chapter:

```
Public Class Form1
Inherits System.Windows.Forms.Form

Dim Agent As AgentObjects.IAgentCtlCharacterEx
Const DATAPATH As String = _
        "C:\WINDOWS\MSAGENT\CHARS\merlin.acs"
Dim Number As Integer
Dim FirstTime As Boolean

Private Sub Form1_Load(ByVal eventSender As System.Object,
ByVal eventArgs As System.EventArgs) Handles MyBase.Load
        Me.Text = "Number Guess"
        FirstTime = True
        InitializeAgent()
    End Sub

    Private Sub Button1_Click(ByVal sender As System.Object,
ByVal e As System.EventArgs) Handles Button1.Click
        Dim Temp As Integer
```

```
            Temp = CInt(lblGuesses.Text)
            Temp = Temp + 1
            lblGuesses.Text = CStr(Temp)
            Agent.StopAll()
            CheckGuess(CInt(TextBox1.Text))
        End Sub

        Private Sub InitializeAgent()
            If FirstTime Then
                Agent1.Characters.Load("Merlin", DATAPATH)
                Agent = Agent1.Characters("Merlin")
                Agent.LanguageID = &H409S
                Agent.MoveTo(Me.Left + Me.Width - Agent.Width,
Me.Top, 10)
                FirstTime = False
                With Agent
                    .Show()
                    .Play("Wave")
                    .Speak("Hello, I am " & Agent.Name & ".")
                    .Speak("Welcome to our guessing game.")
                    .Speak("I will pick a random number")
                    .Speak("between 1 and 10.  Your job will be")
                    .Speak("to guess the number with as few
guesses")
                    .Speak("as possible.")
                    .MoveTo(Me.Left + Agent.Width, Me.Top, 5)
                    .Play("GestureRight")
                    .Speak("This area will display the number of
guesses.")
                    .MoveTo(Me.Left, Me.Top, 5)
                    .Play("GestureLeft")
                    .Speak("You can type your guess into ")
                    .Speak("this box and then click the Guess
Button.")
                    .MoveTo(Me.Left + Me.Width - Agent.Width,
Me.Top, 10)
                    .Speak("Good luck!")
                End With
            End If

            TextBox1.Text = ""
            GenerateNum()
        End Sub
```

```
Private Sub GenerateNum()
    Randomize()
    lblGuesses.Text = "0"
    Agent.Think("I am generating the number now.")
    Number = CInt(Int((10 * Rnd()) + 1))
    Agent.Play("Process")
    Agent.Speak("I have a number, please guess.")
End Sub

Function CheckGuess(ByVal X As Integer)
    Dim Temp As String
    If X = Number Then
        Agent.Speak("You are correct!")
        Agent.Play("Pleased")
        Agent.Speak("The number was " & CStr(X))
        Temp = InputBox("Would you like to play again
(Y/N)?")

        If Temp = "Y" Then InitializeAgent()
        If Temp = "N" Then End
    ElseIf X < Number Then
        Agent.Speak("Sorry, you are too low.")
    ElseIf X > Number Then
        Agent.Speak("Sorry, you have guessed too high.")
    End If
End Function
End Class
```

CHAPTER REVIEW

In this chapter, we looked at some of the methods and properties that make the Agent so valuable to a developer. We proceeded to use a few of these items in making a number-guessing game.

In the next and final chapter, we're going to look at using DirectX in Visual Basic.NET.

DIRECTX GRAPHICS
IN VB.NET

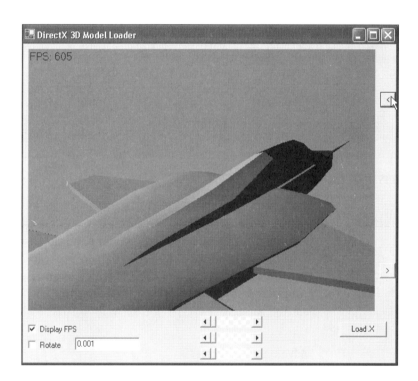

Prior to DirectX Version 7, Visual Basic programmers didn't have direct access to the powerful libraries developed by Microsoft. DirectX 8.1 continues to support Visual Basic, and with components such as DirectSound, DirectInput, and Direct3D, programmers interested in multimedia or game programming will find the tools a necessity.

PROJECT OVERVIEW

In this chapter, you'll be introduced to Direct3D and will build an application to display a DirectX binary model (*.x* extension). You'll have the ability to rotate the object and zoom in and out to change the color of the lighting. The DirectX software development kit (SDK) is available from Microsoft free of charge. You can download it from their Web site (*www.microsoft.com*) or you can order a CD-ROM and pay only a few dollars for shipping fees. In order to do run any samples in this chapter, you must first install the SDK.

WHAT IS DIRECT3D?

Direct3D is a single aspect of DirectX, which in turn is a collection of high-performance APIs written by Microsoft to produce sound, graphics animation, and multimedia. Direct3D is the three-dimensional graphics part of DirectX.

In versions prior to DirectX 7.0, DirectX was available only to VB programmers via third-party controls or type libraries. As a result, most VB programmers simply ignored it. Beginning with Version 7.0, Microsoft started to include a type library written specifically for VB programmers.

Advantages of Direct3D

While there are a plethora of advantages to Direct3D, it's important to understand the most basic of these. First, Direct3D provides transparent access to different hardware devices without the need to understand the intricacies of the different chipsets. As a result, applications become independent of the hardware and allow the developer to know immediately that all the drivers supporting Direct3D will support a certain set of instructions and capabilities. Applications developed using such features will work on all hardware platforms.

Direct3D also provides a standard programming interface for 3D applications, which results in applications that can be developed much easier and faster. Lastly, Direct3D provides some basic protection if a hardware platform doesn't support a certain feature by substituting a software equivalent implementation of the intended feature. Thus, the application can simply detect the hardware capabilities and use them; otherwise, it can render in software mode. Obviously, software substitutions do make applications run more slowly but that's better than not running at all.

The SDK

Before we begin the tutorial, it's important to realize the vast amount of information available to you in the DirectX SDK. The following list includes some specific areas that you should visit to become more familiar with DirectX and Direct3D. The list also assumes that you've installed the software to drive C using the default *mssdk* installation path. If you installed the SDK to another directory or hard drive, you'll need to change the drive letter and root directory. Here's the list:

- *C:\mssdk\DXReadme.txt*: A file that's particularly useful for navigating the rest of the CD-ROM.
- *C:\mssdk\doc\DirectX8\directX_vb.chm*: This is a compiled help file containing information about DirectX 8.1–the most important entry on the entire CD-ROM.
- *C:\mssdk\samples\Multimedia\VBSamples*: This directory contains Visual Basic samples utilizing all the DirectX components.

Direct3D Coordinate System

There are several ways that you might arrange the X, Y, and Z coordinate axes in a given three-dimensional space. Direct3D uses a system that like the one that appears in Figure 32.1 where the X- and Y-axes are parallel to the computer monitor and the Z-axis is going into the screen.

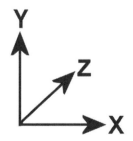

FIGURE 32.1   Direct3D uses this coordinate system.

Using Figure 32.1 as a reference, if you tried to imagine your position when you're sitting at your computer desk, relative to the point x0, y0, z0 in a Direct3D space, you would be at some point in space with a positive z coordinate.

DIRECT3D MODES

DirectX 8.1 provides a single mode, called Immediate mode, to programmers. This mode is a high-level interface to Direct3D that can be cumbersome and confusing to a beginner. Previous versions of DirectX offered the option of using Retained mode, which was a low-level implementation. It was much easier to access and understand, especially for someone new to 3D programming. Taking this into consideration, the sample being developed in this chapter will utilize Retained mode, which can still be accessed by taking advantage of the backward compatibility of DirectX. As a result, we'll be using Direct3D Version 7.

If you don't have any experience with Direct3D, Retained mode is definitely the easiest place to start. A great deal of the more difficult stuff is hidden from you and what's left is a much easier to use Direct3D implementation. What you learn in Retained mode can also act as a stepping stone for future work.

There's a trade-off that occurs with the use of Retained mode. Application frame rates will be much lower with Retained mode. This would cause a problem if you were developing a large project, but if you're after quick-and-easy development, Retained mode is the way to go.

The final disadvantage of Retained mode is the fact that Microsoft has discontinued it. It remains to be seen if Microsoft will continue supporting it in future editions, although there are some persistent rumors that it'll be making its way back into DirectX 9 or 10. It's an interesting thought, although it probably isn't going to happen. You'd probably be better off learning Retained mode in an earlier version and then moving on to Immediate mode.

3D VOCABULARY

For our sample, you must understand some basic 3D vocabulary. The following are very simple explanations of some of the basics:

- Camera: To do something in 3D space, you must have a way to represent where you are. This is the sole responsibility of the camera.

- Rotation: Rotating an object in a 3D world works very similar to a tire rotating on a car's axis. Simply stated, *rotation* is the movement of an object around a coordinate that's referenced to the whole screen but not on the local object.
- Scenes: *Scenes* are comprised of the many objects that you'd like to display including lights, 3D objects, and backgrounds.
- Render modes: To display the 3D information, you must render it in 2D. There are three main render modes: Wireframe, Solid, and Gouraud. *Wireframe* displays only a set of lines and is the simplest. *Solid* rendering fills the spaces between the lines with color while *Gouraud* adds shading to enhance the appearance of objects.
- Lights: A *light* simply does what you would expect it to. If you don't place a light in a scene, you'll see nothing.

CREATING AN APPLICATION

Using DirectX in VB.NET is a bit cumbersome. We won't go into all of the details as to why this is the case, but Version 9, which is currently in beta, will take care of this. Until then, we're stuck with what we have. In this chapter, we're going to use a class that was created for you. We're not going through the various aspects of this class, but you can feel free to use it for other projects that you're working on. If you'd like, you can open up this project on the CD-ROM to look at the class called `DXGraphics8`.

 In order to use the class in another application, you'll first need to add a reference to the DirectX 8 Type library, which is included with the SDK.

This application will display 3D models in DirectX (*.x*) format. We'll begin it by creating a couple of variables:

```
Dim dxg8 As DXGraphics8
Dim ActiveRender As Boolean = True
```

The interface for this application is simple and uses a variety of controls that you've become familiar with throughout the book. We aren't going to spend much time on this part of the application. It consists of the controls listed in Table 32.1.

Table 32.1   Controls for our Application

TYPE	NAME	TEXT
PictureBox	PictureBox1	n/a
CheckBox	CheckBox1	Rotate
CheckBox	CheckBox2	DisplayFPS
HScrollBar	Red	n/a
HScrollBar	Green	n/a
HScrollBar	Blue	n/a
Button	Button1	Load .X
Button	Button2	<
Button	Button3	>

You can copy the layout of the interface from Figure 32.2.

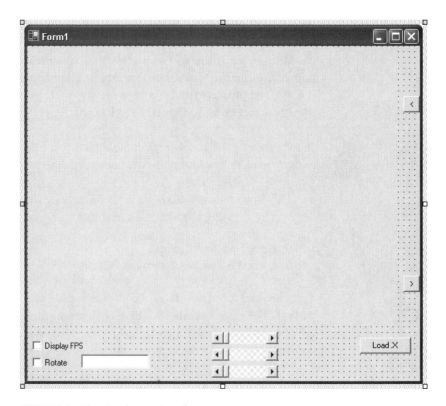

FIGURE 32.2   The simple user interface.

The `PictureBox` and the `Form1_Load` event comprise the first control we're concerned with. It'll be used to render the scene, and ultimately, our object. We're going to use its `Handle` property, which will need to be converted to an `Int32` value. We'll also set the `Text` property of the form to "DirectX Model Loader" and the `Text` property of txtAmount to "0.001".

Here's the code for the `Sub` procedure:

```
Private Sub Form1_Load(ByVal sender As System.Object, ByVal e
As System.EventArgs) Handles MyBase.Load
     dxg8 = New DXGraphics8(PictureBox1.Handle.ToInt32)
     Me.Text = "DirectX 3D Model Loader"
     txtAmount.Text = "0.001"
End Sub
```

The next step will be to create the code for loading a model. The `Button1_Click` event will be used for this step. We'll use a standard `OpenFileDialog` box to browse for a model and then take the results of this. If the OK button is clicked, we can then set the `Boolean` variable called `ActiveRender` to `True`. We can then load the mesh and begin rendering. If Cancel is clicked in the `FileDialog`, the procedure will be exited.

Assuming that the user clicked OK, the next step is to use a loop to continue rendering until stopped. We'll check the value of `CheckBox1` continuously to see if it's checked. If so, we can use the value of txtAmount to rotate the 3D model on the screen. Otherwise, the object is rendered normally.

Here's the code:

```
Private Sub Button1_Click(ByVal sender As System.Object, ByVal
e As System.EventArgs) Handles Button1.Click
     Dim FileDialog As New OpenFileDialog()

     FileDialog.Filter = "DirectX Graphics | *.x"
     If FileDialog.ShowDialog(Me) = DialogResult.OK Then
         ActiveRender = True
         dxg8.LoadMesh(FileDialog.FileName)
     Else
         Exit Sub
     End If

     Do While ActiveRender
         dxg8.Render()
         Application.DoEvents()
```

```
            If CheckBox1.CheckState = CheckState.Checked And
txtAmount.Text <> "" Then
                dxg8.Rotate(CSng(txtAmount.Text))
            End If
        Loop
    End Sub
```

There are only a few more things that we need to do to finish the application. This involves a very small series of one-line Sub procedures dealing with changing the color of the lights and zooming in and out. These concepts are very easy to grasp, so a quick glance at the code should suffice:

```
    Private Sub CheckBox2_CheckedChanged(ByVal sender As
System.Object, ByVal e As System.EventArgs) Handles
CheckBox2.CheckedChanged
        dxg8.ShowFrameRate = Not dxg8.ShowFrameRate
    End Sub

    Private Sub Red_Scroll(ByVal sender As System.Object, ByVal
e As System.Windows.Forms.ScrollEventArgs) Handles Red.Scroll
        dxg8.InitLights(1, Red.Value, Green.Value, Blue.Value)
    End Sub

    Private Sub Green_Scroll(ByVal sender As System.Object,
ByVal e As System.Windows.Forms.ScrollEventArgs) Handles
Green.Scroll
        dxg8.InitLights(1, Red.Value, Green.Value, Blue.Value)
    End Sub

    Private Sub Blue_Scroll(ByVal sender As System.Object,
ByVal e As System.Windows.Forms.ScrollEventArgs) Handles
Blue.Scroll
        dxg8.InitLights(1, Red.Value, Green.Value, Blue.Value)
    End Sub

    Public Sub DXZoom(ByVal percent As Single)
        dxg8.CameraPoint = dxg8.v3(dxg8.CameraPoint.x +
(dxg8.CameraPoint.x - dxg8.ViewPoint.x) * percent,
dxg8.CameraPoint.y + (dxg8.CameraPoint.y - dxg8.ViewPoint.y) *
percent, dxg8.CameraPoint.z + (dxg8.CameraPoint.z -
dxg8.ViewPoint.z) * percent)
        End Sub
```

```
    Private Sub Button2_Click(ByVal sender As System.Object,
ByVal e As System.EventArgs) Handles Button2.Click
        DXZoom(-0.1)
    End Sub


    Private Sub Button3_Click(ByVal sender As System.Object,
ByVal e As System.EventArgs) Handles Button3.Click
        DXZoom(+0.1)
    End Sub
```

TESTING THE APPLICATION

You can run the application at this time but you should probably save it before doing so. Next, click on the Load.X button and from the dialog box that appears (see Figure 32.3), you can browse to the *C:\DXSDK\ samples\Multimedia* directory, which contains several *.x* files. Opening one of them should display a screen similar to the one you see in Figure 32.4. You can change settings to make sure everything works correctly such as rotating an object (Figure 32.5), displaying the FPS (Frames Per Second)

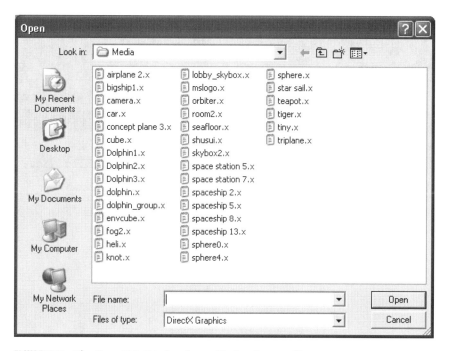

FIGURE 32.3   The `OpenFileDialog` is used to locate an `.x` file.

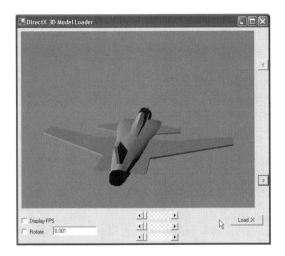

FIGURE 32.4   Once opened, you should see the file in the `PictureBox`.

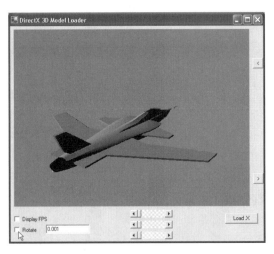

FIGURE 32.5   Rotate the object.

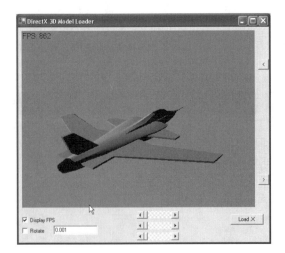

FIGURE 32.6   Display the Frames Per Second (FPS).

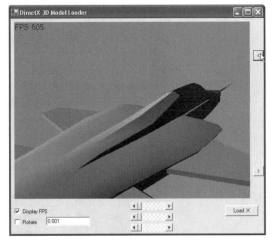

FIGURE 32.7   Zoom in.

(Figure 32.6), zooming in (Figure 32.7), zooming out (Figure 32.8), and changing the color of the lights (Figure 32.9).

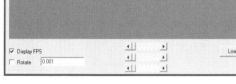

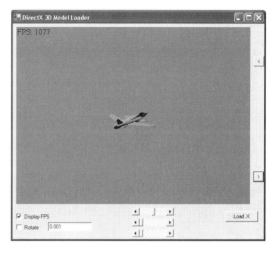

FIGURE 32.8   Zoom out.

FIGURE 32.9   Change the color of the lights. (Full-color images can be found on the book's companion CD-ROM.)

FINAL CODE LISTING

This is the complete code listing for the application:

```
Public Class Form1
Inherits System.Windows.Forms.Form

Dim dxg8 As DXGraphics8
Dim ActiveRender As Boolean = True

Private Sub Form1_Load(ByVal sender As System.Object, ByVal
e As System.EventArgs) Handles MyBase.Load
    dxg8 = New DXGraphics8(PictureBox1.Handle.ToInt32)
    Me.Text = "DirectX 3D Model Loader"
    txtAmount.Text = "0.001"
End Sub

Private Sub Button1_Click(ByVal sender As System.Object,
ByVal e As System.EventArgs) Handles Button1.Click
    Dim FileDialog As New OpenFileDialog()

    FileDialog.Filter = "DirectX Graphics | *.x"
    If FileDialog.ShowDialog(Me) = DialogResult.OK Then
        ActiveRender = True
        dxg8.LoadMesh(FileDialog.FileName)
```

```vb
            Else
                Exit Sub
            End If

            Do While ActiveRender
                dxg8.Render()
                Application.DoEvents()
                If CheckBox1.CheckState = CheckState.Checked And
txtAmount.Text <> "" Then
                    dxg8.Rotate(CSng(txtAmount.Text))
                End If
            Loop
        End Sub

        Private Sub CheckBox2_CheckedChanged(ByVal sender As
System.Object, ByVal e As System.EventArgs) Handles
CheckBox2.CheckedChanged
            dxg8.ShowFrameRate = Not dxg8.ShowFrameRate
        End Sub

        Private Sub Red_Scroll(ByVal sender As System.Object, ByVal
e As System.Windows.Forms.ScrollEventArgs) Handles Red.Scroll
            dxg8.InitLights(1, Red.Value, Green.Value, Blue.Value)
        End Sub

        Private Sub Green_Scroll(ByVal sender As System.Object,
ByVal e As System.Windows.Forms.ScrollEventArgs) Handles
Green.Scroll
            dxg8.InitLights(1, Red.Value, Green.Value, Blue.Value)
        End Sub

        Private Sub Blue_Scroll(ByVal sender As System.Object,
ByVal e As System.Windows.Forms.ScrollEventArgs) Handles
Blue.Scroll
            dxg8.InitLights(1, Red.Value, Green.Value, Blue.Value)
        End Sub

        Public Sub DXZoom(ByVal percent As Single)
            dxg8.CameraPoint = dxg8.v3(dxg8.CameraPoint.x +
(dxg8.CameraPoint.x - dxg8.ViewPoint.x) * percent,
dxg8.CameraPoint.y + (dxg8.CameraPoint.y - dxg8.ViewPoint.y) *
percent, dxg8.CameraPoint.z + (dxg8.CameraPoint.z -
dxg8.ViewPoint.z) * percent)
        End Sub
```

```
        Private Sub Button2_Click(ByVal sender As System.Object,
ByVal e As System.EventArgs) Handles Button2.Click
            DXZoom(-0.1)
        End Sub

        Private Sub Button3_Click(ByVal sender As System.Object,
ByVal e As System.EventArgs) Handles Button3.Click
            DXZoom(+0.1)
        End Sub

        Private Sub Form1_Closing(ByVal sender As Object, ByVal e
As System.ComponentModel.CancelEventArgs) Handles MyBase.Closing
            ActiveRender = False
            Application.DoEvents()
        End Sub
    End Class
```

CHAPTER REVIEW

Now that DirectX 9 is right around the corner, the problems that are associated with using DirectX 8.1 will no longer exist. Much of the same functionality will be present, so getting it to work with VB.NET is still worth the trouble. You should spend a little time with the class that's included with this project as it will help you immensely in developing your DirectX applications. Congratulations, you have finished the entire book! You have built several different types of applications using VB.NET and you should now be well on your way to having a good grasp of the powerful features it provides. You can refer to the appendices for additional information on learning resources for your future projects.

A

WHERE TO LOOK FOR HELP

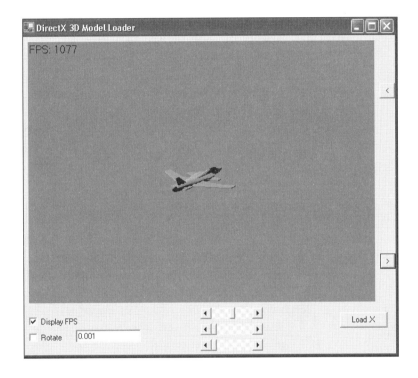

A t this point in time, you should give yourself a big pat on the back. If you've followed through the book, you've created several useful applications that provide a good foundation for the future. Unfortunately, as you learn more about Visual Basic, you'll undoubtedly have a need for answers on specific problems that you'll inevitably encounter.

Given the large number of Internet resources and newsgroups available, you can probably find someone willing to help in those times of crisis. The following list will be a great place to start:

Internet Sites

http://www.vbinformation.com/
http://www.beadsandbaubles.com/coolvb/boards.shtml
http://www.cgvb.com/
http://www.vbhow.to/
http://www.microsoft.com/

Newsgroups

comp.lang.basic.visual.announce
comp.lang.basic.visual.database
comp.lang.basic.visual.misc
comp.lang.basic.visual.3rdparty
microsoft.public.activex.controls.chatcontrol
microsoft.public.activex.programming.control.webdc
microsoft.public.activex.programming.control.webwiz
microsoft.public.inetexplorer.ie4.activex_contrl
microsoft.public.windows.inetexplorer.ie5.programming.activexcontrol
microsoft.public.vb.3rdparty
microsoft.public.vb.6.webdevelopment
microsoft.public.vb.addins
microsoft.public.vb.bugs
microsoft.public.vb.com
microsoft.public.vb.controls
microsoft.public.vb.controls.creation
microsoft.public.vb.controls.databound
microsoft.public.vb.controls.internet
microsoft.public.vb.crystal
microsoft.public.vb.database
microsoft.public.vb.database.ado

microsoft.public.vb.database.dao
microsoft.public.vb.database.odbc
microsoft.public.vb.database.rdo
microsoft.public.vb.dataenvreport
microsoft.public.vb.deployment
microsoft.public.vb.enterprise
microsoft.public.vb.general.discussion
microsoft.public.vb.installation
microsoft.public.vb.ole
microsoft.public.vb.ole.automation
microsoft.public.vb.ole.cdk
microsoft.public.vb.ole.servers
microsoft.public.vb.setupwiz
microsoft.public.vb.syntax
microsoft.public.vb.vbce
microsoft.public.vb.visual_modeler
microsoft.public.vb.webclasses
microsoft.public.vb.winapi
microsoft.public.vb.winapi.graphics
microsoft.public.vb.winapi.networks

B

ABOUT THE CD-ROM

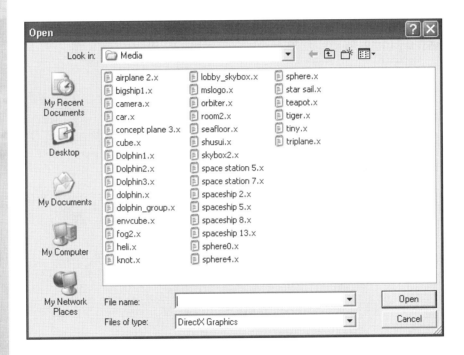

The CD-ROM included inside *Learning Visual Basic.NET through Applications* includes all of the necessary tools (with the exception of Visual Basic) to write the programs that are developed in each chapter. It also includes full color images of all the figures in the book plus the source code and executable files for the sample projects.

The folders contain the following items:

- Figures: Full-color version of all the figures in the book.
- Projects: Arranged by chapter; includes the source code and executable files for every sample in the book.

SYSTEM REQUIREMENTS

Microsoft Visual Basic.NET
Windows 98, NT, 2000, XP
Pentium
CD-ROM
Hard drive: 200MB of free space to install the examples
32MB of RAM

INSTALLATION

To use the programs on the CD-ROM, your system should match at least the minimum system requirements. The image files utilized are TIFFs.

INDEX